D1332381

KINGSTON COLLEGE

00086366

ADRIAN TURNER *on*

GOLDFINGER

WITHDRAWN
FROM
LEARNING RESOURCES
CENTRE
KINGSTON COLLEGE

Bloomsbury Movie Guides

ADRIAN TURNER *on*

GOLDFINGER

Bloomsbury Movie Guide No.2

BLOOMSBURY

KINGSTON COLLEGE
LEARNING RESOURCES CENTRE

Class No.	791·43 4286 TUR
Acc. No.	0008366
Date Rec.	3/3/00
Order No.	k52/2 B854523

First published in 1998

Copyright © Adrian Turner 1998

The moral right of the author has been asserted

Bloomsbury Publishing Plc, 38 Soho Square, London W1V 5DF

A CIP catalogue record for this book is available from the British Library

ISBN 0 7475 3888 3

10 9 8 7 6 5 4 3 2 1

Typeset by Palimpsest Book Production Limited,
Polmont, Stirlingshire

Printed in Great Britain by
Clays Ltd, St Ives plc

A

ab initio i

Turner was given a table on the outdoor terrace, where he treated himself to a delicious, wasteful breakfast of fresh orange juice, and a plate of raspberries and Charantais melon, followed by fried eggs done over-easy with bacon and English muffins. After conducting some extensive research into the subject, he believed that American hotels did the best breakfasts in the world, certainly the best bacon, which was always crisp and juicy. Turner abhorred British bacon, which was flabby and salty, and even the thought of it lying in a layer of grease made him give an involuntary shudder.

Turner could never understand why American coffee was so awful and why they made such a fuss of decaff or, worse, decaff with a twist. Whichever way it came, it always tasted of bilge water. Just as Turner would never order tea in France – or even fried eggs, unless he was at the Crillon or the Château de Bagnols – he never ordered coffee for breakfast in America. Instead, he asked for boiling water and produced from his pocket a small bottle of Yemeni Grande instant coffee granules. He put two heaped teaspoonfuls into his cup and poured just enough boiling water over the granules to create a fair facsimile of espresso. People did stranger things in southern California.

Turner lit his first cigarette of the day, an unfiltered Pall Mall king size, which was the only real cigarette left in the world and which was banned in England. He took a deep lungful of the strong, pungent smoke, picked up his copy of the *Los Angeles Times* and then threw it down again. The headline concerned an earth tremor which had rocked Santa Rosa the previous night; otherwise, the paper was full of tedious Hollywood gossip and full-page advertisements for discount furniture.

When Turner was in Los Angeles he always chose the Ritz-Carlton, which was far from the glamour of the more obvious places like the Beverly Wilshire or the Four Seasons. The Ritz-Carlton was a modern building which somehow exuded the cosiness of a English country club. It also combined a degree of anonymity with the absolute professionalism which Turner always demanded from the hotels he stayed in. Although he could never get used to that which passes in Los Angeles for personalised service – all those 'Have a nice days' and 'Hi, Mr Turner, I'm Steven and I'll be your waiter this morning' – he nevertheless preferred it to the starchiness of Europe. Americans might be preposterous in so many ways, but their friendliness, efficiency and their insistence on giving you value for money was not matched anywhere else.

Marina Del Rey was beautiful this May morning, the water sparkling and the yachts bobbing gently at anchor, their rigging jangling against their masts like Tibetan chimes. A young blonde jogged past, her beautiful firm breasts rippling under her grey sweatshirt. Catching Turner's admiring glance, she smiled and waved. Turner could have sat there for hours, gazing idly as the yacht owners and their crews arrived to spit and polish the brass work and to ready the ships for their voyage into the distant Pacific. It all looked so innocent, all these pleasure craft and gin palaces lined up on the quays, yet Turner knew that many were illicitly gotten gains, paid for by drug runs from Mexico.

Turner had a mission that morning. Usually he would have called on friends in the movie business, gone skeet shooting with John Milius or driven alone up the coast in search of lunch. But this morning was different. He called for his check, to which he added a generous tip, and returned to his room, where he changed into cream trousers, a crisp blue Sea Island cotton shirt and a dark blue blazer. He made a single call to confirm his appointment, retrieved his passport, credit cards and a brown package from the wall-safe, and ensured that his room was tidy. Turner disliked people who left wet towels on the bathroom floor and their clothes strewn across the bed and sofas.

Thirty minutes later Turner took the lift to the lobby. His car was already waiting for him. He tipped the valet five dollars, carefully set the brown package on the passenger seat and switched on the ignition of his rented silver Mercedes SL320. As he turned on to Admiralty Way he glanced down at the package and wondered if he had made a mistake. He had become extremely fond and proud of the contents of the package and even though he had not needed them in several years he suddenly regretted the thought of not owning them any more.

Turner drove the Mercedes along Santa Monica Boulevard, past Westwood and across Beverly Hills. He never ceased to be amazed by how the city had developed since his first visit in 1979. The economy now depended on Japanese tourists and Japanese corporations, which were buying everything from film studios to hotels. Everybody seemed to be driving a Lexus and talking into mobile phones as they did so.

Turner found Melrose Avenue without difficulty and pulled up outside the Heritage Bookstore. It did not look like a bookstore at all; more like one of those discreet fashion houses on Rodeo Drive whose windows are empty except for a card which simply requests that customers make an appointment if they wish to buy a pair of socks.

Turner rang the bell.

'Hi. Can I help you?' said a voice on the intercom.

'The name is Turner. Adrian Turner.'

'Oh, yes, Mr Turner,' said the voice.

The door opened and Turner could see that the voice came from a young man, blond, tanned and immaculately dressed.

'Please, go inside and I'll get your car validated,' he said.

Turner entered the bookstore, which, as he already knew, had once been a morgue. The air was cool and there was the scent of gardenias. The books, thousands of them, stood on shelves behind glass doors, many of them padlocked, as if they were **gold** bullion, which, in a way, they were. In another room there were still more books and soaring above them was a vaulted wooden roof. The windows were stained glass, in the style of Tiffany. Turner heard the door close behind him. The owner introduced himself. His handshake was warm and dry.

'Well, let's see what you've brought us.'

Turner could sense the tension in the air as he carefully slid his fingernail through the tape and removed the brown paper. Beneath that was a shoebox from Ferragamo. He removed the lid and then took out several layers of tissue paper.

'Ah,' said the owner.

Now open to view was a copy of a first edition of *Casino Royale*, immaculate in its battleship grey cover with the cherry-coloured hearts. Turner put the slim volume down on the gleaming table as if it were a beloved cat or dog which had reached the end of its life and was about to be put to sleep for ever.

'I haven't seen one as good as this for a long time,' said the owner, who was gingerly studying the volume for the slightest sign of foxing.

Turner took out the rest of the contents of the package. There were copies of *Live and Let Die*, *Moonraker*, *Diamonds Are Forever*, *From Russia With Love* and **Goldfinger**. These, he knew, were fairly commonplace; it was *Casino Royale* that was the prize. Only 4750 copies were printed and most of them had gone to libraries. No one knew how many had survived the forty-three years since *Casino Royale* was first published, on 13 April 1952, though in this condition – virtually mint – there would certainly be fewer than a hundred in the world. The book had cost Turner £400 in 1982, a price he could afford but which still startled him.

The bartering which followed was not to Turner's taste. He was already upset and the last thing he wanted was a prolonged haggle. But at last it was over and a deal was struck.

Turner left the shop with a cheque for $6000, which he folded and placed in his passport. He drove to a bank in Beverly Hills and was shown to a private booth where he exchanged the bookshop's cheque for traveller's cheques. He then drove back to the Ritz-Carlton and did twenty lengths of the pool before checking out. He drove to the airport, returned the Mercedes, and had a ham and rye sandwich, generously spread with mustard, and a double Jack Daniel's at the airport restaurant. He cursed the fact that he could not smoke inside the terminal, not even in the First Class lounge, so he strolled about outside, lit a Pall Mall and waited for the Air New Zealand flight to Papeete and Rarotonga.

Casino Royale had paid for two weeks in the South Pacific, and Turner convinced himself that it was a fair exchange and that he would not miss the familiar sight of those first editions on his bookshelf at home. After all, the man Bond had been a teenage obsession. Turner had seen *Dr No* on its release in 1962, at the Essoldo in Leigh-on-Sea, and had never seen a British movie quite like it before.

He adored its insolent style – the glamour of Jamaica, the way that **Sean Connery** padded like a leopard through hotel lobbies or casinos, the flash of a blue fiver as he tipped a doorman, the way the actor could make his nostrils flare, the way he emptied his **Walther PPK** into Anthony Dawson. Yes, this was quite different, an American picture with an English and Scots accent, filled with an elegance of scene yet having the low-budget quaintness that one associated with Merton Park studios. It was a heady mixture and a smash hit.

Turner read the novel on which the film claimed to be based and was startled by how much better it was than the movie. He quickly devoured Fleming's other novels, then bought *You Only Live Twice* in hardback, thereby initiating his collection of first editions. Like so many boys of his age, he had found a role model – in the Bond

of the novels and in Sean Connery, even though they existed in
separate if parallel worlds. He smoked the fags with the three gold
rings, he drank vodka martinis and he wore black knitted ties, though
his balls were never assaulted by a carpet beater and he never battled
a giant squid.

Inevitably, the obsession faded, though the interest always remained.
What had begun as a schoolboy fantasy turned into a financial
investment which finally paid off in Los Angeles. And within a
month or two of his return from the South Pacific, Turner had all
but forgotten he had ever owned those **Flemings**.

Two years later his agent, Laura Morris, called.

'Bloomsbury would like you to write a book about *Goldfinger*,'
she said.

'I once owned a first edition of that,' said Turner ruefully.

Somehow his old and battered paperback, which he would have
to use for reference, wasn't the same at all. But Turner did as he was
told. He switched on his Umax computer and his NEC Multisync
Pro P750 colour monitor and started to write from A–Z.

ab initio ii

EYES ONLY
September 14th, 1964
From: Sir Miles Meservy
To: Prime Minister and First Lord of the Treasury
            Foreign and Commonwealth Secretary
            Secretary of State for Defence
            Governor of the Bank of England (item 2 only)
1.   You will recall, Sir, that a year ago we received an infor-
mal request for assistance from the Élysées Palace regarding a
perceived threat against the life of President de Gaulle. Our
Department became briefly involved when one of our agents
suspected that the name of the potential assassin might be Mr

Charles Calthrop, of 10 Mount Street, Mayfair. When this suspicion was passed on to MI5, it resulted in the French police eliminating a suspect whose real identity was never ascertained (I believe he subsequently posed as a Danish schoolteacher and a French war veteran). Unfortunately, the source of this information was acting without authority and he has since been transferred to clerical duties. But in view of the continuing investigation into this matter by MI5 and by the French police, who are acting under the personal supervision of the French President, I must advise you that 'Mr Calthrop' was an alias used by several members of my Department and that the real 'Mr Calthrop,' who returned from 'a fishing holiday' to find his apartment ransacked, was in fact an agent of ours – Number 007 – whom we thought could successfully execute the deception, which he did, at a moment's notice. Naturally, the Head of MI5 has not been informed about this and I respectfully suggest he be required to discreetly retreat from this investigation to save further embarrassment and to minimise what has already become a very serious breach of security. You may rest assured, Sir, that my Department no longer uses the name 'Calthrop.'

2.   This is a report on a recently concluded operation conducted by my Department in conjunction with the Central Intelligence Agency. A fuller account will be delivered to you in due course, when we have had an opportunity to debrief the agent, though his present whereabouts are unknown. However, I thought you should be in possession of a preliminary report in view of your Summit meeting tomorrow with President Johnson and because I believe that certain details of this operation will soon be made public in the pages of the Daily Express.

The facts are as follows:

An agent of ours, Number 007 (see also above report),

had successfully concluded an operation in Latin America by
destroying a plant used for the manufacture of heroin. Our
agent then flew to Miami where we ordered him to put
under surveillance Mr Auric Goldfinger (see earlier Reports
6502A, 7522B, FCO1163) whom we know to be involved
in international **gold** smuggling on a scale that threatens the
United Kingdom's economy and general financial stability.
We also believe Mr Goldfinger to be an agent of hostile
governments, specifically Red China and their client state,
North Korea.

Our information suggested that in Miami Mr Goldfinger
was committing a crime by cheating at cards another guest
at the hotel. Since our agent is an expert card player, we
ordered him to investigate. On entering Mr Goldfinger's suite,
he discovered a secretary, Miss **Jill Masterson**, spying on
the game below with a pair of binoculars and advising Mr
Goldfinger by radio communication. Our agent took control of the situation and spoke directly to Mr Goldfinger
through the radio, ordering him to lose and thus reimbursing
his stool pigeon with his losses. The next morning, Miss
Masterson was found dead in her room. Her body had been
covered with **gold paint** which resulted in death from suffocation. Our agent had been knocked unconscious in the
same room.

The unfortunate death of Miss Masterson had an emotional
impact on our agent – a weakness which has undermined
previous missions – and I warned him once again that his
work should never become a personal vendetta. Nevertheless,
I ordered him to resume his surveillance of Mr Goldfinger.
Following a briefing with the Governor of the Bank of England,
our agent was issued with a bar of gold bullion and authorised to
pose as a gold smuggler and engage Mr Goldfinger in a game of
golf, using the gold bar as bait. Again, Mr Goldfinger was found

to be a cheat though our agent successfully won the game and dutifully returned the gold bar to the Bank.

Our agent then tracked Mr Goldfinger across Europe to his factory in Switzerland which we believed was the centre of his smuggling operation. Our agent discovered Mr Goldfinger's modus operandi – his vintage Rolls-Royce (a familiar sight at the air ferry port at Lydd) was made of gold, melted down and rebuilt for the next illicit run – and the operation might have ended there were it not for the unfortunate intervention of the late Miss Masterson's sister [**Tilly Masterson**] who was intent on assassinating Mr Goldfinger. In the ensuing chase, Miss Masterson was murdered by Mr Goldfinger's henchman – a Korean mute known as **Oddjob** – and our agent was taken prisoner. This was at considerable cost to the tax payer since our agent's Aston Martin **DB5**, modified by our Department, was destroyed during the chase.

These events have only become apparent since our Department's search of Mr Goldfinger's premises in Switzerland where we discovered gold in the process of being melted down, the wreck of the Aston Martin and the body of Miss Masterson. At the time, though, we had no way of knowing what had happened; indeed, we believed that our agent had successfully infiltrated Mr Goldfinger's organisation and had been flown to Kentucky (USA) as his guest. But we must now assume that our agent was always Mr Goldfinger's prisoner and was in considerable personal danger. It is now clear that our agent also gained the confidence of a close associate of Mr Goldfinger's – a Miss **Pussy Galore** – who piloted the plane from Switzerland to Kentucky where Mr Goldfinger owns a stud farm.

While at Mr Goldfinger's stud farm, our agent fortunately overheard a briefing in which Mr Goldfinger announced his intention to mount an armed assault on **Fort Knox** (see attached papers on Fort Knox and **Major-General Henry Knox**) with the intention of exploding a nuclear device in the gold vault. This operation appears to have been underwritten by the government of Red China. The intention was clear: the gold reserves of the USA would be rendered valueless while Mr Goldfinger's personal horde would monopolise the world market.

Present at the stud farm briefing were almost all the leaders of America's crime syndicates who had been coerced into assisting Mr Goldfinger on various aspects of his plan. Our contacts at the FBI and the CIA have advised us that only one major crime boss – Mr Michael Corleone of Lake Tahoe, Nevada – declined Mr Goldfinger's invitation to attend. However, for reasons yet to be fully understood, all but one of these crime bosses were gassed to death during Mr Goldfinger's briefing. The remains of one further crime boss, **Mr Solo**, were later found in the wreckage of a Lincoln Continental car which had been crushed.

Also for reasons not yet fully understood, Miss Pussy Galore betrayed her employer and enabled the CIA and the FBI to perpetrate an elaborate hoax on Mr Goldfinger. His raid on Fort Knox, preceded by an aerial nerve gas attack, was effectively foiled and although he gained access to the gold vault, the nuclear device was disarmed only seconds before it was timed to detonate. Many of Mr Goldfinger's gang were killed in the action as well as several American servicemen. Forensic reports suggest that Dr Ling, the Chinese nuclear physicist, was shot and killed by friendly fire.

Mr Goldfinger himself evaded capture (my views on American military efficiency need no embellishment here) by posing as a US military officer aboard the plane which subsequently flew our agent to Washington. That plane crashed shortly afterwards and we must assume that Mr Goldfinger is dead. However, our agent has been found safe and well in a remote wildlife refuge in South Carolina in the company of Miss Pussy Galore. His arrival in Washington is now imminent. We have respectfully declined the President's offer of conferring upon our agent the Medal of Merit. However, in view of the circumstances, might I suggest a letter of commendation from Her Majesty?

See **Connery, Sean**.

Adam, Ken (b. 1921)

The Bond movies are a machine, a franchise, and, without denigrating the achievements of the producers, directors and other members of the team, the series owes most to two men: **Sean Connery** and the production designer Ken Adam. If Connery gave the films a palpably human superhero, Adam gave them their visual identity, their architectural foundations and their style. Though his best work is to be found in the two very different films he made for Stanley Kubrick – *Dr Strangelove*, which used studio sets throughout, and *Barry Lyndon*, for which Adam adapted many stately homes in Britain and Ireland – he has become so closely associated with the success of the Bond films that, as a consequence, he is quite possibly the only production designer people have ever heard of.

Ken Adam was born in 1921 in Berlin, at a time when the German cinema was about to enter its richest phase with the birth of Expressionism, which saw Fritz Lang and F. W. Murnau at the height of their powers. But in 1934, a year after Hitler came to power, Adam's family moved to England, enrolling him at St Paul's and then the Bartlett School of Architecture. He was an RAF fighter pilot during World War II.

He got his first film job in 1947, working as a draughtsman on *This Was a Woman*, and over the next decade he worked his way up through the ranks – as assistant art director and associate art director, in which capacity he worked on **Guy Hamilton**'s sophomore feature *The Intruder*. In 1956 he got his first film as art director – a B-movie called *Soho Incident* which featured the American actor Martin Benson, who later played **Mr Solo**.

In 1959 Adam started calling himself a production designer, and thus began his long and illustrious career. He worked twice for **Broccoli**'s Warwick Films – *In the Nick* and *The Trials of Oscar Wilde* – before designing the sets for *Dr No*. Apparently, it was his work on *Dr No* that attracted the attention of Stanley Kubrick and it was because he was working on *Dr Strangelove* that he missed out on *From Russia With Love*.

His work is distinguished by a clever use of light and perspective, as well as strong architectural shapes and forms – the triangular War Room in *Dr Strangelove*, for instance, which is oddly mirrored by **Goldfinger**'s 'Rumpus Room', and the dazzling **gold** vault of **Fort Knox**. His sets are also notable for a sense of irony and humour; the sets themselves seem to match not only the laconic humour of Bond but also the fascist fantasies of his adversaries. Literally and artistically, Adam is a child of Expressionism.

Although the Bond films gave Adam some bizarre challenges, he found working for the team of **Saltzman** and **Broccoli** rather depressing at times. 'On *Goldfinger*,' he said, 'I had a completely free hand and hardly any comment on my designs, which isn't very satisfying. The Bond films are the spectacles of the twentieth century. They present things slightly larger than life and this concept was important in designing the sets. On all films I like to be guided almost entirely by my imagination.'

For *Goldfinger* Adam was presented with a formidable challenge. Cubby Broccoli asked him to create 'a cathedral of gold':

I reproduced the outside of Fort Knox exactly and invented the inside,' Adam recalled. 'A bank vault, even if it happens to be the biggest gold depository in the world, is not interesting visually to an audience. Gold is never stored very high because it's very heavy. I came up with the idea of having a gigantic 40-foot-high arch: a grill with gold stacked high behind it to separate it from the audience and make them immediately aware of the gold. It was completely impractical but as so often happens, UA [**United Artists**] got over three hundred letters which asked how were we allowed to film inside Fort Knox when the President of the United States was not allowed inside.

Adam designed the sets for seven Bond movies, creating the vast volcano set for *You Only Live Twice* as well as the interior of the supertanker for *The Spy Who Loved Me*, which were the undoubted stars of the films. He ended his association with *Moonraker*, a feeble **rip-off** of *Stars Wars* and arguably the worst film in the series.

'They were an enormous amount of work,' said Adam, explaining his retirement from the series.

They're not only a design challenge, which didn't worry me, but the whole logistics and organisation did – when you had sometimes four units shooting all over the world at the same time and you had to service those units with props, with sets, whatever. The production team had changed and, in my opinion, not for the better – except for Cubby Broccoli who is an old friend and who I worked for even before the Bonds. I just would not have felt comfortable being associated with some of the new people involved. Also, I like to think that by then I had reached a stage in my career when, as a rule, I only do the films I want to do.

The movies which Adam has designed since *Moonraker* are a mixed bunch, many of them for friends like Herbert Ross and Norman Jewison. He won an Oscar in 1975 for *Barry Lyndon* and a second Oscar in 1995 for performing a similar job on *The Madness of King George*.

Filmography

- *Feature films as draughtsman:*
1947 *This Was a Woman* (dir. Tim Whelan)
1948 *Lucky Mascot* (dir. Thornton Freeland)
1948 *Queen of Spades* (dir. Thorold Dickinson)
1948 *Third Time Lucky* (dir. Gordon Parry)
- *Feature films as assistant art director:*
1948 *Obsession* (dir. Edward Dmytryk)
1950 *Your Witness* (dir. Robert Montgomery)
1951 *Captain Horatio Hornblower RN* (dir. Raoul Walsh)
1953 *The Intruder* (dir. Guy Hamilton)
1953 *Star of India* (dir. Arthur Lubin)
1955 *Helen of Troy* (dir. Robert Wise)
- *Feature films as associate art director:*
1952 *The Crimson Pirate* (dir. Robert Siodmak)
1953 *The Master of Ballantrae* (dir. William Keighley)
- *Feature films as art director:*
1956 *Soho Incident* (dir. Vernon Sewell)
1956 *Child in the House* (dir. Cy Endfield)
1957 *Around the World in Eighty Days* (dir. Michael Anderson)
1958 *Gideon's Day* (dir. John Ford)
1958 *Ten Seconds to Hell* (dir. Robert Aldrich)
1959 *Beyond This Place* (dir. Jack Cardiff)
1959 *The Angry Hills* (dir. Robert Aldrich)
- *Feature films as production designer:*
1959 *The Rough and the Smooth* (dir. Robert Siodmak)
1959 *In the Nick* (dir. Ken Hughes)
1960 *Let's Get Married* (dir. Peter Graham Scott)

1960   *The Trials of Oscar Wilde* (dir. Ken Hughes)
1961   *Sodom and Gomorrah* (dir. Robert Aldrich)
1962   *Dr No* (dir. Terence Young)
1962   *In the Cool of the Day* (dir. Robert Stevens)
1963   *Dr Strangelove* (dir. Stanley Kubrick)
1964   *Woman of Straw* (dir. Basil Dearden)
1964   *Goldfinger* (dir. Guy Hamilton)
1965   *The Ipcress File* (dir. Sidney J. Furie)
1965   *Thunderball* (dir. Terence Young)
1966   *Funeral in Berlin* (dir. Guy Hamilton)
1967   *You Only Live Twice* (dir. Lewis Gilbert)
1968   *Chitty Chitty Bang Bang* (dir. Ken Hughes)
1969   *Goodbye Mr Chips* (dir. Herbert Ross)
1970   *The Owl and the Pussycat* (dir. Herbert Ross)
1971   *Diamonds Are Forever* (dir. Guy Hamilton)
1972   *Sleuth* (dir. Joseph L. Mankiewicz)
1973   *The Last of Sheila* (dir. Herbert Ross)
1975   *Barry Lyndon* (dir. Stanley Kubrick)
1976   *The Seven Per Cent Solution* (dir. Herbert Ross)
1977   *The Spy Who Loved Me* (dir. Lewis Gilbert)
1979   *Moonraker* (dir. Lewis Gilbert)
1981   *Pennies From Heaven* (dir. Herbert Ross)
1985   *Agnes of God* (dir. Norman Jewison)
1985   *King David* (dir. Bruce Beresford)
1986   *Crimes of the Heart* (dir. Bruce Beresford)
1988   *The Deceivers* (dir. Nicholas Meyer)
1989   *Dead Bang* (dir. John Frankenheimer)
1990   *The Freshman* (dir. Andrew Bergman)
1991   *Company Business* (dir. Nicholas Meyer)
1991   *The Doctor* (dir. Randa Haines)
1993   *Addam's Family Values* (dir. Barry Sonnenfeld)
1993   *Undercover Blues* (dir. Herbert Ross)
1994   *The Madness of King George* (dir. Nicholas Hytner)

1996   *Bogus* (dir. Norman Jewison)
1997   *In And Out* (dir. Frank Oz)

advertising

See **product placement**.

Æon, eon

1647. [-eccl. L. *æon*] 1. An age, or the whole duration, of the world, or of the universe; an immeasurable period of time; eternity. 2. The personification of an age. In *Platonic philosophy*, A power existing from eternity 1647.

   1. Æons of æons CARLYLE. 2. The Valentinian thirty Gods and Æons CUDWORTH. Hence Æonial, Æonian *adjs.* everlasting. (*The Shorter Oxford English Dictionary*)

Aston Martin

See **DB5**.

B

Barry, John

See **title number**.

Bassey, Shirley

Singer who performed the **title number**.

Benson, Martin

Actor who played **Mr Solo**.

Blackman, Honor

Actress who played **Pussy Galore**.

Bond, James

See **Connery, Sean; dealers**.

Bond girls

See **Masterson, Jill; Masterson, Tilly; Miss Moneypenny; Pussy Galore**.

bowler hat

See **Oddjob**.

brand names

See **DB5**; **Johnson, Paul**; **Morland & Co.**; **product placement**.

Broccoli, Albert R. (Cubby) (1909–96)

Albert R. Broccoli was a tall, imposing figure who, unlike his partner **Harry Saltzman**, was happy just to make Bond movies. While Broccoli never attempted to expand or diversify, which may betray a narrow outlook and belies his addiction to gambling, Saltzman was always buying companies and dreaming up new schemes and movies. Perhaps Broccoli was the shrewder of the two; the franchise was safely bland in his hands and he successfully steered it right up until *Goldeneye* and his death in 1996.

Albert Romolo Broccoli was born in Queens, New York, on 15 April 1909. A second-generation American, his father was a bricklayer, even though he was a qualified engineer. His uncle, a native of Calabria in the south of Italy, once had the idea of crossing the cauliflower with the rabe, and thus broccoli was born and given the family name. It was that same uncle who was the first to export broccoli to America, and as a child Albert would wash and pack his uncle's vegetables in Long Island and take them by horse-drawn cart to the market in Harlem.

However, vegetable farming was not for him, and he later discovered that his forbears were not farmers but affluent writers and politicians from Lombardy. As a young man, Broccoli managed a firm which made coffins and then, in San Francisco, he sold cosmetics and jewellery, and shared a pokey one-room apartment with a rat. 'I really looked forward to seeing that rat,' he once said. 'He became a friend.'

At least, this is the official biography. Broccoli knew that movie moguls invariably started out by making gloves or dealing in scrap metal or selling coffins (after all, **Sean Connery** polished them in Scotland). Movie moguls started small, humbly, and they lived with vermin, which was fine training for a career in the movie industry.

Moving to Hollywood in the 1930s Broccoli sold Christmas trees (his future wife, Dana, bought one) and landed himself a job in the mailroom at 20th Century-Fox. Exactly how Broccoli inveigled himself into the upper echelons of Hollywood is not entirely clear, but the story goes that he was in a bar when a man stood next to him, spun a silver dollar and asked Broccoli to call heads or tails. Broccoli called and lost. The man spun again and Broccoli lost another dollar. But he gained a friend – Howard Hughes – and was put to work on Hughes's current film, *The Outlaw* (1943), with Jane Russell. It was perhaps this film which began Broccoli's obsession with tits, since the whole movie was a celebration of Russell's pendulous pair, which had been corralled into a special bra, designed by Hughes himself.

After his war service, which he finished with the rank of lieutenant, Broccoli joined Famous Artists, a talent agency run by Charles K. Feldman, who, coincidentally, wound up owning the screen rights to *Casino Royale*. Broccoli got the job through his cousin, Pat de Cicco, who also gave him the nickname 'Cubby,' from a cartoon character of the 1920s called Ish Kabibble. At first Broccoli was called Kabibble, then Kabby, then Cubby. It's said that his teddy-bear looks made the name stick.

As an agent, Broccoli was finally making some money, which he'd gamble away in Las Vegas, often in the company of Hughes. But his goal – to become an independent producer – was always beyond his reach. Maybe there were too many producers in Hollywood, but few had Broccoli's connections. But Broccoli also lacked 'vision'. Regarded as trustworthy, he was not a man who got fired up; what he needed was a moribund climate in which his modest ideas could be realised.

So Broccoli teamed up with Irving Allen and moved to Britain, rather in the manner of Peachy and Dravot in Kipling's *The Man Who Would Be King*. The British were slow and retrograde: these two Americans would run rings around them. But there were also tax loopholes, and the common language meant that Hollywood stars whose careers were on the slide could make movies in Britain for modest fees and maximum publicity. And because all the major Hollywood studios had profits locked in Britain, Broccoli's safe pair of hands enabled the studios to spend their money prudently, on what Broccoli later called 'profitable crap'. He was therefore the Gerald Ratner of movie producers.

Thus Warwick Films was born, the name coming from the hotel where Broccoli and Allen stayed when they were in New York. Howard Hughes bankrolled their first picture, *The Red Beret*, which was directed by Terence Young, and then Columbia came in as Warwick's principal distributor and partner.

Broccoli's partner at Warwick, Irving Allen, was another light-weight opportunist, though he had won Oscars in the 1940s for two short films, *Forty Boys and a Song* and *Climbing the Matterhorn*. He came into contact with Broccoli on *Avalanche* (1946), a snowbound adventure which was produced by Broccoli's cousin Pat de Cicco. Allen followed it with another dud called *High Conquest*, which he produced himself and which was a fictionalised version of his Matterhorn documentary. But after two further forgotten action films Allen quit as a director and turned producer. That way he could order directors around and not leave his office. Allen, it is said, could be brusque; Broccoli was quieter and got on with the paperwork. Everybody loved him.

The movies they made – around twenty of them in seven years – were slick, unpretentious packages with brawny heroes like Victor Mature and busty heroines, like Anita Ekberg in *Zarak*. There is not a minor classic, much less a *film maudit* amongst them, not even the marvellously titled *Odongo*. But Warwick was a team with a house writer, **Richard Maibaum**, and a house cameraman, **Ted Moore**, to whom Broccoli was unswervingly loyal.

Warwick's sole bid for a classier market, *The Trials of Oscar*

Wilde, was designed by **Ken Adam** and shot by Moore in 70 mm Technirama. Despite its qualities, notably the performance of Peter Finch, the picture was hamstrung by a rival film about Wilde and by its unjudicious release in New York on the Jewish Day of Atonement, which guaranteed empty theatres. The movie flopped and Warwick was virtually put out of business. Broccoli and Allen went their separate ways, Allen into the wilderness for four years and Broccoli into the Bond business with another volatile partner, Harry Saltzman.

Filmography

(All titles as producer or co-producer. Where Warwick Films is listed as producer, Allen and Broccoli took no personal screen credit.)

1953　*The Red Beret* (co-prod. Irving Allen; dir. Terence Young)

1954　*Hell Below Zero* (co-prod. Irving Allen; dir. Mark Robson)

1954　*The Black Knight* (co-prod. Irving Allen; dir. Tay Garnett)

1954　*A Prize of Gold* (co-prod. Irving Allen; dir. Mark Robson)

1955　*Cockleshell Heroes* (co-prod. Irving Allen; dir. Jose Ferrer)

1955　*The Gamma People* (Warwick Films; dir. John Gilling)

1956　*Safari* (co-prod. Irving Allen; dir. Terence Young)

1956　*Odongo* (Warwick Films; dir. John Gilling)

1956　*Zarak* (co-prod. Irving Allen; dir. Terence Young)

1957　*Fire Down Below* (co-prod. Irving Allen; dir. Robert Parrish)

1957　*High Flight* (Warwick Films; dir. John Gilling)

1957　*Interpol* (co-prod. Irving Allen; dir. John Gilling)

1957　*How to Murder a Rich Uncle* (Warwick Films; dirs Nigel Patrick [uncredited], Max Varnel)

1958　*No Time to Die* (Warwick Films; dir. Terence Young)

1958　*The Man Inside* (Warwick Films; dir. John Gilling)

1959　*The Bandit of Zhobe* (Warwick Films; dir. John Gilling)

1959　*The Killers of Kilimanjaro* (co-prod. Irving Allen; dir. Richard Thorpe)

1959　*Idle on Parade* (Warwick Films; dir. John Gilling)

1959   *In the Nick* (Warwick Films; dir. Ken Hughes)

1959   *Jazzboat* (Warwick Films; dir. Ken Hughes)

1960   *The Trials of Oscar Wilde* (co-prod. Irving Allen; dir. Ken Hughes)

1961   *Johnny Nobody* (co-prod. Irving Allen; dir. Nigel Patrick)

1962   *Dr No* (co-prod. Harry Saltzman; dir. Terence Young)

1963   *Call Me Bwana* (co-prod. Harry Saltzman; dir. Gordon Douglas)

1963   *From Russia With Love* (co-prod. Harry Saltzman; dir. Terence Young)

1964   *Goldfinger* (co-prod. Harry Saltzman; dir. **Guy Hamilton**)

1965   *Thunderball* (co-prod. Harry Saltzman; dir. Terence Young)

1967   *You Only Live Twice* (co-prod. Harry Saltzman; dir. Lewis Gilbert)

1968   *Chitty Chitty Bang Bang* (sole prod.; dir. Ken Hughes)

1969   *On Her Majesty's Secret Service* (co-prod. Harry Saltzman; dir. Peter Hunt)

1971   *Diamonds Are Forever* (co-prod. Harry Saltzman; dir. Guy Hamilton)

1973   *Live and Let Die* (co-prod. Harry Saltzman; dir. Guy Hamilton)

1974   *The Man With the Golden Gun* (co-prod. Harry Saltzman; dir. Guy Hamilton)

1977   *The Spy Who Loved Me* (sole prod.; dir. Lewis Gilbert)

1979   *Moonraker* (sole prod.; dir. Lewis Gilbert)

1981   *For Your Eyes Only* (sole prod.; dir. John Glen)

1983   *Octopussy* (sole prod.; dir. John Glen)

1985   *A View to a Kill* (co-prod. Michael G. Wilson; dir. John Glen)

1987   *The Living Daylights* (co-prod. Michael G. Wilson; dir. John Glen)

1989   *Licence to Kill* (co-prod. Michael G. Wilson; dir. John Glen.)

See **dealers**.

C

cars

See **DB5**.

Collins, Michael

See **his** *Meister's* **voice**.

come again? (1)

Within the film [*Goldfinger*], the sexuality of Bond/**Connery** is
established in a number of ways. The first and most obvious way
is through the main narrative in which Bond is sexually attractive
to a number of women. The film shares this in common with the
book. Here the role of women operates precisely to signify Bond's
sexuality, but the Bond/Connery figure is also privileged as the
object of the look. As we have already remarked, existing work
in this area suggests that in the complex interaction of different
looks from different places in the cinema, it is the body of the
woman or women which constitutes the point of spectacle. [Laura]
Mulvey suggests two ways in which the spectator is implicated
in the system of looks established in the cinema. In the first
place, the spectator can be in direct scophilic contact with an
object of desire. In the second place, he or she can be fascinated
with the image of his or her like, identifying with his ego ideal
and thus gaining control and possession of the desired object in

the diegesis. In *Goldfinger*, while women undoubtedly constitute one direct object of scophilic desire, the Connery/Bond figure is also inscribed within the looks of the film as a direct object of desire.

(Tony Bennett and Janet Woollacott, *Bond and Beyond: The Political Career of a Popular Hero*, Macmillan Education, 1987)

come again? (2)

In the majority of cases, **Bond** is sent on his mission either symbolically castrated, without a gun, or as the bearer of a gun-cum-phallus donated by **M** and heavily invested with his phallic authority. The threat which the villain articulates is that of real castration . . . . Of course, in such instances, it is not merely Bond's vitals that are threatened, but Bond himself and everything that has been invested in him. The threat posed by the villain is that Bond, as emissary of the English phallus, extended for 'overseas duty,' might be cut off.

(Tony Bennett and Janet Woollacott, *Bond and Beyond: The Political Career of a Popular Hero*, Macmillan Education, 1987)

come again? (3)

Tatiana's role [in *From Russia With Love*] is not merely that of cunt-bait set to trap the English cock . . . . she is also the centre of the enigma within a narrative, a disturbance in the world of signs, a point where word and meaning fail to coincide . . . . Her behaviour constitutes an enigma which **Bond** has to resolve . . . . Drawn forth from England, then, solely in order to be killed in circumstances that will compromise England as he withdraws with his prize, Bond frustrates the villain's conspiracy by an unexpected piece of phallic improvisation.

(Tony Bennett and Janet Woollacott, *Bond and Beyond: The Political Career of a Popular Hero*, Macmillan Education, 1987)

Connery, Neil

Neil Connery looks almost exactly like his older brother, **Sean Connery**, which is both a glory and a curse. Occasionally pestered by the press, and often mistaken for his brother by people in the street, he lived through the Bondmania era with his wife and two daughters in a council house in Clermiston, a suburb of Edinburgh.

Neil Connery liked to mind his own business, which was plastering walls of newly built houses. But brothers, even plasterers, are susceptible. Like Terry Major Ball, the brother of the ex-Prime Minister, Neil Connery was lured into the limelight and promptly made a fool of himself. What he needed was sound advice; what he had was a name, a face and a bottomless reservoir of gullibility.

When he mislaid his plastering kit he was promptly fired by the firm of builders he worked for. Inevitably, the story leaked out to the newspapers, even as far as Rome, where a minor producer, Dario Sabatello, had what he might have considered a brainwave. If James Bond had a brother, well, the possibilities were endless . . .

What followed was a minor classic of movie hype. Having secured Neil Connery, Sabatello got himself a director, a script and a title: *Operation Kid Brother*. **United Artists** financed the package and somehow veterans of earlier Bond adventures were pressed into service – Bond regulars **Bernard Lee** and Lois Maxwell were joined by Anthony Dawson from *Dr No*, Adolfo Celi from *Thunderball* and Daniella Bianchi from *From Russia With Love*, who, like so many of the **Bond girls**, found that being Bond's girlfriend led merely to a life of fleeting celebrity.

Operation Kid Brother, or *OK Connery*, as it was also known, had a music score by Ennio Morricone and a plot about world domination, plastic surgery, half the world's gold reserves, radioactive carpets, hypnotism and Scottish archers dressed in kilts. Critics at the time were unusually kind, admiring the film's spirit if not its technical finesse. Every movie is made for money, they seemed to say, but not every movie has the temerity to come out and say so. Needless to say, it tanked.

Neil Connery busked it afterwards, getting roles in schlock like *The Body Stealers* and TV series like *Taggart*, and giving his brother not so much a run for his money as a round of golf whenever he was in Scotland. Rumours that it was Neil, not Sean, who appeared in the pre-credit sequence of *From Russia With Love* have yet to be substantiated.

See **rivals and rip-offs**.

Connery, Sean (b. 1930)

Picture the scene. It is late 1963 and *The Sunday Times* colour magazine has commissioned a photo-shoot in a studio in Kensington. Lord Snowdon is crouched behind his camera, checking the focus and lighting as eight young men stand smiling or glowering in front of a dark grey-blue sheet. The object of the photograph is to illustrate a feature article written by the paper's film **critic**, Dilys Powell, about the new stars of the British cinema.

The eight men are roughly the same age and they have juggled ruthlessly for position in the picture. They are Alan Bates (29), Michael Caine (30), Sean Connery (33), Tom Courtenay (26), Albert Finney (27), James Fox (24), Richard Harris (33) and Terence Stamp (24). All of them have become stars, some more recently than others, and Miss Powell will write about their backgrounds, note each of their achievements and rashly speculate on which of them will still be a star in thirty-five years' time.

Miss Powell plumps for Finney, Harris and O'Toole, a safe choice since all of them have already starred in some prestigious films – Finney's *Tom Jones* has proved to be a box-office bonanza; *Lawrence of*

Arabia made Peter O'Toole a household name overnight; and Harris
has already appeared opposite Marlon Brando in *Mutiny on the Bounty*,
while his starring role in Lindsay Anderson's *This Sporting Life* has
received rave reviews.

All eight of them are perceived to have swept away an entire
generation of British movie stars – the Richard Todd–Kenneth More
anyone-for-tennis, chocks–away, up-periscope generation. All but
the aristocratic James Fox, who made his mark in *The Servant*,
come from either middle-class, working-class or underclass backgrounds, and all but two are allied to the social-realist movement,
which produced films such as *Saturday Night and Sunday Morning,
The Loneliness of the Long Distance Runner, A Kind of Loving* and
Term of Trial.

Caine and Connery are the outsiders since neither has had a
classical training, nor aligned himself to social realism. Caine has
been a B-movie actor, though his role in *Zulu*, in which he played
a foppish officer, has made him a star and **Harry Saltzman** has hired
him to play an off-the-peg James Bond in *The Ipcress File*. Which brings
us to Connery, another B-movie actor, who rocketed to fame as 007
in *Dr No* and *From Russia With Love*. As popular as these films are, it
is thought likely he will be typecast for the remainder of his career
and that when the Bond films fall from public favour Connery will
be unable to reinvent himself.

Born in 1930 in the drab Edinburgh suburb of Fountainbridge, a
place which smells of breweries, Connery was christened Thomas,
and was the son of a delivery driver and a charlady. His progress
from the Edinburgh slums, through menial jobs like milkman and
coffin polisher, then the Navy, needs no reiteration here. He became
an artists' model, then a body-builder, and came second in a Mr
Universe competition, but without any obvious fetishisation of his
own physique. He changed his name to Sean (as a kid he was
nicknamed Shane) and turned down Matt Busby, who offered him
£25 a week to play for Manchester United – he might have perished

at Munich. Instead, he turned to acting, sang in the chorus of *South Pacific*, did some plays, a little TV and some movies before he was considered for *Dr No*.

Saltzman and **Broccoli** liked the way Sean Connery moved. After one early meeting at their offices, they went to the window and watched him as he crossed the street. There was a purposefulness and a cat-like grace that appealed to them and which sealed Connery's fate as a film star. Afterwards, when the producers held meetings with financiers from **United Artists**, they would summon Connery to their office and ask him to turn around and pace the room – just like a model, or an actress auditioning, or a piece of meat. Connery never forgave Saltzman for that and his relations with him quickly soured. And as the Bond movies became a goldmine, Connery took Saltzman and Broccoli to court, claiming he was being chiselled out of his proper dues. It took years for the matter to be settled, expensively and, eventually, amicably. During the production of *Thunderball* he said:

> The only real difficulty I found in playing Bond was that I had to start from scratch. Not even **Ian Fleming** knew much about Bond. He has no mother. He has no father. He doesn't come from anywhere and he hadn't been anywhere when he became 007. He was born, kerplump, 33 years old. Bond is very much for breaking the rules. He enjoys freedom that the normal person doesn't get. He likes to eat. Likes to drink. Likes his girls. He is rather cruel, sadistic. He takes in a big percentage of the fantasies of lots of people.

It was when Connery was in Japan filming *You Only Live Twice* that he decided he was through with Bond. Paparazzi pursued him into the lavatory and photographed him taking a leak, and the clamour was simply unbearable. And by then, of course, the special effects and **gadgets** had taken over, and Connery shrewdly saw that he was becoming an extra in his own movie. He had also become a cult, denied any kind of private life. He was public property.

'I had no idea of that scale of reverence and pressure,' he said. 'It was around the same time as the Beatles. The difference of course was that there were four of them to kick it around and blame each other.'

So after *You Only Live Twice* he said 'Never again'. Then he did it again, in *Diamonds Are Forever*, having negotiated a massive fee, which he donated to the Scottish International Educational Trust. After *Diamonds Are Forever* he said 'Never again' again. Then he made *Never Say Never Again*, which was *Thunderball* all over again, and even now they are thinking of remaking it once more.

When Ian Fleming first met Connery he was dismissive; he thought the actor was an 'overgrown stuntman'. But later on Fleming warmed to Connery, though of course it was in his interest to do so. They met in London and then in Jamaica when *Dr No* was in production. Fleming took Connery to meet Noël Coward, who said, 'So you're going to play Bond. Dreary slob, isn't he?' Then Coward asked Connery if his plentiful pectoral fur was going to be shaved off. Connery admitted this was a possibility. 'Be assured they will, dear boy. Ian will insist. You see, he'll be terribly jealous because he hasn't got any.'

Connery grew into the role and made it his own. In sections of *Dr No* he is clearly uncertain, most notably in the early scenes, where he just has to sit, hold a drink in his hand and ask dumb questions at the country club in Jamaica. But at the gambling table, or when he's required to walk, or fight, or kill, or flare his nostrils at Dr No himself, Connery is attractively insolent and a real physical and sexual threat. By the time of *Goldfinger* he had the part to a tee, handling with ease the awkward stud farm terrace dialogue scene with **Goldfinger** and the long passages when he has nothing to do.

But Connery's greatest achievement is not any one individual performance but his Houdini-like escape from the straitjacket, or dinner jacket, of Bond. Because he lacked his own hair, he was able to forge parallel careers – a bald one and a bewigged one, until it no longer mattered. Hitchcock saw the sadism of Bond (and his commercial potential) and used it to powerful effect by casting Connery as Mark Rutland in *Marnie*. Then Connery followed *Goldfinger* with *The Hill* for Sidney Lumet, the director who saw most clearly the fine character actor behind the popular image. Unlike his mate Michael Caine, Connery has always been fairly discriminating in his choice of roles, only appearing in a few outright duds.

Then in 1975 came his *annus mirabilis*. Connery starred in three magnificent historical epics – John Milius's Arabian swashbuckler *The Wind and the Lion*, John Huston's *The Man Who Would Be King*, in which he was superbly teamed with Caine, and Richard Lester's melancholic *Robin and Marian*, arguably the greatest of the three. Whether brandishing a sabre in Arab robes, or scratching his arse as he wakes in Sherwood Forest, or literally losing his head to a daft notion of imperialism, Connery gave life to historical characters and carried a deep nobility as well as his trademark laconic humour. These three movies showed his maturity as an actor, nourished his own nationalist idealism, and did little for his career. None of them were exactly flops, but none made more than marginal profits.

In 1979 Connery became the first major actor to sign with Creative Artists, the newly formed talent agency run by Michael Ovitz. It is said that CAA transformed Connery's career, but it took a little time because *The Man With the Deadly Lens* and *Five Days One Summer* were box-office disasters. And the commercial success of *Never Say Never Again* seemed to belong to another actor entirely.

His fortunes changed in 1986, when he starred in the film version of Umberto Eco's *The Name of the Rose*, playing a monk who investigates a series of murders at a monastery – a sort of Sherlock Holmes in a cassock. Then the following year Brian De Palma cast him as an Irish cop in his gangster saga *The Untouchables*. Playing opposite Kevin Costner, Connery was a father figure, showing the younger man how to shoot straight and how to outwit Al Capone's prohibition scams, and he was granted a hero's death, drenched in blood and nobility. It was a tremendous, charismatic performance which won Connery an Academy Award as Best Supporting Actor.

Connery had now entered his final phase, as eminence grise and as one of the few older actors the young audience could look up to and respect. Steven Spielberg shrewdly noted this and cast Connery as Harrison Ford's father in *Indiana Jones and the Last Crusade*, a colossal hit everywhere. Almost 60, Connery was one of the most popular and highest paid stars in the world: he worked hard and consistently well, unlike Michael Caine, who merely worked.

He played celebrity golf and caused a mild controversy when a casual remark led people to believe that he had walked off the set of *Medicine Man* to play a round. He gave relatively few interviews and was known as a stickler for professionalism, for never being cheated out of his dues and for possessing a deep understanding of his own image. He would bring in writers to restyle his dialogue – John Milius for *The Hunt For Red October*, Dick Clement and Ian Le Frenais (who are writing a Lockerbie project for Connery) for *The Rock*. He was loyal, steadfast, a pillar of the Hollywood establishment, even though he had sued every studio in town.

Connery's relationship with Britain was always difficult. He has seemingly always been a tax exile, living with his second wife, Micheline, in Spain and the Bahamas. He espoused Scottish nationalism yet he appeared in advertisements for Japanese whisky. He has 'Scotland Forever' tattooed on his right arm and in recent years has played a significant role in the devolution debate. 'My allegiance to the Scottish National Party [SNP],' he said, 'is because they are the only ones who definitely want independence.'

Appearing in an SNP party political broadcast on TV, Connery echoed Mel Gibson's William Wallace in *Braveheart* when he said, 'We fight not for glory nor for wealth nor for honours, but only and alone we fight for freedom.'

The Tory party, led by John Major, wished to confer upon Connery a knighthood, though it fell to the newly elected Labour government to confirm it. However, because of Connery's passionate support for the SNP, the new Scottish secretary, Donald Dewar, a shrivelled, birdlike and repressed-looking man, decided that no Royal sword should ever dub this man a knight. The story leaked out to the press and became confused when Connery's Scottish nationalism seemed to be less of a problem to New Labour than some remarks he made to a *Playboy* interviewer in 1964: 'I don't think there is anything particularly wrong in hitting a woman – although I don't recommend doing it in the same way that you'd hit a man. An open-handed slap is justified if all other alternatives fail and there has been plenty of warning.'

Speaking from the Bahamas, Connery told BBC Radio 4's *Today* programme that he would have liked a knighthood despite it being an honour bestowed by the English establishment. The country agreed with him and Dewar looked very churlish. Had Dewar's boss, Tony Blair, been asked for a statement he might have smiled broadly and said, 'Look, we're tough on Connery and on the causes of Connery.'

Imagine the scene again . . . It is late 1998 and Lord Snowdon has in front of him the same eight actors. Miraculously, they have all survived, even Peter O'Toole, much of whose insides are missing and whose outside resembles an earthquake; his career is deeply mourned. Finney beams insouciance, portly but still handsome, stinking rich on fine racing stock, and only acting when the mood takes him. Bates and Courtenay skulk, wiry and hardly a presence at all, content to do the odd play and bathe briefly in the gleam of rave reviews. Fox looks almost the same, having gone through a brief retirement and a lasting commitment to religion, brought on partly by his involvement in *Performance*, that beggar's banquet of drugs and violence. Stamp is imperious in a black cape, his greying, thinning hair not denying his beauty, and, like O'Toole, he has become an autobiographer of note.

Harris looks as rancid as O'Toole and glares at Michael Caine, whom he has called 'a fucking restaurateur' in response to Caine's dismissive remarks about Harris's career. Caine himself stands proudly with his trademark glasses and his crinkly hair that looks like permed pubic. He has nearly a hundred movies behind him, many of them rubbish, yet he won an Oscar for a Woody Allen picture and has become something of an institution, occasionally jousting with the government of the day, moving loudly back to Britain from Beverly Hills and then, just as loudly, moving away to Florida, where he has opened another of his restaurants.

But of the eight, there is only one star, only one man who would be instantly recognised by today's moviegoers. And when, on the night of Monday 23 March 1998, the Academy of Motion Picture Arts and Sciences needed a major star to present the Oscar for Best Picture, they selected Connery from the dozens of previous Oscar winners gathered at the Shrine Auditorium for the seventieth anniversary ceremony. He walked out, tall and languid, silver of beard, laconic yet appreciative of the applause, a complex man. And the orchestra played the James Bond theme.

Filmography

1956   *No Road Back* (dir. Montgomery Tully)
1957   *Hell Drivers* (dir. C. Raker Endfield)
1957   *Time Lock* (dir. Gerald Thomas)
1957   *Action of the Tiger* (dir. Terence Young)
1958   *Another Time, Another Place* (dir. Lewis Allen)
1959   *Darby O'Gill and the Little People* (dir. Robert Stevenson)
1959   *Tarzan's Greatest Adventure* (dir. John Guillermin)
1961   *The Frightened City* (dir. John Lemont)
1961   *On the Fiddle* (US: *Operation Snafu*; dir. Cyril Frankel)
1962   *The Longest Day* (dirs Daryl F. Zanuck, Andrew Marton, Ken Annakin, Bernhard Wicki)

1962   *Dr No* (dir. Terence Young)

1963   *From Russia With Love* (dir. Terence Young)

1964   *Woman of Straw* (dir. Basil Dearden)

1964   *Marnie* (dir. Alfred Hitchcock)

1964   *Goldfinger* (dir. **Guy Hamilton**)

1965   *The Hill* (dir. Sidney Lumet)

1965   *Thunderball* (dir. Terence Young)

1966   *A Fine Madness* (dir. Irvin Kershner)

1967   *You Only Live Twice* (dir. Lewis Gilbert)

1968   *Shalako* (dir. Edward Dmytryk)

1969   *The Molly Maguires* (dir. Martin Ritt)

1969   *The Bowler and the Bunnet* (doc.; dir. Sean Connery)

1970   *The Red Tent* (dir. Mikhail K. Kalatozov)

1971   *The Anderson Tapes* (dir. Sidney Lumet)

1971   *Diamonds Are Forever* (dir. Guy Hamilton)

1972   *The Offence* (dir. Sidney Lumet)

1973   *Zardoz* (dir. John Boorman)

1974   *Ransom* (US: *The Terrorists*; dir. Casper Wrede)

1974   *Murder on the Orient Express* (dir. Sidney Lumet)

1975   *The Wind and the Lion* (dir. John Milius)

1975   *The Man Who Would Be King* (dir. John Huston)

1976   *Robin and Marian* (dir. Richard Lester)

1976   *The Next Man* (dir. Richard C. Sarafian)

1977   *A Bridge Too Far* (dir. Richard Attenborough)

1978   *The First Great Train Robbery* (dir. Michael Crichton)

1979   *Meteor* (dir. Ronald Neame)

1979   *Cuba* (dir. Richard Lester)

1981   *Time Bandits* (dir. Terry Gilliam)

1981   *Outland* (dir. Peter Hyams)

1982   *The Man With the Deadly Lens* (US: *Wrong Is Right*; dir. Richard Brooks)

1982   *Five Days One Summer* (dir. Fred Zinnemann)

1982   *Sean Connery's Edinburgh* (doc.; dir. Sean Connery)

1983   *Never Say Never Again* (dir. Irvin Kershner)

1984   *Sword of the Valiant* (dir. Stephen Weeks)

1986   *Highlander* (dir. Russell Mulcahy)

1986   *The Name of the Rose* (dir. Jean-Jacques Annaud)

1987   *The Untouchables* (dir. Brian de Palma)

1988   *The Presidio* (dir. Peter Hyams)

1988   *Memories of Me* (dir. Henry Winkler)

1989   *Indiana Jones and the Last Crusade* (dir. Steven Spielberg)

1989   *Family Business* (dir. Sidney Lumet)

1990   *The Hunt for Red October* (dir. John McTiernan)

1990   *The Russia House* (dir. Fred Schepisi)

1991   *Highlander II: The Quickening* (dir. Russell Mulcahy)

1991   *Robin Hood: Prince of Thieves* (dir. Kevin Reynolds)

1992   *Medicine Man* (dir. John McTiernan)

1993   *Rising Sun* (dir. Philip Kaufman)

1994   *A Good Man in Africa* (dir. Bruce Beresford)

1995   *First Knight* (dir. Jerry Zucker)

1995   *Just Cause* (dir. Arne Glimcher)

1996   *Dragonheart* (dir. Rob Cohen)

1996   *The Rock* (dir. Michael Bay)

1998   *The Avengers* (dir. Jeremiah Chechik)

1998   *Dancing about Architecture* (dir. William Carroll)

credits

See **gun barrel**; **title number**.

critics

See **history of the cinema**; **Houston, Penelope**; **Johnson, Paul**; *Sweet Movie*; *Time Out*; **Walker, Alexander**; **ugh!**; *Variety*; **whoops!**

Cubby

See **Broccoli, Albert R.**

D

DB5

How boring English cars are today, compared with those on offer in the late 1950s and early 1960s. Lucky indeed is the man who can remember seeing, let alone driving, a Jensen, an Allard or a Frazer Nash. They are all gone now, along with lesser marques like Hillman, Humber and Singer. Jaguar and Aston Martin are owned by the American conglomerate Ford, and as I write, the venerable Rolls-Royce and Bentley have been bought by the boys from Brazil.

Ian Fleming's taste in cars always tended towards the exotic. In 1930, when he was barely 21, he was cruising around Europe in a two-seater Buick. In the early years of his marriage he drove a more sedate and economical Morris Oxford, then a sportier 2.5-litre Riley. But Fleming's passion was always for American cars, which guzzled a year's production of Texan oil every mile and rode on suspension that might have been invented for Jane Russell's breasts. In the early 1950s he owned a Studillac, which was a Studebaker with a Cadillac engine. He later ran a 5-litre Ford Thunderbird convertible, then a 7-litre version and, finally, a black Studebaker Avanti, an amazingly sleak coupé which looked as if it was made on Mars. The fibreglass Avanti was so far ahead of its time and so costly to make that it forced Studebaker off the road and into the memory banks.

So fast, so exotic, so long ago . . . which is perhaps why the recent Bond movies and the novelistic clones by John Gardner have put

007 into cars which reflect the modern age of uniformity and which sacrifice adventure for ABS, amputation for airbags. Fleming's Bond would never have looked twice at a BMW, a car that today exudes Germanic efficiency and belongs to estate agents or travelling salesmen, who hang their Boss jackets in the rear windows. Even the BMW Z3, in which Pierce Brosnan tootles about in *Goldeneye*, is a hideous roadster, a salon hairdryer on wheels. The Z3 is not a car for James Bond; nor is the BMW 7-series which Brosnan drives in *Tomorrow Never Dies*. It's not British for starters. It's a car that BMW thought might be effectively launched on the market with the help of Bond's imprimatur, a slick piece of **product placement** which meant the movie-makers got the car for free and calculated its worth in screen time: about five minutes for the Z3 and a rather more thrilling five minutes for the 7-series. The 'ultimate driving machine' became the ultimate marketing machine, and for a while Bond was little more than an advertisement for the suits in Bavaria.

John Gardner gave Bond filtered cigarettes and accordingly put him into a Saab. Consider this sentence from Gardner's first Bond novel, *Licence Renewed*: 'James Bond changed down into third gear, drifted the Saab 900 Turbo into a tight left-hand turn, clinging to the grass verge, then put on a fraction more power to bring the car out of the bend.' One wants to add 'and into the car park at Safeway on the ring road north of Swindon'. It doesn't matter a hoot that Gardner tells us that the Saab has been personalised; the fact that it's a Saab makes Bond appear to be a cautious man, which he isn't. Saabs are for people who set out every day worrying that they're going to crash. They are identified with safety. They are deadly dull. Just like John Gardner, perhaps; certainly not like Bond.

There's no doubt, though, that Bond is a driver whose intolerance of bad or indecisive or female drivers verges on the psychotic. Take this passage from *Goldfinger*:

Bond saw a chance and picked up fifty yards, sliding into a

ten-yard gap left by a family saloon of slow reactions. The
man at the wheel, who wore that infallible badge of the bad
driver, a hat clamped firmly on the exact centre of his head,
hooted angrily. Bond reached out of the window and raised an
enigmatically clenched fist. The hooting stopped.

A few pages later Bond is discovered tail-gating a man he will later
know as **Oddjob**:

The Ford Popular was doing its forty. Why should anyone want
to go more than that respectable speed? The Ford obstinately
hunched its shoulders and kept on its course. Bond gave it a sharp
blast, expecting it to swerve. He had to touch his breaks when it
didn't. Damn the man! Of course! The usual tense figure, hands
held too high up on the wheel, and the inevitable hat, this time a
particularly hideous black bowler, square on a large bullet head.
Oh well, thought Bond, they weren't *his* stomach ulcers. He
changed down and contempuously slammed the DBIII past on
the inside. Silly bastard!

That's not machismo. That's road rage. The man needs to take a stress
pill and sit his test again. Or maybe drive a Saab.

Fleming gave Bond a Bentley, a grey 1933 convertible with a 4.5-
litre power unit plus an Amherst-Villiers supercharger. This vintage
car marked Bond out to be a bit of a bounder, like Terry-Thomas in
goggles and a leather helmet. The Bentley was a link with the past,
and esoteric enough to match the fancy fags and the other fads. But
when Bond needed a car for a mission Fleming knew the Bentley
wouldn't do, so he gave him an Aston Martin DBII – for *Moonraker*
– and a DBIII for *Goldfinger*. By the time the movie was made, it
was a DB5.

In the novel Bond takes the DBIII in preference to a Jaguar 3.4
because the Aston 'had the advantage of an up-to-date triptyque, an

inconspicuous colour – battleship grey – and certain extras which might or might not come in handy'. Compared to the DB5 in the movie, Fleming's extras are modest: variable front and rear lights, reinforced bumpers (in case Quintus Arrius ordered ramming speed), a Colt .45 in a concealed compartment and a sort of radar device called a Homer, ideal for tracking **Goldfinger**'s Roller across Europe. The car Bond drives in the novel is almost normal, except that it's an Aston Martin, which is as far from normal as you can get.

The Aston Martin has always been the most beautiful machine on the road. Only certain Ferraris and possibly the Mercedes Benz 300SL Gullwing and the Lamborghini Miura have ever rivalled it. The latest model, the DB7, is arguably the most gorgeous of all, a sort of cheetah with its mouth agape and its haunches tensed. It looks lithe and fast, and inside there is enough polished wood and soft leather to make you think the bar at the Connaught Hotel is about to break the sound barrier.

Aston Martin Lagonda Ltd was in deep trouble when **Harry Saltzman** and **Ken Adam** went round to request a couple of cars. The company was always in deep trouble because it had to sell a whopping number of cars every week – four to be precise – to make a profit. The company was built on love, passion and a tradition that stretched back to 1914.

It all started with a man called Lionel Walker Birch Martin, an Old Etonian whose fortune came from his family's granite quarries in Lincolnshire. Born in 1878, Martin himself co-owned a garage, Bamford & Martin, in Kensington and his passion was hill-climbing. On 9 May 1914 he successfully negotiated the then notorious half-mile Aston Clinton climb in Buckinghamshire. Martin's car was a Singer Ten, but when he eventually built his own car he combined his own name with the name of the hill – Aston Martin.

The first Aston Martin was a bizarre hybrid – a 1400cc Coventry Simplex engine was force-fed into the chassis of an Isotta Fraschini. Known as the 'coal scuttle', it was completed in 1915. Although

Martin built another prototype in 1920, it was not until 1923 that the first genuine Aston Martin was offered for sale. By then, Lionel Martin had spent more than £100,000 on the company, plus financial support for its racing cars from Count Louis Zborowski, the inventor of the Chitty Chitty Bang Bang, which Ian Fleming turned into a children's story.

In November 1924 the company was on the verge of bankruptcy and was sold to a Birmingham engineering firm, Renwick & Bertelli. Lionel Martin himself was thrown out of the company and later won damages in court of one farthing per seven counts of slander. Throughout the 1930s Martin was a successful racing driver – he drove Humbers, MGs, Rileys and Wolseley Hornets. After the war he turned to racing pedal cycles and on 14 October 1945 he was riding a tricycle near his home in Kingston-upon-Thames when he was hit by a car. He died a week later, aged 67.

Renwick & Bertelli began its ownership of Aston Martin by buying a new factory in Feltham, Middlesex. With backing from Vauxhall, the firm produced nineteen cars and had some racing successes before financial problems forced a sale to Frazer Nash, then to a shipowner named R. Gordon Sutherland. All of a sudden Aston Martin was a going concern, producing 105 cars in 1933 and maintaining its reputation on the track. A new model designed in 1936 by Bertelli (who had remained with the company) and Claude Hill took the company through to the end of the war.

In 1947 Aston Martin underwent its most significant upheaval when David Brown bought a controlling interest in the company for around £22,000. Born in 1908, Brown had been running his grandfather's firm since he was 28 years old. Based in Yorkshire, the firm specialised in farming equipment, specifically tractors, though the Brown family had always dabbled in cars. Brown was a dabbler, and a visionary.

The same year as Brown acquired Aston Martin, he bought the Lagonda company, which was based in Staines, close to the Aston plant in Feltham. By merging the two companies, Brown envisaged producing traditional Aston Martin sports cars as well as Lagonda saloons, both benefiting from shared technology.

Within a year of Brown's arrival, the Aston Martin DBI made its debut at the London Motor Show. Powered by a four-cylinder, 2-litre engine, the sleak roadster went hesitantly into production. Built 'For the Sportsman', it cost £2331, but only fifteen models were made before it was superceded by the DBII. This car – the prototype for all the DB series – was powered by the six-cylinder, 2.5-litre unit which came from the Lagonda and which had been designed by W. O. Bentley, the founder of the Bentley company before its merger with Rolls-Royce.

The DBII was an immediate success, selling half a dozen a week and clocking up an impressive series of triumphs on the racetrack. The DBIII and the DB2/4 followed when Brown moved the plant from Feltham to Newport Pagnell. The DB4 arrived in 1958 and was a considerable refinement on its predecessors. For those who wanted something a little faster, a version with a shorter wheelbase and cowled front lights, the DB4GT boasted a top speed of 172 mph, making it the fastest production car in the world.

The DB4 was plagued by reliability problems which were largely smoothed out when the DB5 entered production in July 1963. It had the same Superleggera coachwork as its predecessor and almost identical interior trim and instrumentation. Between July 1963 and September 1965, 1018 DB5s were produced. The power unit was a V8, 3995cc engine which developed 240 bhp at 5000 rpm. Top speed was around 145 mph and 0–60 mph was claimed at 8.1 seconds. To you and me, this means the car went quite quickly, though not nearly as fast as today's supercars. The showroom price was £4175, four times the average English person's annual income and more than the cost of most houses. By comparison, the DB5's principal competitor, the slightly faster E-Type Jaguar, cost a mere £1913.

Harry Saltzman demanded a more elaborate box of tricks than the DBIII which Bond drove in the novel. Ken Adam, **Guy Hamilton,**

Paul Dehn and **Richard Maibaum** all contributed ideas for the car. Bond's DB5 was originally red, then was repainted in a regular factory colour called Silver Birch, and it came with revolving number plates (BMT216A; 4711-EA-62; LU-6789), front machine-guns, an oil slick to throw pursuers off the road, a bullet-proof rear shield, a smokescreen and the Homer radar device. Also fitted but never seen in the film was a device which threw out dozens of nails from a rear light, extendable front bumpers for ramming and a special tray fitted beneath the driver's seat which contained an array of handguns. All these extras were fitted by the special effects designer John Stears and were fully functional. The only gadget which was a special effect were the scythes which extended from the wire wheels and which treated **Tilly Masterson**'s Ford Mustang like a can of baked beans. The idea was contributed by Maibaum, whose interest in ancient history had unearthed a similar device attached to Persian and, later, Roman chariots of the sort raced by Messala in *Ben Hur*. With all these louche extras, the completed car cost £15,000 and weighed some 300 lbs more than the standard version.

There was also, most famously, a passenger ejector seat, which meant that the Aston factory had to provide two cars. The second car was constructed with a detachable roof panel, and a seat used by the RAF which was called a Martin Baker was installed in the cabin. Because this seat looked nothing like a regular seat, the first car was used for interior shots and the second car was used for the exterior shot when Bond ejects his unwanted Korean passenger. The film's editor, Peter Hunt, glued them seemlessly together, though aficionados can tell them apart by their different housing for the licence plates and by a gold reflector plate near the air-intakes on the front wings.

Such was the impact of the DB5 that Aston Martin produced two further versions, which accompanied the picture on publicity tours around the world. In conjunction with **Eon**, the company also licensed the James Bond DB5 to Corgi Toys, whose miniature, complete with all the gizmos, sold in millions.

There was no question about it. The DB5 was the sexiest movie prop since Tarzan met Jane, and *Goldfinger* was the best thing that had ever happened to Aston Martin. It made the company not only visible but viable. Sales doubled, then tripled, and, just to keep the car in the public mind, it made a reappearance at the start of *Thunderball*.

The DB5 was superceded by the DB6, then the DBS, which looked nothing like the DB5. In fact, they were ugly brutes and sales started to slide. By the time of the oil crisis of 1973, Aston Martin had racked up losses of nearly £0.5 million. David Brown, now Sir David, sold the marque to Company Developments Ltd and retired. A year later the company was declared bankrupt and seemed destined to join Jensen and Allard in the knacker's yard. Between 1974 and 1986 Aston Martin was owned by a Canadian enthusiast, then by an oil tycoon. In 1987 the company was bought by Ford, which launched the DB7. But by that time Bond was driving a BMW, though his old DB5 was given a thorough service for brief appearances in *Goldeneye* and *Tomorrow Never Dies*.

See **Connery, Sean; Lee, Bernard**.

dealers

Ian Fleming had the Etonian's lofty disdain for everything except money, fast cars, beautiful women, a good drink, male friendship, cards, diving, pornography and England's standing in the world. He was also a bibliophile and a reasonable golfer. But, like the hero he created, he was a philistine with scant appreciation of the arts. He seldom went to the theatre, galleries and concerts, or to the cinema.

Cubby Broccoli claimed that Fleming said he hadn't been to the pictures since *Gone With the Wind*, which was an exaggeration but probably indicative of the writer's indifference to the movies. Fleming's most recent biographer, Andrew Lycett, reveals that Fleming was at least familiar with Lang's *Metropolis*, that he reviewed

Our Man in Havana for BBC radio (his friend Noël Coward was starring in it), that he saw *Hiroshima mon amour* and that he took his young son to see *The Absent-Minded Professor*. And when the deal with Broccoli and **Saltzman** was going through, Saltzman showed him *Saturday Night and Sunday Morning*, which can't have been pleasant.

Fleming's view of the cinema was limited to the money it might make him. As soon as he had completed *Casino Royale* he was always looking for a producer or a studio to make him rich. Raymond Chandler, for instance, whom Fleming admired, had made a fortune by selling his novels to Hollywood. If the morose and seedy Philip Marlowe could light up a screen, why not the glamorous and fearless James Bond? Fleming had set his heart on not merely becoming a rich and famous writer – there were plenty of those. He wanted to be known as the creator of a phenomenon that shook the world like one of SPECTRE's crazy schemes. Why have a golden typewriter if you only made brass farthings?

Early on, Fleming had succeeded in selling the television rights to *Casino Royale* to CBC, which made an hour-long version that was broadcast live on 1 October 1954. The title was changed to *Too Hot to Handle* and Bond became an American spy, played by Barry Nelson. The villain, Le Chiffre, was played by the bug-eyed Peter Lorre, whose climactic death was somewhat marred when Lorre, believing the broadcast was over, got up off the floor and walked out of camera range. Some may have called that Brechtian, others a cock-up of the first order.

The British film industry showed little interest in Bond. In the early 1950s it showed little interest in anything at all, apart from drawing-room comedies and wartime adventures. Fleming used all his social connections to interest producers, but to little avail. Even after four novels he had failed to make the bestseller lists; few people had ever heard of Bond, and by the mid-1950s the cultural trend was towards social realism, as shown in plays like *Look Back in Anger* and novels like *Lucky Jim* and *Room at the Top*.

The British film mogul Sir Alexander Korda, who was the nearest thing Britain had to David O. Selznick, had read *Live and Let Die* in galleys. Although Korda passed on it, he liked Fleming, who told him that he had another story in mind, about a madman who wants to destroy London with a V2 rocket. This eventually became Fleming's third novel, *Moonraker*. 'The reason why it breaks so badly in half as a book,' he said later, 'is because I had to more or less graft the first half of the book onto my film idea in order to bring it up to necessary length.'

The Rank Organisation, though, snapped up the rights to *Moonraker* for £5000 after outbidding and outmanoeuvring a rival offer from the Hollywood actor John Payne. But Rank dawdled and Fleming, amazed that a studio could buy a book and then shelve it, wrote his own screenplay in the hope of getting the project moving. Again, nothing happened and the project went into limbo. 'The company's failure to sign up James Bond,' wrote Andrew Lycett, 'was similar to the Decca record company turning down the Beatles.'

The same year Fleming sold the screen rights to *Casino Royale* to the Hollywood actor-producer Gregory Ratoff for $6000. But Ratoff could find no studio willing to make the picture. Instead of selling the book back to Fleming, Ratoff retained his ownership until his death in 1960.

The dismal TV version of *Casino Royale*, Ratoff's failure and Rank's dithering dismayed Fleming, who simply carried on writing, ever hopeful of the big break. In the summer of 1956 he met an American industrialist called Henry Morgenthau III, whose father, Henry II, had been the US Secretary to the Treasury during World War II and was a friend of Lord Beaverbrook. Henry III fancied himself as a movie producer and had somehow persuaded the Jamaican government to start a fledgling film industry, making films for American TV. Morgenthau met Fleming and during the next six months or so they hatched an outline about a master criminal of Chinese-German origins, though the resulting 26-page treatment was called *James Gunn*

– Secret Agent. When Morgenthau failed to raise the finance, Fleming swiftly converted the outline into a new novel, *Dr No*.

At the same time the Rank Organisation, which still owned *Moonraker*, offered Fleming £13,500 for the rights to *The Diamond Smugglers*, a non-fiction book he published in 1957. Then CBS in America contracted Fleming to write a series of 30-minute original scripts to be made into a TV series. 'It was James Bond he was selling,' wrote John Pearson, 'not the books.' Enticed by the money, Fleming told friends that *Goldfinger* would be his final full-length novel and that he would crank out TV scripts instead, a job he did easily and badly. In a sudden burst of energy he wrote six scripts, and when the CBS deal collapsed he converted three of them – *Risico*, *From a View to a Kill* and *For Your Eyes Only* – into a volume of short stories, which appeared in 1960.

The next film producer to engage Fleming's attention was Kevin McClory, a young Irishman who lived in Belgravia with a black butler, a monkey and a macaw. McClory's energy and enthusiasm so impressed Fleming's oldest friend, Ivar Bryce, that he financed McClory's first film, *The Boy and the Bridge*, a fantasy about a runaway boy, a seagull and Tower Bridge. Fleming was drawn into Bryce and McClory's partnership, and wrote a screenplay for them, which McClory hoped to produce in the Bahamas. This eventually became the novel *Thunderball*, which Fleming wrote when McClory's plans seemed to founder. However, when the novel was published McClory sued Fleming for breach of copyright and won. McClory was left owning the rights to the screenplay and the rights to the novel. Fleming was left with egg on his face.

It was at this time, in early 1961, that Cubby Broccoli came calling. Then a Mr Harry Saltzman came calling. Quite separately, both producers had taken a shine to the Bond novels, envisaging a fairly cheap and hugely profitable series. And when they joined forces Fleming found them hard to resist, especially since he was recovering from his first heart attack. Fleming had no interest in becoming involved in the scripts. He just wanted to take the money and run.

Fleming sold Broccoli and Saltzman all the novels except *Casino Royale*, the rights to which were owned by Broccoli's old agency boss, Charles K. Feldman, who had bought them from Gregory Ratoff's widow. Fleming was to be paid $100,000 for each title, plus a percentage of the net profits from each film; both John Pearson and Andrew Lycett claim that Fleming received 5 per cent, though Tino Balio, whose history of **United Artists** (UA) was based on a thorough study of the studio's legal files, claims Fleming received 2.5 per cent.

The only condition was that Broccoli and Saltzman had to option titles every eighteen months, otherwise the deal would be annulled. Broccoli and Saltzman also shrewdly bought the rights to the character of James Bond, enabling them to continue the series even if the supply of source novels was mined to exhaustion.

When this deal was struck six novels and the collection of short stories *For Your Eyes Only* were available. In June 1961, having secured Fleming's agreement, Broccoli and Saltzman went to see Bud Ornstein, who ran United Artists in London. Ornstein arranged a further meeting with the big brass in New York. Broccoli said:

> It was a mixture of optimism and apprehension that I carried into the meeting with Krim, Benjamin and David Picker. David said, 'I'm familiar with James Bond.' Krim said, 'If David likes the idea, we'll talk.' Frankly, they were reluctant to make the series using an unknown actor but eventually we did get an understanding that the picture would be done, if it could be done cheaply. In short, a million dollar budget, tops.

Broccoli, Saltzman and UA had all wanted to make *Thunderball* first. It was the most recent of the novels and in its story about stolen H-bombs had an undeniable contemporary relevance. But

Kevin McClory's involvement in *Thunderball* ensnared everyone in litigation. The team then decided to make *Dr No*, which had similar ingredients to *Thunderball*, notably the West Indies location which was important not only for its exoticism, but also because it was a British Commonwealth territory which was essential if the film was to qualify for Eady money, the tax on cinema admissions which was designed to help support the domestic film industry but which, in reality, helped buy swimming pools in Beverly Hills.

To direct the first film, Broccoli and Saltzman favoured **Guy Hamilton**, who declined for personal reasons, not wishing to commit himself to a long absence in Jamaica. Guy Green and Bryan Forbes were also said to have turned it down. UA favoured Phil Karlson, a director of sloppy B-movies, some of which would later enjoy cult status in the 1970s, though when Karlson's agent asked for $75,000 Broccoli and Saltzman blinked and settled for Terence Young, who had made some of Warwick's trashy epics, such as *The Red Beret* and *Zarak*. Young received $40,000, as did the screenwriter, **Richard Maibaum**. $140,000 was allocated to the cast, including **Sean Connery**, who received $40,000 (£15,000). Broccoli and Saltzman were paid a producer's fee of $80,000 plus 50 per cent of the net profits.

When *Dr No* proved such a success, grossing $2 million in America and Canada and $4 million abroad, UA approved a budget of $2 million for *From Russia With Love*. Costing twice as much to make as *Dr No*, it accordingly **grossed** twice as much. Broccoli and Saltzman saw their share of the profits rise from 50 to 60 per cent, and in order to minimise their tax liability they formed a company called Danjaq – a contraction of their wives' names, Dana and Jacqueline – which was incorporated in Switzerland. **Eon**, with offices in London, was simply a subsidiary of Danjaq SA.

Continuing the inflation in cost and profit ratio, *Goldfinger* was made on a budget of $3 million and grossed nearly $50 million worldwide. At the Odeon Leicester Square it earned a record-breaking $400,000 in two weeks. Within three months it had not only recouped its entire negative cost in the UK market, but also qualified for a government handout of $1.4 million of Eady Money. In America and Canada, *Goldfinger* opened simultaneously at 150 theatres (a huge number in those days) and quickly passed the $10 million mark. 'No other film in memory has ever performed with such speed for such a volume,' said *Variety*.

Sadly and ironically, Fleming himself would never reap the ultimate rewards. He died of a heart attack in the early hours of 12 August 1964, just a month before the premiere of *Goldfinger*.

See **screenplay**.

Dehn, Paul (1912–76)

Paul Dehn (pronounced Dane) was an elusive figure. Brought in to rewrite **Richard Maibaum**'s **screenplay** of *Goldfinger*, Dehn solved the final problems of the adaptation and added some Britishness. Although Maibaum had disapproved of much of Dehn's work, Dehn sent him a cable on the day of the film's premiere – 'CONGRATULATIONS ON GOLDFINGER AM PROUD TO HAVE COLLABORATED WITH YOU' – which was a nice gesture.

Dehn was born in Manchester on 5 November 1912. His godfather was James Agate, later one of Britain's foremost film **critics**. His parents were monied and sent him to Shrewsbury, a school which Dehn always remembered with affection, even writing a musical masque in 1952 for its 400th anniversary. He studied at Oxford and became a journalist, at first for the *Birmingham Post*, for which he became film critic in 1936. After his war service he became one of Fleet Street's most prolific journalists – his columns and reviews appeared regularly in a wide variety of publications, most notably the left-wing *Daily Herald* and the satirical weekly *Punch*. Alexandera Walker credits Paul Dehn as having taught him how to write film criticism.

But Dehn had more strings to his bow. A gay man with a strong sense of British tradition, he wrote poetry, lyrics for popular songs, plays and libretti for short operas. In 1951 he and his partner James Bernard – a composer who would later write the scores for many of the Hammer horror films – wrote an original story which became the movie *Seven Days to Noon*, a gripping and far-sighted drama about a scientist who threatens to explode an atomic bomb in London to warn the world of its rush to Armageddon. Dehn and Bernard's original story won them an Academy Award, and the threat of nuclear war remained one of Dehn's major concerns and an outlet for his mordant poetry:

> O nuclear wind, when will thou blow,
> That the small rain down can rain?
> Christ, that my love were in my arms
> And I had my arms again.

After the success of *Seven Days to Noon*, Dehn turned more and more to writing movies, plays and revues. He won a British Academy Award for his script of Anthony Asquith's *Orders to Kill*, a moral quagmire set in the time of the French Resistance, and after *Goldfinger* he adapted two of John le Carré's novels for the screen, *The Spy Who Came in from the Cold* and *The Deadly Affair*, both for director Sidney Lumet. He adapted Shakespeare for his friend Franco Zeffirelli and then suddenly became part of the Hollywood production line, turning out the sequels to *Planet of the Apes*. Following his stylish adaptation of Agatha Christie's *Murder on the Orient Express* – again for Lumet and which showed his fondness for literary pastiche – he became seriously ill and died prematurely on 30 September 1976, aged 61.

Filmography

1951   *Seven Days to Noon* (original story with James Bernard; dir. Roy and John Boulting)

1952   *Moulin Rouge* (lyrics; dir. John Huston)

1955 *I Am a Camera* (lyrics; dir. Henry Cornelius)
1958 *Orders to Kill* (screenplay; dir. Anthony Asquith)
1961 *The Innocents* (lyrics; dir. Jack Clayton)
1964 *Goldfinger* (co-scripted with Richard Maibaum; dir. **Guy Hamilton**)
1965 *The Spy Who Came in From the Cold* (co-scripted with Guy Trosper; dir. Sidney Lumet)
1966 *The Deadly Affair* (screenplay; dir. Sidney Lumet)
1967 *The Night of the Generals* (co-scripted with Joseph Kessel; dir. Anatole Litvak)
1967 *The Taming of the Shrew* (co-scripted with Suso Cecchi d'Amico and Franco Zeffirelli; dir. Franco Zeffirelli)
1970 *Beneath the Planet of the Apes* (screenplay; Ted Post)
1970 *Fragment of Fear* (screenplay and assoc. prod.; dir. Richard C. Sarafian)
1971 *Escape from the Planet of the Apes* (screenplay; dir. Don Taylor)
1972 *Conquest of the Planet of the Apes* (screenplay; dir. J. Lee Thompson)
1973 *Battle for the Planet of the Apes* (story; dir. J. Lee Thompson)
1974 *Murder on the Orient Express* (screenplay; dir. Sidney Lumet)

design

See **Adam, Ken**.

dubbing

See **Fröbe, Gert**; **his *Meister*'s voice**.

E

Eaton, Shirley

The actress who played Jill Masterson.

See **painted ladies**.

Eol-, Eon

vars. ÆOL-, ÆON.
(*The Shorter Oxford English Dictionary*)

See **æon**.

F

Felix

See **Leiter, Felix**.

first editions

See *ab initio* **i**.

fish finger

A subversive organisation has been smuggling gold out of the country disguised as Birds Eye Fish Fingers. If, in your next packet you should find a gold finger coated in crispy batter and breadcrumbs please return it to us and we will be happy to send you a voucher for a free packet of double delicious Birds Eye Fish Fingers. Signed, **M**. PS: Eat This.

(advertisement in *Goldfinger* World **Premiere** brochure)

See **product placement**.

Fleming, Ian (1908–64)

I am not an angry young, or even middle-aged, man. My books
are not 'engaged.' I have no message for suffering humanity
and, though I was bullied at school and lost my virginity like so
many of us used to in the old days, I have never been tempted
to foist these and other harrowing personal experiences on
the public. My opuscula do not aim at changing people or
making them go out and do something. They are written for
warm-blooded heterosexuals in railways, trains, aeroplanes
or beds.

(Ian Fleming, 1962)

It is perhaps just as well that Fleming wrote these lines, for to hear him speak might have given an erroneous impression. Like so many well-bred Englishmen, Fleming spoke with an affected accent which might have been mistaken for a lisp or a suppressed stammer, or both. He sounded posh and effete, a bit of a wally, like Prince Charles, really, mimicking Noël Coward. Fleming also dressed theatrically, usually with a bow-tie, and he waved a cigarette holder as if he was only slightly bothered by a buzzing fly. The impression he gave was of a gay man, which was far from the truth, as it was with those two boys, Charles and Sebastian, in Evelyn Waugh's *Brideshead Revisited*. Fleming was a creature of the 1920s who evoked 1930s values in the 1950s and who became a phenomenon in the 1960s. The 1940s were a waste land.

Ian Lancaster Fleming was born in Mayfair on 28 May 1908, the second of four sons born to Valentine and Evelyn Fleming. His background was wonderful training for a spy novelist. He went to Eton, where he excelled at athletics, then Sandhurst, then to the universities of Geneva and Munich. He went to work for the news agency Reuters, and in Moscow in 1933 he covered the trial of six British engineers accused of espionage. His reporting was eloquently perceptive and a glittering career on Fleet Street beckoned.

His wartime involvement with naval intelligence gave him access to the 'secret world' of spies, invisible ink and cipher-speak. He was involved in the setting up of the CIA, as well as an undercover operation in Spain called Goldeneye, the name he later gave his home in Jamaica. His resumed career as a foreign correspondent, too, gave him a political perspective into the post-war, Cold War world, as well as an appreciation of foreign places.

His social life, meanwhile, was an endless round of golf, casinos, parties, exotic cars and romantic failures. But Fleming was never a playboy who squandered inherited wealth. By the standards of the ordinary citizen, he was wealthy and privileged, but by the standards of his friends he was a pauper. He had to dirty his hands by earning himself a living.

Fleming made much of the fact that he wrote his first novel as a reaction against getting married at the age of 43. Writing came easy to him – he had mentally prepared it for years – and in Jamaica he dashed off *Casino Royale* in only four weeks. His social connections led him to the publishing house of Jonathan Cape, which was thought by some to be lowering its standards by publishing such trash. But the fact that it was Cape gave Fleming a degree of kudos, as well as reviews in all the major papers and magazines.

The early novels bristle with energy and, although the plotting is always rudimentary, awkward and downright implausible, Fleming got away with it by artful phrasing, pace, verisimilitude and sharply drawn characters. Fleming wrote with such style that he could make you think you had mastered the arts of baccarat or golf without ever having set foot in Monte Carlo or on the Sandwich golf course. And he created a hero who possessed enough psychological flaws and idiosyncracies to make each novel open-ended. For no matter what happens at the end of each novel, Bond himself continues to develop.

Eventually, Fleming grew bored with the hero and came to resent him, calling him a 'cardboard booby'. Like Sir Arthur Conan Doyle with Sherlock Holmes, Fleming wanted to kill Bond off and almost succeeded in doing so several times. By the time of *Goldfinger*, Bond is becoming morose and suspicious of his motives. In *Thunderball* he starts out as a physical wreck (Fleming himself had recently suffered a heart attack); in *The Spy Who Loved Me* the clearly bored Fleming experiments dismally with the format; in *On Her Majesty's Secret Service* Bond suffers an emotional breakdown when his nemesis, Blofeld (the Moriarty of the novels), murders Bond's wife moments after the wedding ceremony. And then, in the unprecedentedly surreal and doom-laden *You Only Live Twice*, the still traumatised Bond discovers Blofeld by chance and is very nearly killed; in fact, he wishes he *was* killed.

That, as far as Fleming was concerned, was the end of it, except that the movies of *Dr No* and *From Russia With Love* had opened and Bond mania was starting. Just as Conan Doyle was obliged to recover Holmes from the Reichenbach Falls, Fleming grudgingly brought Bond back to life. Now in ill health, he cranked out *The Man With the Golden Gun* and proved an astute critic when he told his editor: 'This is, alas, the last Bond and, again alas, I mean it, for I really have run out of both puff and zest.'

The movies had made Fleming a star. He gave interviews, his

picture was in the papers, often at an airport, and he ingratiated himself with the picture people. He looked busy, riding the whirlwind, though the truth was that he felt distracted, bored and vacant. He was experiencing a hollow victory. But he enjoyed his friends, like Evelyn Waugh, who sent him a roll of Bronco bog paper, imported from America, with a note which said that Ian had not 'revealed as much about Bond's defecations as of his other bodily functions'. He drank, he smoked, he lunched and he golfed.

In July 1964 Fleming made a token visit to the set of *Goldfinger* and was photographed with **Sean Connery** and **Shirley Eaton**. A month later, early in the morning of 12 August, he died of a heart attack. At the time of his death he had sold around 30 million books worldwide. By the time that *Thunderball* was released that figure had doubled. But a surfeit of Morland specials, vodka martinis and platefuls of scrambled eggs had taken their toll. 'Despite all the success,' wrote his first biographer, John Pearson, 'life had cheated Ian Fleming of the one thing he had set his heart on, and James Bond had finally destroyed his only flesh-and-blood victim.'

Bibliography

1953	*Casino Royale*
1954	*Live and Let Die*
1955	*Moonraker*
1956	*Diamonds Are Forever*
1957	*The Diamond Smugglers* (non-fiction)
1957	*From Russia With Love*
1958	*Dr No*
1959	*Goldfinger*
1960	*For Your Eyes Only*
1961	*Thunderball*
1962	*The Spy Who Loved Me*
1963	*On Her Majesty's Secret Service*
1963	*Thrilling Cities* (non-fiction)

1964   *You Only Live Twice*
1964   *Chitty Chitty Bang Bang*
1965   *The Man With The Golden Gun*
1966   *Octopussy*

See **ab initio ii**; **dealers**; **Quiet de Luxe**; **Whicker, Alan**.

Flying Circus

See **Pussy Galore**.

Fort Knox

> Man has climbed Everest. Gone to the bottom of the ocean. He
> has fired rockets to the Moon. Split the atom. Achieved miracles
> in every field of human endeavour. EXCEPT CRIME!!

That's a great speech, lifted almost intact from the novel, and it sums
up **Goldfinger**'s madness as well as his genius. Not only does he want
to monopolise the world's supply of **gold** bullion; by doing so he also
wants to create a work of art. Breaking into Fort Knox would give him
a place in history. Unsurprisingly, Goldfinger's cohorts are sceptical.

'Knock off Fort Knox?' says one mobster, incredulously. 'Tee-hee,
tee-hee,' chuckle the heads of all the families, ridiculing this Germanic
madman with carrot hair and a tweed jacket. 'Tee-hee, tee-hee.' At
first Goldfinger humours them. Then he kills them. One wonders
why he even bothered to tell them about his plan. But then, if he
hadn't Bond would not have been able to overhear, would he?

Only the Bank of England is as famous as Fort Knox. It is a byword for
security and for untold millions. People talk of Fort Knox in the same way
that they say something is as 'safe as houses'. Even in an age when money
is transferred via a modem, Fort Knox retains its mystique as the place
where all the money in all the world is stored. It is **Midas**'s piggy bank.

You can get surprisingly close to it and peer through the railings at
the granite building. You cannot, though, get into it, which ensures

that the layout and design of the underground vaults remain a secret, open only to the imagination, to **Ken Adam** and to popular myth. Not even the President of the United States can take a peek at his country's wealth. He wouldn't pass the security test.

Fort Knox is in Hardin County, near Louisville, Kentucky. Abraham Lincoln's father had a small farm nearby. By the time of the Civil War, the area had an established military presence and in 1862 the 6th Michigan Infantry constructed a permanent base called Fort Duffield. By the turn of the century the area's military importance had increased considerably, and by 1918 there was an artillery training camp which covered more than 40,000 acres. In 1925 this camp was named Camp Henry Knox National Forest, after America's first Secretary of War, **Major-General Henry Knox**. The name was changed to Fort Knox on 1 January 1932.

It was in 1934 that the US Mint decided that Fort Knox should become its principal bullion depository. The huge army base gave it a certain immunity from armed robbers and the subsoil was ideal for excavation – Kentucky is world famous for its caves. Construction of the depository was completed in December 1936, at a cost of £560,000. Fort Knox received its first consignment of gold in January 1937 and was fully stocked by June.

The visible part of the building measures 121 x 105 feet and is 42 feet high. Included in the materials used in this construction were 16,500 cubic feet of granite, 4200 cubic yards of concrete, 750 tons of reinforced steel and 670 tons of structural steel. The door weighs nearly 30 tons and no one person is entrusted with the combination; several staff must dial separate combinations known only to them. The vault itself is made of steel plates encased in concrete and its roof is independent of the main building. Additional security is provided by four permanently manned guard boxes at each corner of the building, and in the event of a sustained assault the building is self-sufficient, having an emergency power plant and water supply. Inside are offices, a pistol firing range, stores and restrooms.

The gold itself is stored in two-storey underground vaults in the form of standard mint bars of almost pure gold or coin gold bars, which are made from the melting down of gold coin. The bars are smaller than the average building brick, measuring roughly 7 x 3 x 2 inches and weighing 27 lbs. They are stored without wrappers and staff must wear gloves when handling them in order to avoid abrasion of the soft metal. In 1991 each bar was estimated to be worth around $17,000 and it's probably fair to say there are a lot of them.

The gold vault is also used for the safe-keeping of the original documents of the Constitution, the Bill of Rights and the Declaration of Independence. On 26 December 1941 the British government shipped the Crown Jewels and the Magna Carta (first edition) to Fort Knox, where they remained for the duration of the war.

Also on the site is the Patton Museum of Cavalry and Armor, named for General George C. Patton, who was born nearby and drove Fort Knox's tanks across North Africa and Europe. This museum also houses a piece of the Berlin Wall. In 1987 the entire site – depository, museum, army base – was placed on the National Register for Historic Places. Visitors are welcome. Check in your laser guns at the entrance.

Fröbe, Gert (d. 1988)

'Bond's first view of Mr **Goldfinger** was startling,' wrote **Fleming**. Fleming's villains are almost always ugly, sometimes disfigured and racially blurred. Because Fleming knew that Bond was only as good as the villains, they had to be flamboyant as well as threatening, hence the garish outfits and the bizarre names – Drax, No, Scaramanga, Blofeld, Goldfinger. Their physical ugliness helped convey their appetite for evil and so did their tell-tale eyes – the pupils invariably surrounded by whites and behind them, a tell-tale glint of red.

Goldfinger was first discovered sunbathing, wearing yellow satin briefs and a pair of tin wings around his neck which reflected the rays of the sun under his chin, which otherwise would have remained a tan-free zone. Fleming wrote:

When Goldfinger had stood up, the first thing that had struck Bond was that everything was out of proportion. Goldfinger was short, not more than five feet tall, and on top of the thick body and blunt, peasant legs, was set almost directly into the shoulders, a huge and it seemed exactly round head.

Goldfinger's shortness inevitably reminded Bond of the world's great despots, like Hitler and Napoleon – 'It was the short men,' he mused, 'that caused all the trouble in the world.' Although Bond knew that Goldfinger claimed to be British, he detected Jewish blood and thought he was – what? 'Not a Slav. Perhaps a German – no, a Balt!' Now, not many men go around claiming they are a Balt, but in Fleming's – and Bond's – xenophobic world Goldfinger's genetic and religious composition was a blueprint for evil. Show me a man without a proper flag to salute or a proper language to speak and I'll show you a monster.

While Fleming takes a full three pages to introduce the villain, **Guy Hamilton** takes five seconds – just two brief shots of Gert Fröbe – the first of which is not of Fröbe at all, but a double – wearing a casual shirt and shorts, in front of a back-projected sky. The location is Pinewood Studios, though the scene pretends to be on the terrace of the Fountainebleu Hotel in Miami Beach.

Right from the start Fröbe makes a splendid impression; barely in control of his temper, he wears a 24-carat chip on his shoulder. And when we later meet his henchman, **Oddjob**, Goldfinger's malevolence is complete. He's the perfect Bond villain; like Drax, he's an outsider who forces his way into the British Establishment by buying a golf club, dressing like a country squire and having a chauffeur with a bowler hat. He's the sort of self-made man who inevitably attracts the contempt of the real Establishment, those men who have not been required to buy their own houses or their own paintings and furniture. Apart from Goldfinger's criminal ambitions and murky political allegiances, he is the sort of man upon whom Harold Wilson might have bestowed a knighthood.

Although Auric Goldfinger is not quite the best villain of the novels (I think the bellicose Sir Hugo Drax in *Moonraker* is that), Fröbe makes Goldfinger the best villain of the films, rivalled only by Lotte Lenya's Rosa Klebb in *From Russia With Love*. The rest are either cartoon nasties (such as Donald Pleasance's Blofeld in *You Only Live Twice*) or so weakly acted and scripted that they offer no serious challenge at all. **Paul Dehn**'s rewrite gave Fröbe some great scenes and some great lines:

'Do you expect me to talk?'
'No, Mr Bond. I expect you to die!'

But most of all there is that marvellous speech about Operation Grand Slam, a heist to be compared to the splitting of the atom or the ascent of Everest. Goldfinger is Hitler, Mabuse, Dr Strangelove and Robert Maxwell all rolled into one. There is real menace and madness in Fröbe's performance, and such is the technical wizardry that one never suspects that his voice is dubbed by the British actor Michael Collins.

There's also an offhandedness about him that's frightening, the way he nods an order to Oddjob and the game he plays with the hoods before gassing them to death. He has a creepy little chuckle and a childish glee at his own audacity. What he lacks is any kind of sexuality and this is not only due to his appearance. While one suspects that **Pussy Galore**'s pilots might pleasure him occasionally, or maybe Oddjob has him on the rack in the middle of the night, silently pummelling Goldfinger's tightened, hairless scrotum, he's probably the sort who gets his kicks from the solitary, single-minded and single-handed pleasures of pornography.

Gert Fröbe was born Karl-Gerhard Fröebe in Planitz, Saxony, on Christmas Day 1912, though some sources claim he was born on 25 February 1913. As he began to act in British and American pictures, he dropped the 'e' and became known as Fröbe. In his early years he was sometimes Gerd, more often Gert. British and American studios usually dispensed with the umlaut.

Initially he was drawn to the theatre and to the opera, hoping to make a career as a scene designer, though he had begun to act before the start of World War II. Like many Germans, he had joined the Nazi Party and spent much of the war in Vienna. His film career began in 1945 and, while his physique was never going to make him a leading man, he became one of the busiest character actors in Europe.

His first real starring role was in *Der Gauner und der lieber Gott* (1960), in which he played a safecracker who, after serving time in prison, is falsely arrested on another charge and sent back to prison. After escaping, he disguises himself as a priest. *Variety* said: 'Gert Fröebe will garner many kudos from crix. [He] never overdoes his role and skilfully avoids slapstick. It's a top-notch portrayal which will further his career.'

Fröbe's career trundled on and across Europe. He made films in his native Germany as well as in Switzerland, Austria and France. According to some sources, Fröbe also started to throw his not inconsiderable weight around. When the imperious and one-eyed Fritz Lang cast him in *The Thousand Eyes of Dr Mabuse*, a sequel to his silent classic, as well as a later 1933 drama which put Nazi slogans into the mouths of master criminals, Lang and Fröbe behaved like a pair of stags during the rutting season. Lang's biographer and friend Lotte Eisner, who blinded herself to Lang's own arrogance, cruelty and murky past, described Fröbe and co-star Peter Van Eyck as 'the scum of the German film industry'.

None of this bothered Fröbe; by the time Lang adjusted his monocle and edited the picture, Fröbe had busked through a couple of others, notably Darryl F. Zanuck's vast D-Day epic *The Longest*

Day, playing a plump and evidently dim German private who wanders along the cliff blissfully ignorant of the approaching armada.

Fröbe was not the first actor to be considered for *Goldfinger*. The Austrian Theodore Bikel, who was Oscar nominated for *The Defiant Ones*, is known to have done a screen test. But Fröbe had been spotted by one of **United Artists'** (UA) sharp-eyed European talent scouts in the Swiss picture *Es geschah am hellichten Tag*, which was sent to **Broccoli** in London. In that film, directed by Ladislao Vajda, Fröbe played a murderous paedophile and his portrayal of evil was unusually chilling. He had the ability to be amusing and innocent and then, in a second, become threatening.

Goldfinger made Fröbe an international . . . well, one cannot really say a 'star'. It certainly made him famous and led to appearances in many all-star comedies, in which he tended to play apoplectic Prussians, most notably in *Those Magnificent Men in Their Flying Machines*, in which he more than held his own against scene-stealers like Terry-Thomas and Benny Hill. People who worked with him – like Guy Hamilton and Sarah Miles, the star of *Those Magnificent Men* – remember him fondly as entertaining the cast and crew with his 'one-man band', a collection of drums, cymbals and horns which he tied around his girth and played like a virtuoso.

The final phase of his career gave him the opportunity to work with major directors such as Bergman (*The Serpent's Egg*), Franju (*Eyes Without a Face*) and Visconti (*Ludwig*), and there were also two dismal collaborations – *Triple Cross* and *Bloodline* – with Terence Young. But the best of his later roles was in Richard Brooks's *The Heist*, in which Fröbe played the manager of a high-security bank robbed by Warren Beatty and Goldie Hawn. It was a role that looked back mockingly to *Goldfinger*, and Fröbe took the joke and ran with it.

Fröbe was briefly embroiled in a distressing controversy about his membership of the Nazi Party. He was especially sensitive about this and, indeed, Guy Hamilton remembered him being 'very, very nervous and very upset' by the prospect of playing the scene in which he orders that the American gangsters be gassed to death. For Fröbe, the scene had explicit connotations with the Holocaust and, as a German, he did not wish to give any offence to the victims of the gas chambers.

In December 1965 *Goldfinger* was running in Israel, having broken box-office records in Jerusalem and Nathanya. As it transferred to Haifa, Ramat Gan and Tel Aviv, news of Fröbe's Nazi past led the Israeli film censorship board to withdraw the picture from distribution. Fröbe had given an interview to the Paris correspondent of an Israeli journal, *Yediot Ahronot*, in which he admitted membership of the Nazi Party from 1934 to just before the outbreak of the war. While he said he approved of the party's social programme, he had never read Hitler's *Mein Kampf*. In any case, he said, his membership fees were paid by his mother. He also claimed to have saved the life of a Jewish woman and her son by giving them sanctuary in his apartment in Vienna in 1941. Two months later Fröbe's story was confirmed when the Jewish boy came forward and named Fröbe as his saviour. The Israeli film censorship board accordingly lifted the ban on *Goldfinger*.

A serial husband (he married five times), Fröbe died in Munich of a heart attack on 5 September 1988.

Filmography

1948	*Berliner Ballade*
1949	*Nacht Regen scheint Sonne*
1952	*Der Tag vor der Hochzeit*
1953	*Arlette erobert Paris*
1953	*Man on a Tightrope*
1953	*Ein Herz spielt falsch*
1954	*They Were So Young/Mannequins für Rio*
1954	*Ewige Waltzer*
1954	*Die kleine Stadt will schlafen gehn*
1955	*Das zweite Leben*

1955	*Morgengrauen*
1955	*Das Kreuz am Jägerstag*
1955	*Der Postmeister*
1955	*Der dunkel Stern/Dark Star*
1955	*Vom Himmel gefallen/Special Delivery*
1955	*Confidential Report/Mr Arkadin*
1955	*Das Forsthaus in Tirol*
1955	*Les Héros sont fatigués*
1955	*Ich weiß, wofür ich lebe*
1955	*Mädchen aus Flandern*
1956	*Waldwinter*
1956	*Ein Herz schlägt für Erika*
1957	*Celui qui doit mourir/He Who Must Die*
1957	*Der tolle Bomberg*
1957	*Typhoon Over Nagasaki*
1957	*Das Herz von St Pauli*
1957	*Robinson soll nicht sterben*
1957	*El Hakim*
1958	*Éche au porteur*
1958	*Charmants garçons*
1958	*Grafatigués*
1958	*I battellieri del Volga*
1958	*Es geschah am hellichten Tag/Assault in Broad Daylight*
1958	*Das Mädchen Rosemarie*
1959	*Nasse asphalt*
1959	*Der Pauker*
1959	*Das Mädchen mit den Katznaugen*
1959	*Nick Knattertons Abenteuer*
1959	*Grabenplatz 17/17 Sinister Street*
1959	*Jons und Erdman*
1959	*Und ewig singen die Wälder/Vengeance in Timber Valley*
1959	*Schüß im Morgengrauen*
1959	*Douze Heures d'horloge*

1959   *Old Heidelberg*
1959   *Tag, als der Geld euch scheidet*
1960   *Menschen im Hotel/ Grand Hotel*
1960   *Bis daß Geld euch scheidet*
1960   *Le Bois des amants*
1960   *Der Gauner und der lieber Gott*
1960   *Das kunstseidene Mädchen*
1960   *Soldatensender Calais*
1960   *12 Stunden Angst*
1960   *Der Tausend Augen des Dr Mabuse/ The 1000 Eyes of Dr Mabuse*
1961   *Der grüne Bogenschütze/ The Green Archer*
1961   *Via Mala*
1962   *Auf Wiedersehen*
1962   *Heute Kündigt mir mein Mann*
1962   *The Longest Day*
1962   *Die Rote*
1962   *The Threepenny Opera*
1963   *Le Meurtrier/ Enough Rope*
1963   *Karussell der Leidenschaften*
1963   *Peau de banane/ Banana Skin*
1964   *Goldfinger*
1964   *100,000 Dollars au soleil*
1964   *Échappement libre/ Backfire*
1964   *Tonio Kröger*
1965   *Is Paris Burning?*
1965   *Those Magnificent Men in Their Flying Machines*
1965   *A High Wind in Jamaica*
1966   *Du Rififi a Paname*
1966   *Ganovenehre*
1966   *Das Liebeskarussell/ Who Wants to Sleep?*
1966   *Triple Cross*
1967   *Rocket to the Moon*

1967	*J'ai tué Rasputine/I Killed Rasputin*
1968	*Caroline Chérie*
1968	*Chitty Chitty Bang Bang*
1969	*Monte Carlo or Bust*
1971	*$/The Heist*
1972	*Ludwig*
1973	*Nuits rouges/Shadowman*
1973	*Der Räuber Hotzenplotz*
1974	*L'Homme sans visage/The Man Without a Face*
1974	*And Then There Were None/Ten Little Indians*
1975	*Mein Onkel Theodore*
1975	*Docteur Justice*
1976	*Profezia per un delitto*
1976	*Les Magiciens/Death Rite*
1977	*Tod oder Freiheit/Death or Freedom*
1977	*Das Gesetz des Clans*
1977	*The Serpent's Egg*
1978	*Der Tiefstapler*
1978	*Der Schimmelreiter*
1979	*Sidney Sheldon's Bloodline*
1980	*Le Coup de parapluie*
1981	*Ein sturer Bock*
1981	*Der Falke*
1982	*Der Garten*
1985	*Alte Sünden rosten nicht*

See **his *Meister*'s voice**.

G

gadgets

See **DB5**; **Hamilton, Guy**; **Lee, Bernard**; **Q**.

Galore, Pussy

See **Pussy Galore**.

gold

See **Fort Knox**; **Hood, Thomas**; **Midas touch**; **painted ladies**.

gold paint

See **painted ladies**.

gold vault

See **Fort Knox**.

Goldfinger

See *ab initio* **ii**; **dealers**; **Fröbe, Gert**.

Goldfinger, Auric

See *ab initio* **ii**.

Goldfinger II

Gert Fröbe may have been sucked out of the aeroplane but he nearly staged a comeback – along with **Sean Connery** – in *Diamonds Are Forever*. In his first stab at adapting **Fleming**'s fourth novel, **Richard Maibaum** quickly recognised that the book's major weakness was its lack of a decent villain. Fleming's fondness for Americans and all things American did not extend to his descriptions of them; Americans in his novels are often crudely drawn, lacking the layers of psychosis which colour his Europeans and Asians. The Las Vegas gangsters Jack and Seraffimo Spang are pathetic spivs when placed beside true megalomaniacs like **Goldfinger** or Dr No.

Maibaum had a clever idea: if Auric Goldfinger was obsessed by gold, why not let him have a brother who was obsessed by diamonds? Better still, why not let him have a twin brother, so that the excellent Fröbe could be cast again? Pleased by his invention, Maibaum developed the story and included a line of dialogue where Bond meets the villain and is told: 'You remember my brother Auric, Mr Bond. Mother always said he was a bit retarded.'

Maibaum also contrived an extravagant climax to replace Fleming's rather lame, sub-Disneyland train chase. He had the Las Vegas crime syndicates ganging up on the usurper Goldfinger and chasing him across Lake Mead in a variety of craft, ranging from Chinese junks to Roman slave galleys which the Vegas hotels had moored on the lake. Maibaum said:

> I had this fleet of boats in pursuit of Goldfinger because he gave the city such a bad name. They wanted to do something patriotic to catch this terrible villain. I thought I had one of the best lines in the entire series when Bond, in the lead boat, broadcasts to the fleet, 'Las Vegas expects every man

to do his duty,' a take-off on what Nelson said at Trafalgar. Just for the sake of that line, I was heartbroken when they rejected it.

Sadly, **Broccoli** had doubts about the whole idea and engaged Tom Mankiewicz to rewrite the screenplay to include all the moon-buggy nonsense as well as establish Blofeld as the central villain. 'And my smash ending,' said Maibaum, 'became an interminable thing on an oil-rig.'

Goldfinger, Erno (1902–87)

When **Ian Fleming** told his friend Cyril Connolly that he was calling his next villain Auric Goldfinger, Connolly said that was wrong; he should be called Goldprick. But taste won the day and, in any case, Fleming had named his villain after a vague acquaintance of his, the architect, Erno Goldfinger.

Like Auric, Erno was a European who settled in England. Born in Budapest on 11 September 1902, he became a relatively famous and influential architect of the post-war era. In 1922 he settled in Paris and studied architecture at the École des Beaux Arts. The fact that his ideas were somewhat revolutionary, even for Paris, delayed his final qualification until 1931.

Goldfinger's mentor was Auguste Perret, who lectured at the Institut d'Urbanisme at the Sorbonne. Perret believed that reinforced concrete was the material from which all great buildings should be built, a belief which found favour among many young architects and contributed to the uglification of many of our cities.

In 1934 Goldfinger brought these ideas to London, where he wrote for the French magazine *L'Architecture d'aujourd'hui*. With Perret and Sir Patrick Abercrombie, he founded the International Union of Architects and other architectural associations. On becoming a British citizen in 1935 he began to plan buildings and housing estates in which the British people might wish to live. In this respect he was like Le Corbusier – he knew what was best for the common people while he himself lived somewhere better.

Or did he? In Hampstead in 1937 Goldfinger built a row of houses on Willow Street which overlooked a disconnected part of the Heath, a crap-trap for passing dogs. Made of concrete, with metal windows, broad balconies and other modernist elements, the four two-storey houses were built over their garages and caused considerable attention and controversy. Fleming himself joined the campaign to stop the construction. To begin with, the local authority disapproved of his design, and only when the London County Council intervened was planning permission given. Goldfinger liked the place so much he took one of the houses for himself and his family, and lived there until his death on 15 November 1987.

While Goldfinger lived in clinical splendour in Hampstead his revolutionary ideas for the proletariat began to take shape. Huge swathes of ageing Victorian terraces were demolished to make way for his high-rise apartment blocks and office buildings, including a vast complex at the Elephant and Castle which included a subterranean and futuristic Odeon Cinema.

His masterpiece is said to be Trellick Tower, a monstrous erection which rises above and therefore crushes shabby, terraced Westbourne Grove. Made of reinforced concrete, with its lift shaft a parallel tower, and crowned by its phallic boiler apparatus, thus bringing Cape Canaveral to West London, it would not disgrace the workers' villages of Ullan Bator or Pyongyang. 'A dinosaur from another age,' is how Nikolaus Pevsner described it shortly after it was completed in 1973. Stung by the criticisms, Goldfinger became a short-term tenant and pronounced it an excellent place in which to live. No one believed him. Needless to say, Trellick Tower is a listed building, preventing its long overdue demolition.

By all accounts, Goldfinger was a difficult customer, intolerant of the opinions of others, hard to work with and harder to work for, a man of baroque tastes and temperament who created monuments of awesome banality. He seems to have been less like Auric Goldfinger than Sir Hugo Drax, the truculent villain of *Moonraker*, a man who would blitz London to remake it in his own image.

gross

The James Bond films are the most profitable franchise in the history of the cinema. What each film grossed worldwide is shown below. The figures have been adjusted for inflation:

1962	*Dr No*	$60m
1963	*From Russia With Love*	$79m
1964	*Goldfinger*	$125m
1965	*Thunderball*	$141m
1967	*You Only Live Twice*	$112m
1969	*On Her Majesty's Secret Service*	$65m
1971	*Diamonds Are Forever*	$116m
1973	*Live and Let Die*	$127m
1974	*The Man With the Golden Gun*	$98m
1977	*The Spy Who Loved Me*	$186m
1979	*Moonraker*	$203m
1981	*For Your Eyes Only*	$196m
1983	*Octopussy*	$188m
1985	*A View to a Kill*	$153m
1987	*The Living Daylights*	$191m
1989	*Licence to Kill*	$157m
1995	*Goldeneye*	$357m
Total		$2554m

(*Source*: United International Pictures; list first published in *Screen International*, 5 December 1997)

gun barrel

A man in a suit walks purposefully from right to left across the screen, his every pace viewed from inside the barrel of a gun. The man turns, pulls a pistol and fires straight at us. Blood fills the screen, the barrel wavers and falls, the music begins . . . and another Bond movie is up and running.

It was Maurice Binder who designed this opening to every Bond movie and Norman Wanstall added the **sound** of the echoing pistol shot. But the man in the suit was not **Sean Connery**; it was stuntman Bob Simmons, who, for *Goldfinger*, choreographed the major fights and the assault on **Fort Knox**. It was also Simmons who executed Kisch's fatal fall in the gold vault.

See **title number**.

H

Hamilton, Guy (b. 1922)

Guy Hamilton has retired. Even if a smashing project were to come his way, he's not sure he could stomach the flight to Los Angeles, much less the bartering with the studios. Long gone are the days of Korda or Selznick, who would sense a director's passion for a story, and long gone are the studio executives who might have heard of Guy Hamilton, the man who directed *Goldfinger*.

So Guy has retired, and he has retired in style. He asked me not to say precisely where; so let us say that he lives on an island in the sun. No, that is not quite precise enough. He lives on the top of an island and his house is almost the sort of place one might expect to see in a Bond picture. It is modern, with acres of polished stone, granite and marble, and there is a pool terrace with majestic views. Although parts of the island have been blighted by tourism, Guy's place stands well above and beyond them.

He lives with his wife, Kerima, whom he met while filming *Outcast of the Islands* in Borneo. After she served me a glass of wine and some deliciously plump black olives, I mentioned the name of Howard Hawks, with whom she made *Land of the Pharaohs* in 1955. She thought Hawks was a lovely man; he drove her around Rome in a new Porsche. Then I said, 'You were born in Algiers, weren't you?' I had come prepared to discuss the anarchy into which the country had slipped. 'No! I was born in France!' she said in her heavily accented English. 'Alex Korda invented the name Kerima for me and told me to say I was born in Algiers. He thought it would make me seem exotic.'

Guy is full of yarns, many of them untapped and unrehearsed, for he is not often interviewed. He's seen it all, done it all, for who can claim to have made pictures in Borneo or the Belgian Congo in 1950; or to have restaged the Battle of Britain; or to have outwitted the Salkinds so that he got paid for directing *Superman* when he didn't shoot a single frame. There is also a modesty about the man and an apparent lack of a chip on his shoulder or any kind of resentment. Let us be frank: Guy Hamilton was never in the same class as, say, David Lean or William Wyler or Howard Hawks. But like so many other British directors – J. Lee Thompson, say, or Basil Dearden or Terence Young – he was a true professional who got the job done as efficiently and as stylishly as possible.

Q: How old were you when you decided you wanted a career in pictures?

A: I fell in love with movies at a very early age and by the time I was 12 or 13 I wanted to be a director. I was born in Paris because my father worked in the British embassy there. So from the age of nought to 8 I lived in France. I didn't care for French movies, but amongst my schoolmates there were some American children whose daddies worked for **United Artists** [UA]. So after 4 o'clock on the Champs Élysées we used to sneak in and see American pictures. My educational career was not very brilliant. I was destined for the diplomatic corps and at 14 or 15 I was solemnly beaten because wanting to be a film director was like wanting to run a brothel. It just wasn't on.

Q: Most people of your age would have thought that movies were all about stars. Who did you like and when did you realise that directors ran the show?

A: Ginger Rogers, dancing with Fred Astaire. She was my first sex symbol. She seemed to me the epitome of elegance, everything.

I twigged that directors ran the show at a very early age. For me, it seemed a well-paid job and you met pretty girls. By the time I was 16 I was very serious. My holidays consisted of trying to see forty pictures in thirty days. I discovered French pictures, fell totally in love with them and thought American pictures were rubbish. I saw films by Renoir, Duvivier, René Clair, all that great period.

Q: How did you enter the industry and why did you become an assistant director? The usual way to become a director was to be a cameraman or an editor.

A: My mother had a flat in the south of France, where I lived with my two younger sisters. I managed to make a deal with my old man that I could have six months in the movie business before I went back to school. So I marched into the Victorine Studios in Nice and said I wanted to be a film director. A wonderful man called René Schwab ran the studio. He was amazed by the cheek of this little idiot English boy, but he said, 'Well, that's all right. You won't get paid and you start on Monday.' I got shoved in the accounts department and spent a week licking wage packets. I thought it was exploitation of child labour, so I complained to Schwab, who said I'd been there a week and that I'd already learnt that there was more to movies than stars and directors. I'd found there were gardeners, boilerhouse men, and of course I'd learnt the composition of a studio.

Duvivier was making a film and I was put into the camera crew, who were delighted to see me because there wasn't a clapper boy. I was taught to load a camera in the dark and I made coffee, so I was extraordinarily popular. One day, the cameraman told me, 'Cinema is a visual art and the way to become a director is to become a cameraman.'

Then I got shoved on the sound crew and held the microphone, which was on a bamboo pole. The **soundman** took me aside and told me, 'Movies were nickelodeons until sound came in. If you want to be a director, you should be a soundman.'

Then I got sent into the cutting rooms. The editor said to me, 'This is where movies are made. If you want to be a director you have to become a cutter.'

At the end of that production Schwab said to me, 'You have learnt the first basic fact of life. If you want to be a director you know that all technicians are bullshitters and your first job is to bang their little heads together.'

Then a Fernandel picture started and off I went as a sort of assistant assistant director. I rushed around the studio doing everything. I absolutely adored it.

Q: This must have been when the war started, when France was invaded. What happened to you then?

A: The Italians came in, which rather spoilt things. I drove an ambulance evacuating people from the south of France. When the Germans broke through, two British colliers were sent to evacuate people from Cannes. I had the great pleasure of driving Rolls-Royces off the jetty into the water. All the evacuees seemed to be a hundred years old. Somerset Maugham was aboard and that was a big thrill because I liked his short stories. When I saw him, his manservant was serving him tea from a bully-beef tin. But Maugham was a big disappointment because he was unshaven and he'd lost the collar of his shirt. He looked like any refugee. It was a terrible voyage and the old ladies were dying like flies. We failed to land in Oran, Algeria, so we went on to Gibraltar, where we passed one of the greatest sights I've ever seen. It was the Mediterranean fleet, which was on its way to shell the shit out of the French navy because Churchill could not afford to let the Germans take the ships over. From Gibraltar we sailed on to Liverpool.

Q: What happened when you got to England? Did you join the services straight away?

A: No, I had six months with Paramount News at Acton. That
was splendid because we did two newsreels a week and I was
a librarian. There was always a lot of film lying about which I
could play with, and that lasted until I joined the Navy. I had
a noisy war, in destroyers on the lower deck and then in MTBs
[Motor Torpedo Boats]. I landed in Norway and got left behind
once in France. I was absolutely determined that if I came out
in one piece the movie business was it.

Q: That sounds easier than it probably was. You weren't really part
of the British film industry and presumably had few contacts.

A: It was difficult because the ACT, the union, was very powerful.
You couldn't get a ticket unless you had a job and you couldn't get
a job unless you had a ticket. But somehow I met John Sutrer at
Autus Films and got a job there as his assistant. Eventually I got my
ticket and started as a second assistant, which was pretty goddamn
easy. The first picture I did as a second assistant was *Mine Own
Executioner*, directed by Tony Kimmins with Burgess Meredith.
It was Kieron Moore's first film. Then I did a lot of pictures out
of Walton Hall, a very nice studio at Isleworth, which had the
biggest silent stage in Europe. It was later dismantled and taken
to Shepperton. There was only one picture made at a time there
so you could run off for a pot of paint and not have to bother
about chits. Everyone knew which production it was. Later on,
we made *The African Queen* there.

Q: When did you become a first assistant?

A: It was *Britannia Mews*, directed by Jean Negulesco. The critic
C. A. Lejeune said, '*Britannia Mews* – as well she might.' That
was also my first experience of American directors. It was the most
boring thing to work on because you covered everything in a master
shot on a crane, which took hours, and then you shot it all over again
for over-the-shoulders shots, then again for close-ups. Negulesco
had no input at all. It all went back to Zanuck in Hollywood,
who ran rushes and cut the picture. I remember we were behind

schedule and Negulesco had to film a gun going off, with some smoke coming out of the barrel and blood on Dana Andrews's shirt. I told Negulesco that he wouldn't need both shots – you'd use either one or the other, you couldn't have both – and that he just needed to choose which one he wanted, the gun or the blood. So he chose and, bugger me, back came the order from Zanuck: 'Where's slate 7926A?' It was a painting-by-numbers job.

Q: I guess your big break came when you were assigned to work for Carol Reed.

A: Carol was a joy to work with and we did *The Fallen Idol* first. I'd sussed out that the way to work was not as an assistant director but as a director's assistant because some directors are particularly interested in specific aspects of a production and less interested in others. And they're very grateful if you take that under your wing. Carol himself had been an assistant to Basil Dean, who ran the studio and was a very tough cookie. Carol was brilliant because he could mimic Basil's voice perfectly, so he'd ring up and say, 'Props? This is Basil Dean speaking, where are my . . . ?' and they'd say, 'Oh yes, Mr Dean . . .' and it would all happen very quickly.

Q: What was Reed not interested in, which he let you do?

A: Well, background action. He didn't care for that, so I would create these little scenes with the extras. While Carol was attending to his actors, I'd shoot off and make the background better. I remember he shot a scene once and called 'Print it' on the first take. When I asked for another take he said, 'What the fuck for?' I said, 'The background's all wrong. You'll hate it when you see it.' So he said, 'All right, one more for Guy.'

Q: What do you remember about *The Third Man*?

A: That was an amazing picture because we had three units. We had a day unit, a night unit and a sewer unit. Carol directed all three units and I had to tag along as well. We used to knock off about four or five in the morning, get three hours' sleep and off again at eight until four in the afternoon. Then another three hours' sleep and we'd be off again. We did that for sixteen weeks and kept going on benzedrine. It was terrific. My main problem was partly getting the equipment from the day unit to the night unit, but mainly the actors who had worked all night and were wanted during the day as well. Carol just couldn't understand why the actors wanted a minimum of eight hours between calls.

Q: What about Orson Welles, who some people have said co-directed the picture, mainly all those lopsided angles and shadowy lighting seem pinched from Citizen Kane.

A: Welles had absolutely bugger all input and I get very angry when people say he directed it. Orson was living in the Excelsior Hotel in Rome and didn't want a fee. He wanted to be bailed out of unpaid hotel bills and laboratory fees where his negatives were stored. We start shooting and Orson is meant to be there for his night shots, when Harry Lime is running all over Vienna. But Orson never showed up, so the location manager, Bob Dunbar, was sent to Rome to get him.

Because Orson wasn't in Vienna, we had to shoot something. This is where the shadows started. Carol said, 'Guy, can you make a shadow running down that wall?' I found I was rather good at running in front of an arc light and moving down the wall. I was a skinny young lad so I was given a big hat and a heavy coat with shoulder padding. So we shot all this shadow stuff and that's me you can see running down the streets at night. Orson finally arrives, and he's quite happy with the hat and the coat I'd worn for the shadow shots. His first scene was in the sewers. All he had to do was stand there as water poured over him. Carol did the shot and said, 'Isn't that wonderful?' Then Orson went into a tirade. He said he was an American, that he might catch typhoid and he said he wasn't going into the sewers again. So when Orson was being chased through the tunnels, we had to use doubles. We did one shot of him running towards the ferris wheel and a shot of him leaving it, and then it was goodbye Orson Welles as far as Vienna was concerned. Some ten weeks later, Orson shows up in London to do the interior ferris wheel sequence, which was back-projection and was totally as per script with the exception of the cuckoo-clock dialogue, which he wrote himself. It was funny and we all laughed. Then we did a bit of Orson in the sewer set and that was about a week and a half, I'd say.

Q: What about the famous shot when we first see Orson in the doorway? There's a stray cat at his feet and when a woman switches on a light we suddenly see his face. I've always wondered where that doorway was.

A: That was a set at Shepperton but the cat was in Vienna and was directed by me, as were all the faces of the Viennese people. I got an unbelievable bollocking for that. I used to go and collect faces at night. There were soup kitchens and I'd look for old people with extraordinary faces, and I'd put them up against something and take a couple of stills to show Carol. One night I found a monstrously deformed human being and photographed him. He'd got no tongue, couldn't speak and his face was all twisted. I showed it to Carol and he said, 'What's this?' I said, 'Isn't he terrific?' Then Carol said, 'Don't ever, ever, make fun of people with a stammer or a deformity.' He was very sensitive about that kind of thing and I've never forgotten it.

After *The Third Man*, Carol became very friendly with William Wyler, who, when he'd seen the picture, sent Carol a present. Carol opened it up and it was a silver spirit level. Wonderful joke, that. I also did quite well when Carol got his knighthood. He'd go round asking people what they should call him, if he'd get better tables at restaurants, that sort of thing. Then he asked me, 'Do you think I dress properly?' I said, 'Well, some of your things are a bit scruffy.' So he asked me to go through his wardrobe and I took armfuls of his clothes away.

Q: Shortly after *The Third Man* you worked on another classic, *The*

African Queen, and then *Outcast of the Islands*. You were getting all the plums.

A: Well, I was a very good director's assistant, though I had to earn my living between Carol's pictures. And I always thought you could learn just as much from bad directors as well as good ones.

Q: Who were the bad directors?

A: Oh, well, Sidney Gilliatt was adorable. He wrote a very entertaining script of *State Secret* which he decided to direct himself, which was basically a slight mistake. He really didn't know the ABC of film-making, but his editor, Thelma Myers, gave him little cribs as he went along. But he still got into terrible technical trouble two or three times a day. He also wasn't firm enough with the actors, who usually get restless after six weeks or so and come up with their own ideas. George More O'Ferrall was another one. We used to call him George More Awful.

Q: *The African Queen* is one of the most legendary shoots in movie history. Clint Eastwood even made a movie about it. Is it really true that Huston wasn't interested in shooting the picture and that he only wanted to shoot an elephant?

A: Oh yes, that's all he cared about. He disappeared in a light aircraft looking for elephant and when he found plenty of them he put a stone into a handkerchief, threw it out of the plane to mark the spot and said that's our location. Water was about a quarter of a mile away so we paid the village ladies about a penny a bucket and all day long they arrived to fill our water tower. The lodgings were primitive but we all enjoyed it. *The African Queen* itself was a real pain in the ass because it was a very small boat, not very powerful, and it towed a pontoon which was four or five very long Belgian Congo pirogues, cut from tree trunks. We laid planks across them and on one of them were bits and pieces of the *African Queen*. You couldn't put a Technicolor camera on the real boat, so we had a mock-up stern where Bogart and Katie Hepburn did their

steering, and there was a bit of the boiler and the sides of the
boat. That's where we did all their dialogue. The next pontoon
contained the make-up and costume department, and the next
had all the electrical and camera equipment. The next pontoon
had the generator and all the cables ran out from there, connected
to little canoes. Finally, there was another pontoon which carried
a little rattan hut which contained Katie Hepburn's private loo.
She had that written into her contract. So, that's the circus, about
two hundred yards long from the *African Queen* all the way back
to Katie's loo. Africans are basically stupid. I have to say this. It's
a joy to work in Ceylon or with the Chinese. They don't speak
our language but they're very quick. Africans are slow and, well,
they don't get it. So there's nobody to help. It was a nightmare
taking this thing along the river.

Q: But worth it, though, surely. A great location.

A: Ah. . . . We'd cruise along the river looking for somewhere to
shoot a scene. Huston would see a likely spot and we'd all pull
up. I said, 'Jesus, we could be shooting this in Marlow on the
Thames.' And it was absolutely true. John saw us all chatting away
and I said, 'John, I can take you twenty minutes from the studio,
along the Thames . . .' He said, 'Oh, you don't think it looks
like Africa?' I said, 'No, I don't.' 'Well,' he said, 'Why don't
you just Africa it up?' So John goes off with his gun, looking for
gnu or whatever, while we got boxes of Kleenex and went into
the bushes and crushed the tissues so they looked like white lilies.
Then we got some fake blood and gave them red centres. That
was how we'd 'Africa it up'. Later on, when we were shooting
at Murchison Falls in Uganda, I went for a walk thinking how
wonderful it was to be where no white man had ever been. But
behind the falls I found some old film tins from Metro's *Trader
Horn*. Terribly disappointing!

Q: It must have been shortly after *African Queen* that you directed
your first picture.

A: Well, I did *Outcast of the Islands* for Carol, which took us to Borneo and Ceylon. You know, Carol was absolutely brilliant at matching scenes. There's a sequence in *Outcast* when we see Trevor Howard standing on a riverbank talking to Robert Morley and to a little boy in a canoe. We shot the boy in Borneo, we shot Trevor in Ceylon and we shot Morley at Shepperton, and no one ever noticed the joins!

Anyway, my contract ended when I was in Ceylon and Carol told me not to renew it unless Korda promised to give me a picture to direct. I duly sent this telegram and waited hopefully for Korda's reply. A few days later a telegram arrived for Carol. Korda had written, 'Dear Carol. You put him up to it. You bastard. Love Alex.'

Q: Korda didn't want you to become a director? Perhaps you were valued too much as an assistant.

A: David Lean and Carol Reed were taking about eighteen weeks to shoot their pictures and Alex Korda started screaming. He was castigating both of them and boasted that he could make a picture in three weeks. They both said, no, he couldn't. So he decided to do it. The picture was *Home at Seven*, with Ralph Richardson, who had starred in the stage version. The idea was to rehearse for two weeks and shoot for three weeks. Alex was going to direct it himself but he had to go to America. So he told Ralphie to rehearse the actors and he asked me to handle the rest. So off we go. It was the story of a bank clerk who has amnesia and is accused of murder. Of course, there were huge cuts made to the stage version but Ralphie would just carry on as if he was on stage. The actors hadn't a clue what he was going on about. We fired the cameraman on day one and reshot on day two. I really just kept an eye on things as it was pretty easy to shoot.

Then Alex put me on *The Holly and the Ivy*, which George More O'Ferrall was going to direct. Korda said to me, 'George can't direct traffic so you'll do all the cameras and the action, and he'll do the actors.' I said, 'No way,' so he said all right and he gave me an Edgar Wallace mystery, *The Ringer*, which was my first film. We had a super cast, with Donald Wolfit, Mai Zetterling and Herbert Lom.

Q: *The Ringer* was a B-picture, what used to be called a Quota Quickie, a humble beginning. Did you have lots of stories you wanted to do or were you simply being assigned pictures. What was your plan?

A: I wanted to get some mileage under my belt and get out of B-pictures. But in those days there were a lot of directors but very few really good assistant directors, so people wanted me to stay as an AD. Sir Arthur Jarrett, the head of British Lion, took me to lunch and asked me to wait another year. 'I said, Sir Arthur, I'm ready now.' He said, 'No, you're not, lad.' So I showed him a telegram. He read it and said, 'You're a nasty little devil and I think you'll make a good film director.' A few years before, Carol had run the rough cut of *The Third Man* for Jarrett and had a telegram from him saying, 'Loved the picture. Please take off the banjo.' And I kept the telegram. So that's how I became a director.

Q: Your next film was *The Intruder*, with Jack Hawkins from Robin Maugham's novel, then *An Inspector Calls* and *The Colditz Story*, which was a huge hit.

A: The one thing I wanted to do was *Dial M For Murder*, which had been done live on television. Alex bought it for a thousand quid, plus five hundred for the script. Freddie Knott [the author of the play] and I got on like a house on fire. We were two-thirds of the way through when I heard that they'd sold it to Hitchcock for a vast sum of money. I threatened to jump off the roof of 146 Piccadilly and in due course Alex sent for me. I went in with a sad look on my face and Alex said, 'In the years to come, my boy, you are going to have so many bigger disappointments, so I don't know why you are making such a fucking fuss now.'

Wandering around Korda's offices was a producer called Ivan Foxwell, who had a script called *The Intruder* from a novel by Robin Maugham. That was a very happy picture, though at first I had to persuade Jack Hawkins to accept me as a director. He'd just come off *The Cruel Sea* and was very hot, and he'd only known me as an assistant. He was also very wary about playing a homosexual. Anyway, Ivan Foxwell and I got on very well; we didn't get in each other's way. So after *The Intruder* he asked me what I wanted to do next. I said *The Colditz Story*, as I was sick and tired of POWs who were captive hearts. I was myself a POW and I thought Colditz was comedy and it was all true. The people were marvellous and you had to be pretty ballsy to get into Colditz, which was like a club. I convinced Ivan but Korda wasn't very helpful. But it was fun to make and we picked some new faces, like Lionel Jeffries.

Q: You next made *Manuela*, about a burnt-out sea captain whose love for a young half-caste girl causes him to ignore his duties and the ship capsizes. It's a strangely doom-laden and unusually erotic movie for its time.

A: After *Colditz* we felt very confident and wanted to make something a bit more serious, and I came across a book called *Manuela*. Elsa Martinelli was very pretty but she wasn't an actress, so Trevor Howard carried the whole thing. It had a downbeat ending, which gave us problems, and in the middle of the night, when we were shooting near Alicante, I suddenly got the giggles when I realised that one shot could alter the whole meaning of the ending. A bit like *Third Man*, you know, when the girl walks past the camera. If she'd stopped and walked off arm in arm with Trevor Howard the whole film would have changed. Anyway, I shot it both ways, just for laughs. The picture got fine notices but did absolutely no business at the box office. We were told it was the downbeat ending, so I said I had another ending but the damage was done. I like the film personally because it was my first taste of melodrama and because it was quite sexy. I also put all my old enthusiasm for French movies into it.

Q: Your next films, *The Devil's Disciple* and *A Touch of Larceny*, were still very much in the British movie tradition, though you now had impressive stars like Olivier, Burt Lancaster and Kirk Douglas. Did you think you were destined for Hollywood?

A: No, I never thought that, or planned for it. *Devil's Disciple* was being directed by Sandy Mackendrick, who'd just done *Sweet Smell of Success* with Burt. But the picture, which I think is absolutely marvellous, had flopped and he was removed from *Devil's Disciple* after shooting for three weeks. I took over reluctantly and I vowed never to do it again. It wasn't a picture I had any involvement in and I just did it to work with major stars, which was interesting because Burt and Kirk were at each other's throats the whole time. But if push comes to shove, I'd have to say that *A Touch of Larceny* is my favourite of all my pictures. James Mason was born to play that part and we had Robert Flemyng, who was marvellous. We also had George Sanders, who hated acting, but he had so many ex-wives that he did it for the money. He was also a fine cocktail pianist so we gave him a piano and he'd sit on the set tinkling away until we were ready to do a take, and he'd sit quietly, then start up again. He was a wonderful man.

Q: This was all in the late 1950s, when the British cinema was in serious decline. Audiences had plummeted since their post-war levels and cinemas were closing down. What was your perspective on the industry at this time?

A: Television had become a huge competitor and financing became trickier. As a result, fewer movies were being made and only movies on safe subjects. The stars were getting a bit long in the tooth – Margaret Lockwood, Anna Neagle.

Q: What did you make of the so-called 'angry young men', the generation inspired by *Look Back in Anger*, which opened as a play in 1957. There seemed to be a cultural revolution taking place in the theatre, which soon spilled into the cinema.

A: I thought, jolly good, very exciting. The combination of angry young men, Michael Caine and the Beatles killed the leading men who all spoke with Oxford accents. 'Who's for tennis?' and Kenneth More went out of the window. Unless you had a Brummy accent, forget it. I think the Beatles and the pop scene in general had a major influence on the cinema at this time.

Q: The Bond films were also a major part of this stylistic and cultural shift. I believe you were offered the first film, *Dr No*.

A: Yes, I was. I'd known **Cubby [Broccoli]** for a long time. He asked me to do *Cockleshell Heroes* but I didn't like the idea of an Americanised Royal Marines or having battles with Cubby's partner, Irving Allen. So I passed on it but I always enjoyed Cubby. He sent me the script of *Dr No*, but I couldn't do it because I had a lot of personal family problems and couldn't go off to Jamaica for ten weeks. Cubby told me there were things in the script that they wanted to fix but I told him not to, that it had a lot of charm. They shot it pretty seriously, but at the preview the audience fell about laughing at things they weren't supposed to. Cubby wised up to this pretty quick, and then they did *From Russia With Love* and got the balance just about right.

Q: Did you know about Bond before the script of *Dr No* arrived? Had you read any of **Fleming**'s novels?

A: That wasn't my sort of reading, really. I think I read the novel of *Dr No* when I got the script, but I wouldn't read a Bond novel for pleasure, though that's neither here or there. Then I was asked to do *Goldfinger* and it was a very good script. It departed from the book in the sense that Fleming never worked out how to get **Goldfinger** into **Fort Knox** or how to get the gold away by train. I don't think there was an atom bomb, either. **Maibaum** had done a very good job but it was very American. Now, I liked my Commander Bond very straight, with short hair, and certainly

when he goes to the Bank of England and in the **M** scenes he had
to be properly English. So we got **Paul Dehn**, who very quickly
wrote some very good scenes, basically the 'English Club' type of
scene. He gave a nice balance between the slam-bang and a bit of
wit. My other concern was, having seen *Dr No* and *Russia*, I felt
Bond was only as good as his villains and there was a great danger
in him becoming Superman. Consequently, tension goes if you
know he's always going to win every time. The villain has to be
a convincing threat.

Q: It's said that Terence Young didn't do *Goldfinger* because after
directing the first two films he wanted a piece of the action and
Broccoli and **Saltzman** wouldn't cough up.

A: I can't confirm that but I'm pretty certain it's damn true. I was
never party to any of those conversations, though, yes, it's pretty
obvious.

Q: How much of the film was set up by the time you arrived? Apart
from **Sean Connery**, were any of the other actors signed?

A: Cubby had already discovered Goldfinger. He asked me to come
and look at a German actor who he thought would be pretty good.
I looked at a German film in which **Gert Fröbe** played a child
molester and he was on a bench talking German, offering sweets
to a small child, making the sweet come from behind his ear.
He was deliciously evil and wicked. I thought he was absolutely
marvellous so I asked Cubby if he spoke English. 'Yeah,' said
Cubby, 'I've talked to his agent.' That of course turned out to
be total rubbish. Fröbe didn't speak a word of English.

Q: Hardly any of Fröbe's films were released in English-speaking
countries. How would Broccoli have discovered him?

A: Well, MCA had agents in Munich and so the call goes out for a
Mr Big. He's fat and Jewish, named Auric Goldfinger, and that's
probably how the office sent the film over.

Q: What was Fröbe like to work with?

A: He was absolutely adorable. He had this music-hall act in which

Artwork for the original *Goldfinger* poster. (James Bond Fan Club)

Director Guy Hamilton on the set with Shirley Eaton. (BFI)

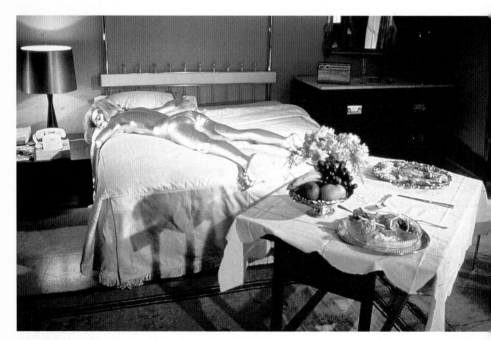

'The girl's dead. She's covered in paint … gold paint.' (BFI)

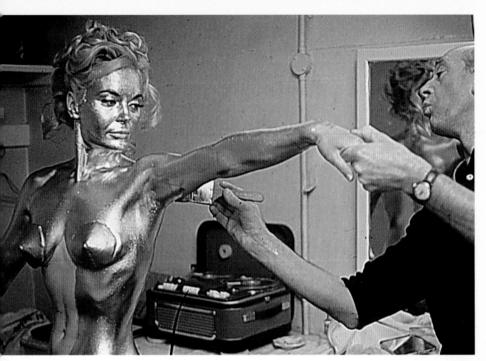

A make-up artist transforms Shirley Eaton into the film's golden girl. (James Bond Fan Club)

Sean Connery confers with lighting cameraman Ted Moore as they shoot the pre-credit sequence of *Goldfinger* at Pinewood Studios. (James Bond Fan Club)

'Ejector seat? You're joking.' 'I never joke about my work, 007.' (James Bond Fan Club)

Gert Frobe relaxes between holes on the golf course. (BFI)

Small-time actor Michael Collins who gave Goldfinger a voice. (James Bond Fan Club)

Ken Adam's set design for Goldfinger's Rumpus Room. (James Bond Fan Club)

'Of course, you know he's quite mad, don't you?' (James Bond Fan Club)

A month before his death, Fleming paid a visit to the *Goldfinger* set to admire Sean Connery in what Shirley Eaton called his Andy Pandy suit. (James Bond Fan Club)

Bernard Lee as M sees this whole gold business turning into another of Bond's personal vendettas. (James Bond Fan Club)

'Do you expect me to talk?' 'No, Mr Bond, I expect you to die!' (BFI)

Honor Blackman as Pussy Galore, admiring Bond's close shave. (James Bond Fan Club)

Not Kentucky but an airfield in Buckinghamshire. (BFI)

Guy Hamilton (with viewfinder), Connery and the crew line-up at the 18th hole as Goldfinger sinks the wrong ball. (BFI)

Harold Sakata and young fans. (BFI)

he played a goalkeeper, and he had his musical act where he did
a one-man German band, which he did on the set, which was
great fun.

Q: How did you first realise he couldn't speak English? That must
     have been a, well, a big problem.

A: European stars have rarely made it in English-speaking movies.
     Catherine Deneuve, Danielle Darrieux . . . they make them in
     industrial quantities. They work hard, they learn their lines but
     when the director says action, they say, 'Will . . . you . . . be . . .
     so . . . kind . . . as . . . to . . . pass . . . me . . . the . . . butter.' Much
     too slowly and deliberately. Now, you can get Sarah Bernhardt
     to dub them but it ain't going to change because if the mouth
     is going at that speed there's nothing you can do. And all these
     poor girls and boys drag the scene down. Gert turned up on the
     set and said, 'How you do you, Mr Hamilton. Very happy to
     meet you. It is a great pleasure to be in the picture.' When I
     asked him where he was staying, he said, 'How do you do, Mr
     Hamilton. Very happy to meet you.' That's all he'd learnt. He
     had a coach and was learning by rote. He worked very hard but
     very, very slow. So I said, 'Gert, we've got to double the speed.'
     So he did that and when Cubby and Harry saw the rushes they
     thought we were insane, even though they knew we were going
     to dub him. But when we had Gert talk at double speed, we had
     the right tempo and it worked very well.

Q: Do you recall who you got to re-voice him?

A: I've totally forgotten. The sound editor would know.

Q: What about the rest of the cast?

A: I'd worked with Shirley [Eaton] before on *Charley Moon*. Honor
     [Blackman] was obvious. **Q** I sorted out in one minute. He
     started out by sucking up to James Bond. I said, 'Q. Have you
     never seen the two pictures? Here's this man who comes and
     borrows all this stuff; he uses it in the wrong way and never
     returns it. You must grit your teeth when this facetious sod

comes into your world and workshop. You hate the bugger.'
So off we went.

Q: What about the Aston Martin **DB5**? Some of the gadgets were
taken from Fleming's original.

A: The ejector seat was interesting. The scene was written with Q
saying, 'Now, 007, if I can have your undivided attention. You
see this little red button . . .' and you faded out on that. So you let
the audience know about the button but they don't know what
it's for. Cubby was sitting around and he said, 'No, you gotta tell
'em what you're gonna do before you do it.' I said, 'No, it will
spoil all the fun if they know what's going to happen.' So I sat
down and scribbled some lines about the ejector seat and how
to operate it. Poor old Q said, 'My God, have I got to learn all
this?' But we shot it and I think on the whole Cubby was right.
The laughs you get when you produce the button; they know
what's going to happen and it's the old Chaplin thing of show
them the banana skin before the fat man slides on it.

Q: It's also the Hitchcock thing, you know, the difference between
surprise and suspense.

A: Yeah, and I give full marks to Cubby on that point, though I
didn't agree with him at the time.

Q: How was Shirley Eaton **painted** gold? When the film opened
the publicity said how dangerous it was and how a small area had
to be left unpainted to avoid suffocation. Was that true?

A: Basically, not. The make-up department spent a lot of time
getting gold paint, and for weeks they had been testing the
colour and ensuring that it stayed on under the lights. Shirley
spent an hour in make-up being sploshed, which can't have
been comfortable, and we shot it in a morning, very quickly
with no fuss. She was wearing a little bikini which I hid with
a pillow to hide her butt. We had no tit problems and that was
about it.

Q: About **Pussy Galore**. In the book she's quite obviously a lesbian.

In the film it's still obvious but more subtle, especially to an audience in 1964.

A: We had to glide over it. And you had to be wary of the censor, who played a very big part in Bond. John Trevelyan, the censor at the time, went bananas when he saw the rough cut and the sound effects of the violence. The American censor was concerned only about sex and the name Pussy. But we conned him in the usual way by inviting him and his wife out to dinner and saying we were very big supporters of the Republican or the Democratic Party. We'd trade a glimpse of tit for something else. Appalling.

Q: What about Harold Sakata and **Oddjob**?

A: I'd been watching some wrestling on Saturday afternoon TV and there were boos and yells at this villain who was fighting the white hero. I thought he was absolutely Oddjob. He was a Hawaiian and had an Olympic medal in wrestling and was earning a poor living. I met him and I always remember he walked away from me and I said, 'Oh, Harold . . .' And he way he turned round, with his whole body, was just marvellous. Cubby and Harry liked him and off we went. Sean was appalled at the squashing the golf ball. He said, 'That's stupid. You can't crush a fooking golf ball. It's fooking stupid.' I said, 'Sean, the whole point is this is a guy you're going to come up against and the audience will think, if he can do that to a golf ball, what can he do to you?' The golf scene itself was quite tricksy to script because you have to go on the basis that the audience doesn't know golf from croquet. You have to explain the rules and how they cheated them. And that's how Sean fell in love with golf. He couldn't play before that and now it almost governs his entire life.

Q: What about the American locations, Fort Knox, Miami and so on. When I saw the picture for the first time in 1964 I just accepted that scenes took place where they claimed to take place. But now when you watch it on video or laser, you can see how ingenious you were. You seemed to have learnt all the old matching tricks from Carol Reed.

A: Before production really started, **Ted Moore**, **Ken Adam** and myself went to Miami and the Fontainebleu Hotel. We shot all the plates for the balcony, when Sean and Shirley Eaton look down at Goldfinger playing cards.

Q: Did Connery go to Miami?

A: No. Nobody went there, so it was quite tricky getting the shots, or plates, which we'd use as back-projection. At the hotel I saw these little planes flying banners and the pool with the glass sides. Living in England, you never saw these things. So I got a plane saying 'WELCOME TO MIAMI', which Ted shot from a helicopter. I was at one end of the pool and our diver was on the diving board. We didn't have any walkie-talkies, so I had a handkerchief and had to guess when Ted was in position. I waved the handkerchief and the diver jumped off the board. It took about three goes before we got it. Then we cut to the shot of the diver underwater, on to **Felix Leiter** and we're in the plot. I guess the Americans would call that 'neat'.

Q: What about the car crusher?

A: We shot that in Miami on a Sunday. We had a deal with Ford – Cubby was friendly with Henry Jr – and he supplied Fords for all the Bond films. We could do what we wanted with them as long as Bond drove in the best one at some point in the film. So we had this actor who was doubling for Oddjob and a Lincoln Continental which we put through the crusher.

Q: I don't think it had an engine. If you look carefully, in one shot you can see right through the bonnet.

A: Ah . . . you could be right. I remember falling around with delight because this scene was supposed to be in Kentucky and just by the crusher's yard was this huge sign which said Kentucky Fried Chicken. I thought this was fabulous luck so we got these CIA guys and shot them by the sign. I had no idea it was a franchise, I just thought God was being kind to me.

Q: So all the shots of driving around in Kentucky were actually done in Miami. Bloody clever, Guy, and cheap, too.

A: That's right. So, after doing the hotel and the car crush, Ted, Ken and I flew to Louisville and drove out to Fort Knox, which was run by Zero Mostel's brother-in-law. We asked him if we could go inside the depository and take pictures. 'No you cannot,' he said. 'Even the President is not allowed inside.' Apparently, this was because of a Congressional Act which protected against a bent President entering Fort Knox and helping himself to some ingots. All we could do was take pictures of the depository from behind the perimeter fence. When we got all the reference stills we could get, I said to Ken, 'This is perfect. Nobody has been inside Fort Knox so we can go bananas with it.' So off he went and it's really one of his best sets.

Q: What about the aerial shots of Fort Knox? Those can't have all been done in Buckinghamshire?

A: Towards the end of shooting we sent a second unit out to Kentucky to get some shots of the real Fort Knox and the shots of Pussy's flying circus squirting their nerve gas. But the stuff they shot was terrible and it wasn't really their fault. After the last day of shooting near Pinewood, when we did the car chase stuff with the Aston Martin, we flew out to Kentucky. It was just Ted, Cubby and me, and we did more shooting the next day than I think I've ever done in my life. We were told we were not allowed to fly less than 3000 feet above the depository, which was hopeless for us. Then we had these crop dusters who smoked cigars who were playing Pussy Galore's pilots. They wore blonde wigs which made them all feel a bit poofy. So, we take off and got down to within 500 feet when we did these flying passes over the bank. Zero Mostel's brother-in-law was going absolutely ape. But Cubby kept him happy and told him it was all an optical illusion.

Then we did the shots of the army base near the depository. Ted and I get into the helicopter and we tell the pilot to buzz all the troops marching around and doing their training. When we go down to reload the camera, we're told the general has complained about us. So I tell Cubby to get a sergeant and a platoon of men and that he's to tell them that the next time we fly over they've got to march, count to five and fall down dead. They thought that was the funniest thing they'd ever heard. Well, Cubby gives them ten bucks and a beer each and they did it. We got the whole thing in two hours. Just the three of us. Absolutely exhausting. After that, it was just a rushed editing job to meet the date of the **premiere**.

Q: Then there were the locations in Switzerland.

A: We did all that in two days, near Andermatt, all the car scenes and the shots of Goldfinger's factory, though not the night scenes and the car chase, which was done in Pinewood with doubles. Most of the Swiss stuff was done with doubles as well because Sean, I think, was still in America, making *Marnie* for Hitchcock.

Q: How did you get the laser?

A: Harry had a good friend, Colonel Charlie Ruschon, who worked at the Pentagon, and he sent us stuff about all the latest toys. At that time the laser beam had no known use. I think they'd sent one up to the Moon but it had no medical use. So we used it to cut Bond's balls off.

Q: What was Ted Moore like to work with?

A: Very quiet man who got on with it. He came from South Africa and had a very distinguished war record. He was in bombers, I think. He was a very tight man, difficult to know. When I came on to *Goldfinger* the crew were very lazy. They were obviously surprised by the success of *Dr No* and *Russia* so they were a bit lazy and arrogant. They thought they were the *crème de la crème*. It was part of my job to put a big boot up all their arses. Ted had huge sets to light and he lit them very well, and he later did a magnificent job on *A Man For All Seasons*.

Q: I wonder if you noticed a big difference in the Connery of *Goldfinger* and the Connery of *Diamonds Are Forever*, which was your second Bond movie.

A: Sean had obviously thought very hard about coming back as Bond. He'd decided that he couldn't stand Harry and said, bollocks, I don't care how much you pay me. But to understand his decision you have to go right back to *Dr No*. Cubby wanted Cary Grant, who was a friend of his. Cary Grant was interested but he wanted residuals and he didn't want to be tied to a three-picture deal. Then Cubby went to David Niven and it was the same thing. So because of the low budget they had to go with someone who was cheap and who would sign a multi-picture contract. Harry was very hot for Sean. I don't think Cubby was quite so hot because of the Scots accent, which was very thick in those days. But Harry was backing Sean and every time some lion tamers from UA arrived he'd call Sean in and ask him to turn around and move about for them. Harry had the subtlety of an ape and he made Sean feel like a complete gorilla. Finally, they went with Sean, who was in debt. He told Harry he wanted an advance of five hundred quid and Harry said sure. Sean collected the money from the accountant and it was four hundred and fifty. Actually it was a genuine mistake, but Sean was convinced he was being screwed. Instead of complaining, he kept schtum and from then on he and Harry were at daggers drawn.

But to answer your question, yes, there was a considerable difference between Sean in *Goldfinger* and Sean in *Diamonds Are Forever*. Sean arrived having made the decision to do it, and was going to do something useful with the money. He liked the script, apart from a couple of minor twidges. Vegas was a fun place; we got the golf organised and he always appreciated that I got the picture finished on schedule. The Sean in *Dr No* shows an actor finding his way. He's a little bit nervous in front of the camera. Less so in *Russia*, and in *Goldfinger* he's pretty solid and confident with dialogue.

Q: *Goldfinger* seems to finesse the formula. It's the Bond film where all the elements came together.

A: Well, I had a couple of good lessons, and you've got to credit Terence Young for getting the ball rolling.

Q: You directed four Bond films. Do you think maybe four was too many?

A: Well, yes, I regret doing the two with **Roger [Moore]**. What happened was dead simple. Lazenby cocked it up and behaved very stupidly on the picture [On Her Majesty's Secret Service]. He got up Cubby's nose. So Lazenby was out and then they asked me to do the new Bond. All sorts of names were bandied about. I was in America and found the perfect Bond, who was Burt Reynolds. He had all Sean's qualities, a nice wit, a little short maybe, but he moved like a dream. But UA said forget it, he's just a stuntman. When no one else came up, they dug deep into their pockets and brought Sean back. So I did that picture happily and said, 'That's it, chaps, thank you, goodbye!' But they said, no, you haven't done the picture with the new Bond. They made me an offer I couldn't refuse, so I hung around for the next one, *Live and Let Die*.

Q: It was then, wasn't it, that Saltzman and Broccoli began to fall out badly?

A: Very much so. The history of that is very, very sad. They'd made no money on *Dr No* or *Russia* because it was all collateralised, but, finally, with *Goldfinger*, they hit the jackpot. If they stood on my terrace and threw their money away all day, they still couldn't have got rid of it. Now their dreams were achieved and they asked themselves what they wanted to do with their lives. Harry wanted to make hundreds of pictures and he saw that MGM was going cheap and wanted to buy it. He said, 'Whaddya think, Cubby?' and Cubby said, 'You're joking. I've been working all my life not to work. For God's sake Harry, we'd have to read scripts!'

Harry had been virtually down and out in Paris after the war, and every week he'd go over to Paris and buy lunch for everyone who'd helped him. That was an attractive side to Harry but he also had to be Mr Big. Cubby and Harry went their own ways and led totally separate lives. They worked together okay until Harry bought Technicolor with 50 per cent of Danjaq's collateral. From that moment on the problems started and they got so bad they couldn't work together. I could work happily with Harry and happily with Cubby, but when they were together it was a nightmare. I mean, Cubby would say, 'I like this scene,' and Harry would say, 'Well, I don't.' He'd say that on principle, even if it was a good scene. It was very sad to witness, so they agreed to produce the films separately. I made a few films with Harry – *Battle of Britain* and *Funeral in Berlin* – but after *The Man With the Golden Gun* I left the Bond business.

Filmography

(All titles as director.)
1952   *The Ringer*
1953   *The Intruder*
1954   *An Inspector Calls*
1955   *The Colditz Story*
1956   *Charley Moon*
1957   *Manuela*
1959   *The Devil's Disciple*
1959   *A Touch of Larceny*
1961   *I due nemici/ The Best of Enemies*

1963	*The Party's Over**
1963	*Man in the Middle*
1964	*Goldfinger*
1966	*Funeral in Berlin*
1969	*Battle of Britain*
1971	*Diamonds Are Forever*
1973	*Live and Let Die*
1974	*The Man with the Golden Gun*
1978	*Force 10 from Navarone*
1980	*The Mirror Crack'd*
1981	*Evil Under the Sun*
1985	*Remo – Unarmed and Dangerous*
1989	*Try This On For Size*

his *Meister*'s voice

Because **Gert Fröbe** could not speak English, someone had to be found to supply **Goldfinger**'s voice. It had to be a voice with an accent which might have engaged Professor Higgins's mind for a minute or two – German? Austrian? No, a Balt! It also had to be a voice which matched Fröbe's physique and character. All **Fleming** tells us about Goldfinger's voice is that it is 'flat, colourless' and, later on, 'calm, authoritative', which is strange considering the lengths Fleming goes to in describing Goldfinger's bizarre physical appearance. For a man with an outsize head and carrot hair, a 'flat, colourless' voice is disappointing. Fleming should have given him a suggestively hysterical falsetto.

The Bond movies used dubbing extensively. Ursula Andress in *Dr No* was dubbed by another actress (Nikki Van Der Zyl) and so, in

---

* Uncredited; Hamilton removed his name from the credits following demands from the British Board of Film Censors that the film's depiction of necrophilia should be modified.

fact, were most of the Bond girls. As far as the men were concerned, the king of the voice-over was Robert Rietty, an actor so skilled in the arts of locution that he often took several roles in the same movie, sometimes even talking to himself. Rietty worked on several Bond movies, providing the voices for Largo in *Thunderball* and Tiger Tanaka in *You Only Live Twice*. But for *Goldfinger* the actor chosen was Michael Collins, whose performance was supervised in the Pinewood dubbing theatre by Norman Wanstall's associate Harry Miller, who once performed a miracle with Laurence Olivier's soliliquy on *Hamlet* which convinced people that Olivier was speaking the lines live, to camera, which was not the case.

Although Fröbe's real voice can be heard in a few scenes, it was Michael Collins who spoke most of the dialogue. So smooth is Miller's dub that you never notice it, and so good is Collins that he deserves at least as much praise as Fröbe himself for bringing Goldfinger so vividly to life.

Collins himself is a shadowy figure. The present writer has been unable even to ascertain the year of his birth and the year of his death, which was around 1977. He always seemed to be a minor player, mainly on television as 'second policeman' or 'third security guard'. He appeared in *Quatermass II* (1955), a number of episodes of *Z-Cars* and *Dr Finlay's Casebook*, as well as the early soap *The Newcomers*, in which he played Farmer Langley. His few feature film roles included *Miracle in Soho* (1957), *Caught in the Net* (1960), *A Prize of Arms* (1962) and *The Court-Martial of Major Keller* (1964). His final role appears to have been in a Canadian film of 1975, *Journey Into Fear*.

See **Hamilton, Guy**.

history of the cinema

The history of the motion picture industry might be summed up as the development of the serials with the blade of the sawmill moving closer and closer to the heroine's neck, to modern movies with the laser beam zeroing in on James Bond's crotch.

(Pauline Kael)

See **dealers**.

Homer

See **DB5**; **Lee, Bernard**.

Hood, Thomas

Thomas Hood (1799–1845) was an English poet and humourist. One of his verses was on the title page of the final screenplay of *Goldfinger*:

> Gold! Gold! Gold! Gold!
> Bright and yellow, hard and cold,
> Molten, graven, hammer'd and roll'd;
> Hoarded, barter'd, bought and sold,
> Stolen, borrowed, squander'd, doled,
> Price of many a crime untold.
> Gold! Gold! Gold! Gold!

hot stink

Her body was more than just desirable – it had that proud mocking beauty that seemed to say, 'Now then, you handsome brute, are you man enough to handle me?' A body that only a man amongst men would ever possess. Passionately. Ruthlessly.

He took stock. He wanted to take the memory of this first moment of possession to keep and cherish – a masculine sentiment. The deep-piled hand-laid carpet underfoot; Wilton, naturally, and in that warm, dark shade that reminded him of Barberesco; but not shop Wilton, surely? Ah, specially woven, of course. He ran his fingers, tenuously, across her seat. They thrilled to the touch of fine leather. Coach hide. Tanned in Lancashire, no doubt.

He was eager, but gentle. She whimpered once, trembled for an instant, then yielded. She was his.

The lightest action on the clutch and he shifted to fourth, settled into a casual sixty. Soon, to try her out, to see if she was as good as her promise, it would be into fifth. His hand glanced at the fascia, and the safety-glass window beside him disappeared effortlessly, electrically. The hot stink of the A2 hit him. He drank it in joyfully, slowed, bridged into the sprawl of Rochester, did a silent change into third.

He nudged open the gun-metal case and took out another cigarette. He thought with pleasure, 'This is driving. This is an Aston Martin **DB5**.'

(advertisement in *Goldfinger* World **Premiere** brochure)

See **product placement**.

Houston, Penelope

Such was the power of the publicity machine and the popularity of the previous films that *Goldfinger* was as impervious to critics as **Fort Knox** was to bombs. If every critic had panned the picture it would probably not have been quite so sucessful, though it would have still cleaned up. The reviews, then, are barometers of popular and intellectual taste at the time, and most of the critics talk about their guilt – or lack of it – in enjoying the Bond films. Reviews from various newspapers and magazines appear elsewhere in this book, but printed below is what remains the best (and certainly the best-written) review of any Bond film and its surrounding context.

The article appeared in the winter 1964/65 issue of *Sight and Sound* and is by the magazine's editor, Penelope Houston, a middle-aged, chain-smoking and tweedy woman whose main passion was for the racetrack. Appointed editor in the 1950s, Ms Houston steered *Sight and Sound* through four decades, espousing the British 'new wave' of social realism spearheaded by Lindsay Anderson, Tony Richardson and Karel Reisz (all of whom were *Sight and Sound* writers), as well as the French 'new wave' led by Jean-Luc Godard, François Truffaut and Jacques Rivette. Published by the British Film Institute, *Sight and Sound* was regarded by many as elitist and irrelevant, and rivals resented the fact that the magazine was state funded. It largely eschewed the popular cinema (for example, the magazine did not bother to review *Lawrence of Arabia*) unless it was a film by a favoured director such as Ford, Wilder or Hitchcock. On its back page it awarded a maximum of four stars to films 'of special interest to *Sight and Sound* readers'. In its issue of Autumn 1964 no film received four stars. Three stars were awarded to Satyajit Ray's *Devi*, Losey's *King and Country*, Demy's *Les Parapluies de Cherbourg*, Truffaut's *La Peau douce* and *Goldfinger*, which would have startled many of the magazine's readers. By contrast, *A Hard Day's Night* received one star.

In her article Miss Houston really gets to grips with what was then only just becoming a phenomenon. And like many who have written about Bond, she clearly finds the novels so much more interesting to write about. But, like the film she is reviewing, her comments have acquired a time-capsule quality:

> The pre-credits sequence of *Goldfinger* ends, as everyone knows, with an impromptu electrocution. Caught for a moment without his revolver [*sic*] (the trusty Beretta? Or the **Walther** with the tailored holster?), Bond catches a glimpse of an advancing assailant reflected in the eyeball of the lady with whom he is temporarily engaged. Casually, he gets her out of the way by flinging her in the path of his opponent. Scuffle; villain tipped into the bath, but still clutching Bond's pistol above the water-line; the electric fire is hurled across the room, with a movement reminiscent of a slip fielder shattering the bails;

and exit, in a cloud of steam, another emissary of Smersh or
Spectre. At which moment, the audience at the London press
show gave that concerted yell of innocent happiness, that great
collective sigh of satisfied expectation, which has become the
standard accompaniment to the exploits of 007.

Joy, of course, was not entirely unconfined. 'One vast,
gigantic confidence trick to blind the audience to what is
going on underneath,' wrote Nina Hibbin, sticking severely
to her guns in the *Daily Worker*. What she detected underneath
was hardly unexpected: sex, sadism, racialism (**Oddjob** and the
Korean bodyguards), and 'a constantly lurking viciousness and
the glamorisation of violence'. But the charm of the Bond
films, for those of us who are charmed, is that nothing is
allowed to lurk for very long, and that the glamorisation is
almost preposterously out in the open. One of the familiar
critical attitudes is a kind of wary protectiveness towards the
audience. We all know, of course, that we ourselves are beyond
corruption. But what about that great innocent mass out there,
subjected to the wiles of mass cult, mid cult, pop cult, seduced
by the advertising campaigns, fodder for the sociological surveys?
One of the reassuring and agreeable things about the Bond films
is that they do practically nothing to encourage or substantiate
such critical paternalism. 'It seems to me,' wrote Philip Oakes
of *From Russia With Love*, 'that audiences not only identify the
elements which go to make up this kind of entertainment, but
also that they pause to consider their effect.' There may hardly
be time for the pause, and I would myself be very hesitant about
analysing the effect, but as far as the identification of elements is
concerned, the reactions of the audience make it clear that they
know precisely what they are watching. The **Aston Martin** in
Goldfinger, with its machine-guns, flamethrower, smokescreen,
and special equipment for forcing pursuing cars off the road
and ejecting unwanted passengers, is a majestically preposterous

agent of destruction. It's no more credible as a car than is **Pussy Galore** as a pilot, or the laser beam as an instrument of torture. These are not the kind of fantasies likely to seduce the unwary.

The film-makers had been warned. 'Without doubt the nastiest book I have ever read,' wrote **Paul Johnson** of *Dr No*: 'The sadism of a schoolboy bully, the mechanical, two-dimensional sex-longings of a frustrated adolescent, and the crude snob-cravings of a suburban adult.' This celebrated broadside was fired from the *New Statesman* in April 1958, a month after Bernard Bergonzi had been harrying Bond in *The Twentieth Century*. 'Mr **Fleming**'s affective superstructure,' wrote Mr Bergonzi in an article almost prim in its distaste, 'is mainly concerned with gambling, potent fantasies of High Life, and, of course, sex and violence . . . The fact that his books are published by a very reputable firm, and are regularly reviewed – and highly praised – in our self-respecting intellectual weeklies, surely says more about the present state of our culture than a whole volume of abstract denunciations.'

No doubt. In 1958, however, the transformation scene was still to come. Bond was still just a character in a series of popular novels; and the critical denunciations, in fact, could be taken as signs that the success machine was getting thoroughly into its stride. Mr Fleming made a fortune, and a contribution to the export drive, he estimated, roughly comparable with the output of a small boot factory. Bond became a symbol and a landmark, along with the Beatles and Lucky Jim, the Angry Young Men and Elizabeth Taylor, and all those ruthlessly over-publicised horses and jockeys on the familiar roundabout. In another context, we've seen this whole process of assimilation into the national fantasy life demonstrated with the demise of the Windmill Theatre, celebrated on television and in the press in tones appropriate to the disappearance of Nelson from his column, with even a glimpse of Richard Dimbleby mourning over a Windmill dancer's fan. At least Bond's place in the fantasy was comprehensible, as a kind of antidote to Blake and Lonsdale, to the villa in Ruislip and the Admiralty files.

All the same, Bond was perhaps more vulnerable to his critics than to the agents of Smersh and Spectre. He was never quite the same, Maurice Richardson has noted, after those near-lethal kicks from Rosa Klebb's poisoned boots – which happened more or less to coincide with the Johnson –Bergonzi attack. Perhaps the charge of suburban snobbery was the most wounding. Certainly Mr Fleming seemed to be gradually tapering off those almost endearingly absurd catalogues of Bond's domestic accoutrements. ('The single egg, in the dark blue egg cup with the gold ring round the top, was boiled for three and a third minutes. It was a very fresh, speckled brown egg from French Maran hens . . . Bond disliked white eggs . . .' and so on, through the Tiptree jam, the wholewheat bread, and the Minton coffee cup.)

A certain studied melancholy, perhaps an inheritance from the world of Raymond Chandler, began to creep into his creator's attitudes. In the brilliant opening chapter of *On Her Majesty's Secret Service*, Bond is found sitting by the sea, looking out at the sunset and reflecting on his long-lost childhood. In *You Only Live Twice* the setting is a rose garden in Regent's Park, and the reflections are on mortality. It seems almost a reflex of the quintessential Bond that he should still carefully note the name-tags on the rose bushes. As the inventory of improbable girls grew longer – Gala, Tiffany, Solitaire, Honey, Pussy, Kissy – even this old enthusiasm seemed to be flagging. Bond when last seen, landed with amnesia and Kissy on a Japanese pearl-fishing island, was a shadow of the adventurer who took on Dr No.

The job of the films was to reinvigorate a formula which was already, one suspects, beginning slightly to pall on its inventor.

But exactly what formula? It's evident that the idea of Bond, the mystique of the double 0 number and the licence to kill, the paraphernalia of guns and cars, is more alluring in screen terms than many of his actual adventures. *Casino Royale*, the first of the novels, in which Bond beat the Soviet paymaster in France at baccarat and fell in love with Vesper Lynd, double agent and reluctant spy for Redland, has the tightest construction and the most credible surface. Most of the plots, however, are just variations on Jack the Giant Killer, with appropriately extreme trimmings. Dispatched by **M**, the Prospero of the Secret Service, Bond stages a one-man assault on a fairytale stronghold furnished out of *House and Garden* and the travel supplements. The ogre (Dr No, Mr Big, Ernst Stavro Blofeld) captures him; there is a great smash-up; and Bond swims, skis or shoots his way out. This is not a magic formula: just a formula.

If the books are compellingly readable, it's for all sorts of non-adaptable reasons. Ian Fleming was not, like Graham Greene in the mood of his 'entertainments', a master of the almost self-consciously cinematic image. The things he did best were mainly things that the cinema does badly – a fact which throws a tolerably revealing light on some of the differences between the bestseller and the hit film. If he wrote, as has often been suggested, like an advertising copywriter, at least it was like a copywriter for those ingeniously esoteric advertisements which bewitch us with technicalities. The brand-name emphasis may be a kind of obsessive window-dressing, a way of hinting at sophistication to the unsophisticated, but when Fleming told us how something actually worked we believed him

He was very good on the sensations of fast driving: the cinema can't cope with this, perhaps because of the problem of just where to fit the camera, so that you are liable to end up with no more than screaming tyres on the **sound** track, close-ups of hands on the wheel, and windscreen views of the road. You can do all sorts of things with cars in the cinema, except communicate the sensation of actually driving one. He was knowing and exact about travel – the cinema prefers the generalities. He wrote greedily about food – film-makers are cautious about what actors eat, presumably since there's felt to be a risk of hungry audiences stampeding from the cinemas. In particular, he wrote with precision and brilliance about games and gambling: about the battles of nerve played out under the casino chandeliers, about bridge and golf and baccarat. Fleming was distinctly old-fashioned about his villains and their shocking ways ('Extraordinary man. There's only one thing . . . Sir Hugo Drax cheats at cards'). He would never, one feels, have encouraged the solecism of Oddjob's outfit as caddy in the screen *Goldfinger*. Writing about games brought out all his feeling for detail, for the technicality as a stimulus to excitement. Popular cinema deals in particularised emotions, but its preference is for generalised fact.

So the film-makers found themselves with a brand-name hero, a conventional line in criminal master-minds (though Blofeld may stalk about his death-dealing Japanese garden in samurai armour, he hasn't even the mad Mabuse's wits), a lot of skilful, unassimilable detail, and the legend of sex, violence, etc., which they had somehow to steer past the censor. The conversion of all this into box-office gold can't have been quite as easy as it now seems. Was it Mr **Broccoli** or Mr **Saltzman**, the screenwriter **Richard Maibaum** or the original director Terence Young, who hit on the entirely contemporary solution to any otherwise insoluble problem – to turn it into a frantic joke?

A legend has somehow grown up that *Dr No*, the first of the films, is still the best. Seeing it again, however, one realises that here the film-makers were feeling their way. There is plenty of cool, callous fun, like the scene in which Bond traps the geologist spy into emptying his Smith and Wesson into a dummy, or the calm welcome given the fugitives by the receptionists at Dr No's establishment. The sequence in which Bond fights his way along Dr No's assault course of pain is gingerly toned down, perhaps in deference to the censor, but Bond still bleeds real blood. The problem of how to kill without hurting remains to be solved. And it's an interesting sidelight on the risks encountered by films whose jokes are resolutely up to the minute that the best of the lot – the discovery of the National Gallery's lost Goya as an adornment of Dr No's island – now leaves the audience cold. Out of the headlines, out of mind.

From Russia With Love had a much better story, a richer choice of locations, Lotte Lenya in maid's cap and apron, the shooting of one of the villains as he pops out of Anita Ekberg's mouth on a poster, and the best pre-credits sequence of any thriller on record. The manhunt around the formal garden, ending with the blaze of light on the château terrace as Spectre's head of operations comes down the steps to congratulate his chief executioner, displayed a throwaway elegance not found elsewhere. It is *Goldfinger*, however, which perfects the formula – and does it so conclusively that it is hard to see what Mr Broccoli and Mr Saltzman have left themselves in hand for the future. A new director (**Guy Hamilton**) and a new script collaborator (**Paul Dehn**) must be assumed to have something to do with the greater finesse, although on the face of it one can think of few films in which the director's contribution seems to subordinate to a total production strategy. *Goldfinger* allows nothing to impede its sense of humour: it converts Bond into a human equivalent of the cat in Tom and Jerry cartoons, with the same ghastly resilience and the same capacity for absorbing punishment; it can't bring itself to take Pussy Galore, with her hockey team of pilots ('Dress rehearsal went like a dream, skipper') as anything but a joke. There is an assumption –

which you find, at quite the other end of the spectrum, in the Godard films – that we all know the clichés and can have a little fun with them.

A key sequence is that in which the car, with newly shot corpse inside, is scrunched and pulped into a tidy little cube of scrap metal. Not for Mr Saltzman and Mr Broccoli some tired old motor due in any case for the breaker's yard. They put a gleamingly polished Thunderbird through the works, inflicting on the machine a torture far more agonising (because, for once, it is really happening; and to a status symbol at that) than the consciously risible sequence in which Bond is nearly carved up by the laser beam. Another example of impudence raised almost to the level of art is the scene of dinner at the Bank of England, where the camera pulls slowly back down the room to reveal that the set really is as big and rich as we thought it was.

Ken Adam's sets have their own kind of wit, like extensions of the power game into steel and concrete. It is a total dream world, a larger version of Goldfinger's revolving room, in which the mechanical accessories look entirely and formidably real, and it is assumed (rightly, I think) that we will accept the advertising and strip cartoon origins of the people. It helps if there can be a suggestion that machines are getting on top of people, as when Bond, tied to the ticking bomb in the Fort Knox vaults, cracks open the casing but can't pick out the time fuse from among the maze of wires. It would be impossible to sustain the whole mood of the film in a novel, because it becomes essentially a matter of playing off one set of associations against another, allowing a geniality in the acting to undercut the brutality, using humour as a disinfectant and exaggeration as a calculated effrontery. Where Hitchcock manipulates a response, *Goldfinger* assumes a mood of good-humoured complicity with the audience, from the first absurd sight of 007 emerging from the waves wearing a toy seagull on his head.

As thrillers, the Fleming trilogy won't stand up in the same company as classics like *The Man Who Knew Too Much* or *The Maltese Falcon* or *The Big Sleep*. They have the speed but not the urgency; the fun but not the cutting edge. Bogart would have demolished 007 long before he drew the Walther from its specially tailored holster, and Sydney Greenstreet would hardly have found Goldfinger a worthy companion on the trail of the Falcon. In a few years time the films will seem dated by their assumptions as much as by the lines of their cars, or by Pussy Galore's extravagantly leathery wardrobe. At the moment, however, and for the moment, it's all sufficiently here: 'the brassy, swinging, ungallant taste of the Sixties', to quote Penelope Gilliatt. Ian Fleming's Bond could still be considered – was in fact considered by Mr Bergonzi – in terms of the ethics of Richard Hannay. The screen's Bond is at once the last of the clubman buccaneers and the first of the joke supermen. The transformation has earned the film-makers their place in the annals of public taste. One must give the sociologists best and admit that *Goldfinger* really is a rather symbolic film.

See **history of the cinema**; **Johnson, Paul**; *Sweet Movie*; *Time Out*; **Walker, Alexander**; **ugh!**; *Variety*; **whoops!**

J

Jill

See **Masterson, Jill**.

Johnson, Paul

Up to 1956 the Bond novels had enjoyed a modest success. Even though each new title outsold its predecessor, **Fleming**'s readers could still be classified as affluent, professional and literary, people who enjoyed a bit of rough trade, a bit of slumming, a joke – even when the novels lacked a sense of humour, which is, of course, what made them funny.

Public perception began to change when the *Daily Express* serialised *Diamonds Are Forever* and *From Russia With Love*. What had started as harmless entertainment for the Establishment and for those who clung to its coat-tails now appealed to the general masses, the unread and the unwashed, those who lived in suburban semis, had a fridge and not a scullery, and polished their chrome-heavy Ford Consuls and Vauxhall Wyverns every Sunday morning.

Because of his growing fame – helped, too, by the prime minister's sojourn at Goldeneye – Fleming found himself analysed by various academics and invariably left-wing journalists, who, while remaining immune to Fleming's virus of sex and violence, worried about the ordinary man's risk of infection. Professor Bernard Bergonzi opened the hunting season on Fleming in an article for the obscure monthly *Twentieth Century*, which took issue with Fleming's obsession with

brand names, his crude sadism and his vulgar treatment of sex. Rallying
to Bergonzi's call, the *Manchester Guardian* editorialised, stating that
Fleming's work was 'symptomatic of a decline in taste'.

But it was Paul Johnson, then a left-winger who wrote for
the *New Statesman*, the unofficial parish gazette of Britain's Labour
Party, who fired the most armour-piercing critical salvo, taking a
stridently moral line, questioning Fleming's treatment of sex and
violence, his evident snobbery and, inevitably, his penchant for
brand names. It was Johnson's article, published on 5 April 1958
under the alluring title 'Sex, Snobbery and Sadism', which firmly
established the critical line on Fleming and, in due course, on
the Bond films and the Bond phenomenon. If Fleming's novels held up a mirror to the age, then so did Johnson's critique
of them:

> I have just finished what is, without doubt, the nastiest book
> I have ever read. It is a new novel entitled *Doctor No* [*sic*]
> and the author is Mr Ian Fleming. Echoes of Mr Fleming's
> fame had reached me before, and I had been repeatedly urged
> to read his books by literary friends whose judgment I nor-
> mally respect. When this new novel appeared, therefore, I
> obtained a copy and started to read. By the time I was a
> third of the way through, I had to suppress a strong impulse
> to throw the thing away, and only continued reading because
> I realised that here was a social phenomenon of some impor-
> tance.
>
> There are three basic ingredients in *Doctor No*, all unhealthy,
> all throughly English: the sadism of the schoolboy bully, the
> mechanical, two-dimensional sex-longings of a frustrated ado-
> lescent, and the crude, snob-cravings of a suburban adult. Mr
> Fleming has no literary skill, the construction of the book is
> chaotic, and entire incidents and situations are inserted, and then
> forgotten, in a haphazard manner. But the three ingredients are

manufactured and blended with deliberate, professional precision; Mr Fleming dishes up his recipe with all the calculated
accountancy of a Lyons Corner House . . . .

Fleming deliberately and systematically excites and then satis-
fies the very worst instincts of his readers. This seems to
me far more dangerous than straight pornography. In 1944,
George Orwell took issue with a book which in some ways
resembles Fleming's novels – *No Orchids for Miss Blandish*.
He saw the success of *No Orchids*, published in 1940, as part
of a discernible psychological climate, whose other products
were Fascism, the Gestapo, mass-bombing and war. But in
condemning *No Orchids*, Orwell made two reservations. First,
he conceded that it was brilliantly written, and that the acts
of cruelty it described sprang from the subtle and integrated,
though perverse, view of human nature. Secondly, in contrasting
No Orchids with *Raffles* – which he judged a healthy and harmless
book – he pointed out that *No Orchids* was evil precisely because
it lacked the restraint of conventional upper-class values; and
this led him to the astonishing but intelligible conclusion that
perhaps, after all, snobbery, like hypocrisy, was occasionally
useful to society.

What, I wonder, would he have said of *Doctor No*? For
this novel is badly written to the point of incoherence and
none of the 50,000 people who, I am told, are expected to
buy it, could conceivably be giving the publishers, Cape, 13s
6d to savour its literary merits. Moreover, both its hero and
its author are unquestionably members of the Establishment.
Bond is an ex-Royal Navy Commander and belongs to Blades,
a sort of super-Whites. Mr Fleming was educated at Eton and
Sandhurst, and is married to a prominent society hostess, the
ex-wife of Lord Rothermere. He is the foreign manager of that
austere and respectable newspaper the *Sunday Times*, owned by
an elderly fuddy-duddy called Lord Kemsley, who once tried to

sell a popular tabloid with the slogan (or rather his wife's slogan) of 'clean and clever.' Fleming belongs to the Turf and Boodle's and lists among his hobbies the collecting of First Editions. He is also the owner of Goldeneye, a house made famous by Sir Anthony Eden's retreat from Suez. Eden's uneasy slumbers, it will be remembered, were disturbed by giant rats which, after they had been disposed of by his detectives, turned out to be specially trained ones kept by Mr Fleming.

Orwell, in fact, was wrong. Snobbery is no protection: on the contrary, the social appeal of the dual Bond–Fleming person- ality has added an additional flavour to his brew of sex and sadism. Fleming's novels are not only successful, like *No Orchids*; they are also smart. The *Daily Express*, pursuing its task of bringing glamour and sophistication to the masses, has serialised the last three. Our curious post-war society, with its obsessive interest in debutantes, its cult of U and non-U, its working-class graduates educated into snobbery by the welfare state, is a soft market for Mr Fleming's poison. Bond's warmest admirers are among the Top People. Of his last adventure, *From Russia With Love*, his publishers claim, with reason, that it 'won approval from the sternest critics in the world of letters.' The *Times Literary Supplement* found it 'most brilliant,' the *Sunday Times* 'highly polished,' the *Observer* 'stupendous,' the *Spectator* 'rather pleasant.' And this journal, most susceptible of all, described it as 'irresistible.'

It has become easier than it was in Orwell's day to make cruelty attractive. We have gone just that much farther down the slope. Recently I read Henri Alleg's horrifying account of his tortures in an Algiers prison; and I have on my desk a documented study of how we treat our prisoners in Cyprus. I am no longer astonished that these things can happen. Indeed, after reflecting on the Fleming phenomenon, they seem to me almost inevitable.

Johnson's broadside brought about a passing comment from none other than Hugh Gaitskill, the leader of the Labour Party, who said: 'The combination of sex, violence, alcohol and – at intervals – good food and nice clothes is, to one who lives such a circumscribed life as I do, irresistible.'

Fleming himself countered Johnson's assault in two ways: he arranged for a fan of his, name of Raymond Chandler, to give *Dr No* a rave review in The *Sunday Times*; and then he buggered off to the Seychelles to write a travel piece and to research a story which became *The Hildebrand Rarity*.

See **history of the cinema**; **Houston, Penelope**; *Sweet Movie*; *Time Out*; **Walker, Alexander**; **ugh!**; *Variety*; **whoops!**

judo

See **Pussy Galore**.

K

Knox, Major-General Henry

Henry Knox gave his name to **Fort Knox** and thus to a simile for security. He was a lousy businessman, though it was not his financial or business prowess which he was valued for. It was for his military brilliance and for his establishment of the security of the nation.

Henry Knox was born on 25 July 1750 in Boston, the seventh of ten children. His father, William, was a shipmaster who came from Scotland and his mother, Mary Campbell, came from the north of Ireland. When Henry was 12 his father was bankrupted and died in the West Indies, leaving the boy to support his mother. But he was bright and energetic, and on leaving school he worked in the bookstore of Wharton & Bowes in Boston. By the time he was 21 Henry had set up his own business, the London Book-Store, and was making enough money to live on.

Henry was already interested in military and political affairs, though a hunting expedition robbed him of the third and fourth fingers of his left hand when a fowling-piece exploded. Nevertheless, he joined the Boston Grenadier Corps and was soon made second-in-command. A striking and flamboyant figure, he successfully wooed a British diplomat's daughter, Lucy Flucker, whom he married on 16 June 1774. Her family, it is said, was much displeased, though that in itself did not cause the War of Independence, which broke out two years later.

Henry had become an expert in military engineering and tactics.

He served under General Ward and quickly became a confidante and close friend of George Washington, alongside whom he fought in New York. He was especially adept at devising schemes for capturing enemy artillery and then putting it to good use in the destruction of its previous owners. He started an arsenal and was in the thick of things at the Battles of Brandywine, Germantown and Monmouth. In 1779 he proposed a military academy – later named West Point – and at the Siege of Yorktown in 1781 his cannon emplacements won the day. Washington said that the 'resources of his genius supplied the deficit of means'. On 15 November 1781 Washington promoted him to major-general, and when, in 1783, the War was finally at an end and the army disbanded it was Henry's hand that Washington shook first. From 1787 to his retirement in 1794 Henry served as America's first Secretary of War, responsible for forging treaties with warmongering Indian tribes and for creating a serious navy and coastal defences.

The security of the nation was in his pudgy hands. For Henry was huge. By 1783 he weighed 300 lbs and was known as the Philadelphia Nabob, for the lavishness of his receptions as well as his girth. His wife, Lucy, was almost as corpulent as he was, and they were also known as 'the largest couple in the city'. Henry himself was often ridiculed for his size, for his truculence and for his exaggerated swagger.

He entertained grandly, treating the likes of Talleyrand, Louis Philippe and Alexander Baring (founder of the bank) to opulent banquets. He spent vastly more than he earnt, mainly on property in New England. He was into many things – brick-making, livestock, shipbuilding and timber, as well as incipient debt. He fathered twelve children, nine of whom died young, and he died himself on 25 October 1806, at the relatively young age of 55. He choked on a chicken bone.

He was, perhaps, worth his weight in **gold**.

L

Lee, Bernard (1908–81)

As Bond's boss, M, Bernard Lee is generally seen behind his desk, gruff and irritable, not so much envious at Bond's adventures in the field as disdainful of his sexual weakness. M is a moral barometer and represents a traditional ploy of British thriller writing; M is to Bond what Dr Watson is to Sherlock Holmes, a sort of buffoon redeemed by unfailing loyalty and barely concealed love. A retired admiral and confirmed bachelor, M is far too straightlaced to fancy Bond, even though **Ian Fleming**'s friend Cyril Connolly once wrote a pastiche called 'Bond Strikes Camp' (*London Magazine*, 1963) in which M orders Bond to wear a dress and then tries to seduce him.

Bernard Lee fitted the role like the proverbial glove. There is a bit of the Basil Radford about him (just as there is a bit of the Naunton Wayne to **Q**) and although he only has one or two brief scenes per picture, he created a vivid character which was very close to the M of Fleming's novels.

Although one never went to see a picture because Bernard Lee was in it, one was often grateful that he was. His face, which looked like a chunk of limestone cut with a blunt chisel, and the gravelly voice which went with it, distinguished many a threadbare British B-movie of the 1950s.

Lee was born in London on 10 January 1908 and by the age of 6 he was appearing with his father in music hall. Having made the decision to become an actor, Lee enrolled at RADA and paid his fees by working as a porter in Covent Garden's fruit and vegetable market. He toured the reps, worked as an understudy in the West End and slowly inched his way on to the bottom of the cast list, which led to minor appearances in movies. After war service he began to get more significant roles, notably in Carol Reed's *The Fallen Idol* and *The Third Man*, where he worked with **Guy Hamilton**, the assistant director.

He invariably played policemen or military types, such as Captain Dove in Powell and Pressburger's *The Battle of the River Plate*. Powell later called Lee a 'shaggy dog' and counted him among the greats he had known and worked with. But his range was considerably extended in *The Angry Silence*, in which he played an embittered factory worker who incites a strike. Lee agreed to play the role for a token £1000 to assist producer Richard Attenborough and writer Bryan Forbes to get it made. Attenborough and Forbes then returned the favour by casting Lee in *Whistle Down the Wind*, as the Yorkshire farmer whose children are convinced that the convict in their barn is in fact Jesus Christ. Lee's performance was another feather in his cap; despite the gruffness, his despair for his children is written all across his weathered face. It is a deeply touching performance in a minor classic.

At this point – in the early 1960s – Lee might have become one of the British cinema's most enduring character actors, a sort of Trevor Howard without the romantic appeal. But when he took the role of M in *Dr No* he became a household face instead. However, he resisted being typecast and often chose movies which explicitly flew in the face of the Bond machine.

Lee's best role by far was as the British traitor Harry Houghton in *Ring of Spies*. Based closely on the real-life Portland Spy Ring, when Gordon Lonsdale blackmailed Houghton into passing on files from the Admiralty's Underwater Weapons Establishment, the picture is remarkably convincing in its treatment of espionage – the underpaid resentment of records clerks, the fear of being found out and the incongruity of a Soviet spy nest in a bungalow in Ruislip which, the spymaster's wife says, is 'more like **Fort Knox** every day'.

Lee had already made two appearances as M when this picture was released in June 1964, so audiences may well have appreciated the irony of seeing him betraying Her Majesty's government for the price of a cottage and a flash Ford Zodiac. But two years later, in the film version of John le Carré's *The Spy Who Came in From the Cold*, Lee's appearance as a shopkeeper who is thumped on the nose by Richard Burton's seedy secret agent can only have been a casting joke.

Although Lee – as well as Lois Maxwell, who played **Miss Moneypenny** – was part of the general embarrassment called *Operation Kid Brother*, which started **Sean Connery**'s brother **Neil Connery**, he had a good role in *10 Rillington Place*, as one of the detectives in the grisly Christie murder case, and in *The Raging Moon*, another film for the ever-loyal Bryan Forbes.

In 1973 tragedy struck when Lee's wife died in a fire which destroyed their home. He married again but his appetite for work understably left him. Mainly he contented himself with playing M, which he did until *Moonraker*. By the time **Broccoli** had settled for an anti-inflationary policy with the next film, Lee was dead. He died of cancer on 16 January 1981. Somehow those interviews with 007 behind the green baize door were never the same again.

Filmography

1934	*The Double Event* (dir. Leslie Howard Gordon)
1935	*The River House Mystery* (dir. Fraser Foulsham)
1936	*Rhodes of Africa* (dir. Berthold Viertel)
1937	*The Black Tulip* (dir. Alex Bryce)
1938	*The Terror* (dir. Richard Bird)
1938	*Murder in Soho* (dir. Norman Lee)
1939	*The Frozen Limits* (dir. Marcel Varnel)
1940	*Let George Do It* (dir. Marcel Varnel)
1940	*Spare a Copper* (dir. John Paddy Carstairs)
1941	*Once a Crook* (dir. Herbert Mason)
1946	*This Man Is Mine* (dir. Marcel Varnel)

1947	*The Courtenays of Curzon Street* (dir. Herbert Wilcox)
1948	*The Fallen Idol* (dir. Carol Reed)
1948	*Quartet* (dirs Ralph Smart, Harold French, Arthur Crabtree and Ken Annakin)
1948	*Elizabeth of Ladymead* (dir. Herbert Wilcox)
1949	*The Third Man* (dir. Carol Reed)
1949	*The Blue Lamp* (dir. Basil Dearden)
1949	*Morning Departure* (dir. Roy Baker)
1950	*Odette* (dir. Herbert Wilcox)
1950	*Last Holiday* (dir. Henry Cass)
1950	*Cage of Gold* (dir. Basil Dearden)
1950	*The Adventurers* (dir. David Macdonald)
1951	*Calling Bulldog Drummond* (dir. Victor Saville)
1951	*Appointment With Venus* (dir. Ralph Thomas)
1951	*Mr Denning Drives North* (dir. Anthony Kimmins)
1952	*Gift Horse* (dir. Compton Burnett)
1952	*The Yellow Balloon* (dir. J. Lee Thompson)
1953	*Single-Handed* (dir. Roy Boulting)
1953	*Beat the Devil* (dir. John Huston)
1954	*Father Brown* (dir. Robert Hamer)
1954	*Seagulls Over Sorento* (dir. Roy Boulting)
1954	*The Purple Plain* (dir. Robert Parrish)
1955	*Out of the Clouds* (dir. Basil Dearden)
1955	*The Ship that Died of Shame* (dir. Basil Dearden)
1956	*The Battle of the River Plate* (dirs Michael Powell and Emeric Pressburger)
1956	*The Spanish Gardener* (dir. Philip Leacock)
1957	*Fire Down Below* (dir. Robert Parrish)
1957	*Across the Bridge* (dir. Ken Annakin)
1957	*High Flight* (dir. John Gilling)
1958	*Dunkirk* (dir. Leslie Norman)
1958	*The Key* (dir. Carol Reed)
1958	*Nowhere to Go* (dir. Seth Holt)

1958	*The Man Upstairs* (dir. Don Chaffey)
1958	*Danger Within* (dir. Don Chaffey)
1959	*Beyond this Place* (dir. Jack Cardiff)
1959	*Kidnapped* (dir. Robert Stevenson)
1960	*The Angry Silence* (dir. Guy Green)
1960	*Cone of Silence* (dir. Charles Frend)
1960	*Clue of the Twisted Candle* (dir. Allan Davis)
1960	*Fury at Smuggler's Bay* (dir. John Gilling)
1961	*Partners in Crime* (dir. Peter Duffell)
1961	*Clue of the Silver Key* (dir. Gerald Glaister)
1961	*The Secret Partner* (dir. Basil Dearden)
1961	*Whistle Down the Wind* (dir. Bryan Forbes)
1962	*The Share Out* (dir. Gerald Glaister)
1962	*The L-Shaped Room* (dir. Bryan Forbes)
1962	*Dr No* (dir. Terence Young)
1962	*Vengeance* (dir. Freddie Francis)
1963	*Two Left Feet* (dir. Roy Baker)
1963	*From Russia With Love* (dir. Terence Young)
1963	*A Place to Go* (dir. Basil Dearden)
1963	*Ring of Spies* (dir. Robert Tronson)
1963	*Saturday Night Out* (dir. Robert Hartford-Davis)
1964	*Who Was Maddox?* (dir. Geoffrey Nethercott)
1964	*Goldfinger* (dir. Guy Hamilton)
1964	*Dr Terror's House of Horrors* (dir. Freddie Francis)
1965	*The Legend of Young Dick Turpin* (dir. James Neilson)
1965	*Thunderball* (dir. Terence Young)
1965	*The Spy Who Came in From the Cold* (dir. Martin Ritt)
1967	*You Only Live Twice* (dir. Lewis Gilbert)
1967	*Operation Kid Brother* (dir. Alberto de Martino)
1969	*Crossplot* (dir. Alvin Rakoff)
1969	*On Her Majesty's Secret Service* (dir. Peter Hunt)
1970	*10 Rillington Place* (dir. Richard Fleischer)
1971	*The Raging Moon* (dir. Bryan Forbes)

1971   *Danger Point!* (dir. John Davis)
1971   *Diamonds Are Forever* (dir. Guy Hamilton)
1971   *Dulcima* (dir. Frank Nesbitt)
1973   *Live and Let Die* (dir. Guy Hamilton)
1973   *Frankenstein and the Monster From Hell* (dir. Terence Fisher)
1974   *Percy's Progress* (dir. Ralph Thomas)
1974   *The Man With the Golden Gun* (dir. Guy Hamilton)
1976   *Beauty and the Beast* (dir. Fielder Cook)
1977   *The Spy Who Loved Me* (dir. Lewis Gilbert)
1979   *Moonraker* (dir. Lewis Gilbert)

Leiter, Felix

James Bond is a man without a social life. In the books we hardly ever see him doing anything in his spare time and even if he's on holiday, as he was in *The Hildebrand Rarity*, Bond somehow contrives to turn it into a case. This secret agent appears to be on call twenty-four hours a day. He has no friends, only professional relationships. He responds emotionally to very few people – notably Kerim Bey in *From Russia With Love*, Henderson and Tiger Tanaka in *You Only Live Twice*, and the European gangster Draco who becomes his father-in-law at the bleak conclusion to *On Her Majesty's Secret Service*. These friendships are borne out of common enthusiasms for drink, cigarettes, fast cars, strong-minded women and professional efficiency. Bond likes men who are good at their jobs. One could call him Hawksian, but we won't.

An exception of sorts is Felix Leiter, who appears in six of the novels and eight of the films. Leiter works for the Central Intelligence Agency and patently isn't much cop at his job. He looks at Bond walking arm in arm with **Pussy** and assumes everything's just hunky dory. 'That's my James,' he says, misreading the situation completely. Leiter, though, has a significant role to play: he is there to be bland, boring and stupid, and to show how resourceful and charismatic Bond is. More importantly, Leiter is there to be simply an *American*. This way, Bond makes the CIA and America itself look foolishly amateur, dependent on the brains and brawn of the old imperial power.

Fleming chose the name Felix Leiter from the names of two of his close friends – Ivar Felix Bryce and their mutual friend Tommy Leiter, an American businessman. In the novels Leiter remains consistent; having lost an arm to a shark in *Live and Let Die* – 'he disagreed with something that ate him' – he has a hook in subsequent adventures, the effect of which is curiously charming and not at all sinister.

In the movies Leiter is played by different actors (only David Hedison has played the part twice, in *Live and Let Die* and *Licence to Kill*) and is treated even more cursorily than he was by Fleming. For *Goldfinger*, the original idea was to have Jack Lord play Leiter again, after his first appearance in *Dr No*. This would have given the films some continuity, but Lord's demand for joint billing, as well as a huge fee, put paid to that idea. Then Austin Willis was hired to play Leiter. But in January 1964, when **Guy Hamilton** was shooting the Miami exteriors, he made a switch: Willis became **Goldfinger**'s card opponent, Simmons, while the actor hired to play Simmons, the Polish-Canadian Cec Linder, suddenly found himself playing Felix Leiter.

Richard Maibaum had his own view of Leiter. 'I've never liked another Leiter,' he said of the original, Jack Lord, 'and as time went on they hired older and fatter men to play the part in order to make James Bond look younger and more handsome.'

lesbianism

See **Pussy Galore**.

Llewelyn, Desmond (b. 1914)

Actor who played **Q**.

M

M

See **Lee, Bernard**.

Maibaum, Richard (1909–91)

One searches in vain through Richard Maibaum's long filmography to find a famous title before he wrote *Dr No*. Of course there is *The Great Gatsby*, though Maibaum's version, starring Alan Ladd as Scott Fitzgerald's suave and enigmatic hero Jay Gatsby is hardly revered as even a minor classic. Maibaum was associated with Ladd on other films, yet possibly because Ladd himself never attracted a cult following after his death – like Bogart, say – the movies he made have slipped into critical limbo. Today Ladd is remembered only for being the man who said 'Or Rosebud' at the end of *Citizen Kane* and for *Shane*, that buckskinned paean to pacifism; and Maibaum scripted neither of those.

There is also *Bigger Than Life*, a key 1950s melodrama directed by Nicholas Ray, who threw out Maibaum's script but was contractually obliged to retain his name on the credits. And there are the films Maibaum produced and wrote for Mitchell Leisen, a distinctive stylist and flamboyant gay man, though these are reckoned to be amongst Leisen's duds. 'You might say Maibaum and I were friendly enemies,' said Leisen. 'We didn't dislike each other personally, it was just that we didn't see eye to eye about anything. The pictures I made with him were pretty disastrous for my money.'

It is, in fact, a list which bespeaks hard graft more than ambition and inspiration. There were literally hundreds of men like Maibaum, men who could produce the required number of pages per week for studios which turned out pictures by the yard.

Yet Maibum must be regarded as a key contributor to the Bond ethos and the Bond machine; its creation surely owes nearly as much to him as it does to **Ian Fleming**, or to **Saltzman** and **Broccoli**, or to **Sean Connery** and **Ken Adam**. It was Maibaum who took the novels and turned them into movie stories; he cut and tucked where necessary, modernised and modified, transformed the momentum on the page to pace on a screen, and he added a modicum of humour. Very often the most stylish bits were added by others, such as **Paul Dehn**, Maibaum's co-writer on *Goldfinger*. But who was Richard Maibaum?

He was born on 26 May 1909 in New York City and studied Speech and Dramatic Art at the University of Iowa. While he was a student his play *The Tree*, about lynch-law, opened on Broadway. He told Peter Haining:

> I wrote my first play when I was nine years old. It was about cowboys. At college I took up acting as well as writing and in 1933 I joined the Shakespearean Repertory Theater in New York. Between the ages of twenty-three and twenty-six I had three plays running on Broadway, *The Tree*, *Birthright* and *Sweet Mystery of Life*.

Maibaum was also an actor of some note, becoming the youngest Iago ever seen on Broadway.

He married Sylvia Kamion in 1935 and, like so many Broadway talents, Maibaum was quickly lured to Hollywood. As soon as pictures acquired a voice the studio executives realised that in order to make the actors talk they had to hire people who could write. So they turned to New York and rounded up anyone with their name on a theatre marquee. To these playwrights the California sun, the ocean, the waving palm trees and the money seemed irresistible, as did the thought of writing for studio executives who could barely read. Wasn't it Herman J. Mankiewicz, the brother of Joseph L. and later the contested author of *Citizen Kane*, who sent a cable in 1929 to the impoverished playwright Ben Hecht saying:

> Will you accept three hundred per week to work for Paramount Pictures? All expenses paid. The three hundred is peanuts. Millions are to be grabbed out here and your only competition is idiots. PS: Don't let this get around.

Maibaum found a home at MGM. Although MGM prided itself on its roster of stars, its vast art department and its seemingly limitless resources, the studio was not above making a lot of low-budget trash which kept its theatres ticking over. Maibaum earned an honest dollar at the MGM factory, seeing his work rewritten by others and changed again to suit the paternalistic, patriotic foibles of Louis B. Mayer.

In 1942 Maibaum enlisted in the US Army, and, like many a Hollywood figure, he worked in wartime documentaries and finally achieved the rank of lieutenant-colonel. After the war he was offered a job at Paramount as a producer and screenwriter – an unusual combination – and started with the espionage thriller *OSS*, starring Alan Ladd. This led to *The Great Gatsby*, and when Ladd was offered work in Britain with Broccoli, Maibaum went along as Ladd's preferred writer. So impressed was Broccoli that Maibaum became Warwick's in-house writer.

Maibaum received $40,000 for *Dr No*, though **United Artists'** Bud Ornstein was worried about the writer's talent as shown by his previous films for Warwick. 'I must tell you,' Ornstein wrote to David Picker, 'I have not been impressed with Maibaum's work and only hope that he will come up with something much better this time.'

Maibaum wrote thirteen of the Bond films, and those that he didn't write – such as *You Only Live Twice*, which was scripted by Roald Dahl – are no different from those that he did write. That says much about the role of the producers and the strength of the formula. 'The most difficult thing,' Maibaum told *Starlog* magazine in 1983, 'is coming up with a great caper for the villains. That's the thing that drives us up the wall.'

If it is possible to heap praise on Maibaum's co-writers, it should be stressed that he wrote the script of *On Her Majesty's Secret Service* alone and that might well have the best script of all the Bond pictures. It sticks closely to Fleming's original and does not compromise the novel's pessimism. It is likely that with a new actor playing Bond – George Lazenby – Saltzman and Broccoli felt able to experiment a little with the mood. And *On Her Majesty's Secret Service* is the only Bond movie which allows its hero some humanity as well as the luxury of thought. It's just a shame that Lazenby has problems conveying this.

When **Roger Moore** took over Maibaum thought the films became increasingly enslaved to the gadgetry and, without Fleming's plots to fall back on, Maibaum had to invent his own, which meant recycling the old ones – principally Dahl's reinvention of *You Only Live Twice* – and ripping off movies like *Superman* and *Star Wars*. It was a sad spectacle. And while Maibaum had admired Connery's performances, he thought that Moore brought an unwarranted flippancy and an eagerness to rewrite his own dialogue. 'Sean would come up with pretty witty lines at times,' he said. 'Sean is a witty man. And so is Roger. But, God, *the lines*, please.'

Maibaum's last Bond film was *Licence to Kill*, for which he produced a complete script, set in the Far East, only to have it rejected and relocated in Mexico, where the locations were easier and cheaper. He had long since moved back to America and lived in Pacific Palisades, where he died, a rich man, on 4 January 1991.

Filmography

1936   *We Went to College* (co-scripted with Maurice Rapf; dir. Joseph Santley)

1936   *Gold-Diggers of 1937* (co-play basis only; dir. Lloyd Bacon)

1937   *They Gave Him a Gun* (co-scripted with Cyril Hume and Maurice Rapf; dir. W. S. Van Dyke)

1937   *Live, Love and Learn* (co-scripted with Charles Brackett and Cyril Hume; dir. George Fitzmaurice)

1938   *The Bad Man of Brimstone* (co-scripted with Cyril Hume; dir. Walter Ruben)

1938   *Stablemates* (co-scripted with Leonard Praskins; dir. Sam Wood)

1939   *Coast Guard* (co-scripted with Albert Duffy and Harry Segall; dir. Edward Ludwig)

1939   *The Amazing Mr Williams* (co-scripted with Dwight Taylor and Sy Bartlett; dir. Alexander Hall)

1940   *20 Mule Team* (co-scripted with Cyril Hume and E. E. Paramore; dir. Richard Thorpe)

1941   *I Wanted Wings* (co-scripted with Lt Beirne Lay Jr and Sid Herzig; dir. Mitchell Leisen)

1942   *Ten Gentlemen From West Point* (screenplay; dir. Henry Hathaway)

1945   *See My Lawyer* (co-play basis only; dir. Eddie Cline)

1946   *OSS* (prod. and screenplay; dir. Irving Pichel)

1947   *The Big Clock* (prod. only; dir. John Farrow)

1948   *The 'Sainted' Sisters* (prod. only; dir. William D. Russell)

1949   *The Bride of Vengeance* (prod. only; dir. Mitchell Leisen)

1949   *The Great Gatsby* (prod. and co-scripted with Cyril Hume; dir. Elliott Nugent)

1949   *Song of Surrender* (prod. and screenplay; dir. Mitchell Leisen)

1949   *Dear Wife* (prod. only; dir. Richard Haydn)

1950   *Captain Carey, USA* (prod. only; dir. Mitchell Leisen)

1950   *No Man of Her Own* (prod. only; dir. Mitchell Leisen)

1953   *The Red Beret* (co-scripted with Terence Young; dir. Frank Nugent)

1953   *Hell Below Zero* (adaptation only; dir. Mark Robson)

1955   *Cockleshell Heroes* (co-scripted with Bryan Forbes; dir. Jose Ferrer)

1955   *Ransom!* (co-scripted with Cyril Hume; dir. Alex Segal)

1956   *Bigger Than Life* (co-scripted with Cyril Hume; dir. Nicholas Ray)

1956   *Zarak* (screenplay; dir. Terence Young)

1958   *No Time to Die* (co-scripted with Terence Young; dir. Terence Young)

1959   *The Bandit of Zhobe* (story only; dir. John Gilling)

1959   *The Killers of Kilimanjaro* (co-story only with Cyril Hume; dir. Richard Thorpe)

1960   *The Day They Robbed the Bank of England* (co-adaptation only; dir. John Guillermin)

1961   *The Battle at Bloody Beach* (prod. and co-scripted with Willard Willingham; dir. Herbert Coleman)

1962   *Dr No* (co-scripted with Joanna Harwood and Berkely Mather; dir. Terence Young)

1963   *From Russia With Love* (co-scripted with Joanna Harwood; dir. Terence Young)

1964   *Goldfinger* (co-scripted with Paul Dehn; dir. **Guy Hamilton**)

1965   *Thunderball* (co-scripted with John Hopkins; dir. Terence Young)

1968   *Chitty Chitty Bang Bang* (additional dialogue; dir. Ken Hughes)

1969   *On Her Majesty's Secret Service* (screenplay; dir. Peter Hunt)

1971   *Diamonds Are Forever* (co-scripted with Tom Mankiewicz; dir. Guy Hamilton)

1974   *The Man With the Golden Gun* (co-scripted with Tom Mankiewicz; dir. Guy Hamilton)

1977   *The Spy Who Loved Me* (co-scripted with Christopher Wood; dir. Lewis Gilbert)

1980   *S*H*E* (screeplay; dir. Robert Lewis)

1981   *For Your Eyes Only* (co-scripted with Michael G. Wilson; dir. John Glen)

1983   *Octopussy* (co-scripted with George Macdonald Fraser and Michael G. Wilson; dir. John Glen)

1985   *A View to a Kill* (co-scripted with Michael G. Wilson; dir. John Glen)

1987   *The Living Daylights* (co-scripted with Michael G. Wilson; dir. John Glen)

1989   *Licence to Kill* (co-scripted with Michael G. Wilson; dir. John Glen)

See **screenplay**.

Mallet, Tania

Actress who played **Tilly Masterson**.

Masterson, Jill

The character, played by Shirley Eaton, who is painted gold. See **painted ladies**.

Masterson, Tilly

If you qualify as a 'Bond girl' by being a girl in a Bond film, then Tania Mallet qualifies. But if being a 'Bond Girl' means sleeping with Bond, then Miss Mallet escaped by the skin of her ice-skates.

The role of Tilly, sister of **Jill Masterson**, expanded and contracted with every rewrite. (Her surname was Masterton in the book, Masterson in the film) A lesbian in the novel, who takes a shine to **Pussy Galore** and whom Bond pigeon-holes as 'one of those girls whose hormones need straightening out', Tilly was written in and out of the script, and eventually became that dread thing – hero's encumbrance, a stupid girl who fancies taking a vengeful pot-shot at **Goldfinger** but merely hits the trip-wire with her **gun barrel**. That one stupid move gets 007 into a lot of trouble.

Tania Mallet, who is half Russian, had already done a screen test for the role of Tatiana in *From Russia With Love*. But someone at **Eon** thought she 'looked like a Bond girl' and they called her back for *Goldfinger*. In the early 1960s she adorned the pages of many a fashion magazine, but her acting ambitions fell short of her achievements; she said she failed get into RADA because she could never remember her lines. A monied, horsy type who dressed in silk shirts and cardies, Ms Mallet never made another movie and thus avoided the brief celebrity status conferred upon that sad legion of Bond girls.

Maxwell, Lois

Actress who played **Miss Moneypenny**.

Midas touch

There are two Midases. There is the King Midas of legend and myth and there is the real person, whose name was Midacritus or Mita of Mushki. He ruled the Phrygian Empire – in present-day northwestern Turkey – and was said to have been a far-sighted, warmongering ruler with expansionist and commercial interests who married the daughter of the king of Cyme.

Two major legends have attached themselves to his name. In the first, he captured a wild nature spirit named Silenus, from whom he wanted to learn the secrets of the world and the universe. And when Midas returned Silenus to the wild, Dionysus offered Midas anything he desired. Midas asked that everything he touched was turned to gold but as soon as his wish was granted, Midas realised he had made a mistake – as he touched his food and drink it turned into gold. He begged Dionysus to remove the gift and Dionysus agreed, instructing Midas to wash his hands and face in the waters of the River Pactolus. The destructive Midas touch flowed into the river, which ran golden for eternity.

The second legend concerns Midas's ears. He was asked to officiate at a musical contest between Pan and Apollo. Choosing Pan as the winner, he was rewarded with the ironical gift of donkey's ears. Embarrassed by his disfigurement, Midas covered his ears with a turban, though his barber could not keep the royal secret. He told a hole in the ground, whereupon the ground sprouted a bunch of reeds which, when the wind blew, told anyone listening that Midas had ass's ears.

It is thought that Midas died in 696 BC, following the sacking of his capital, Gordium, by the Cimmerians. There is a large excavated tomb near the site of Gordium which is thought to be Midas's final resting place. His name is clearly visible on an inscription, and a skeleton, thought to be Midas's, was discovered inside. However, the skeleton showed no signs of deformed ears.

Moneypenny, Miss

What was Miss Moneypenny's first name? Was she a Dolores or a Doris? A seductive Charlotte, a glum Edna, a country-set Polly or just a plain Jane? Most definitely not, we hazard, a Sharon or a Tracy, let alone a Sue. We shall christen her Elizabeth because most English girls of her age (born, shall we say, in 1927) were named after the young princess and her mother, the queen. In the novels she's such an easy-going, jolly-hockey-sticks sort of girl that she was probably happy to be called Liz. Not that M called her anything other than Miss Moneypenny or just Moneypenny.

Andrew Lycett reveals that **Fleming** chose the name Moneypenny after a character in an unfinished novel, *The Sett*, by his brother Peter. Fleming often did this sort of thing; for instance, his secretary at *The*

Sunday Times was called Una Trueblood (a Bond girl's name if ever there was one), and it was a Mary Trueblood who was Strangway's unfortunate secretary in *Dr No*.

Lois Maxwell, formerly Lois Hooker, made the role of Moneypenny very much her own and was noticeably hurt when she was pensioned off after fourteen appearances. A Canadian, Miss Maxwell had a brief Hollywood career before moving to Italy and then to England in the early 1950s. Along with other Canadian emigrés, such as Robert Beatty and William Sylvester, she coasted along in B-movies and supporting roles in A-movies, such as Kubrick's *Lolita*.

When the casting call went out for *Dr No* she was in the throes of a family tragedy – her husband had suffered a heart attack – and needed money to raise her children. Although Terence Young thought she 'smelt of soap' he offered her a choice of two roles – Miss Moneypenny or Sylvia Trench, who was Bond's first screen conquest. Unwilling to appear dressed only in one of Bond's shirts, Miss Maxwell chose Moneypenny. She was paid £200 and told to wear her own clothes.

Miss Moneypenny makes no appearance in the novel of *Goldfinger*. She is said to be 'desirable' but 'off duty' when Bond goes to see M. Because Lois Maxwell had cleverly asserted her presence in the earlier films, she could not possibly be 'off duty' now. **Maibaum** wrote two scenes for her, the first when Bond is en route to Q branch and another after the laser torture. When **Goldfinger** decides to take Bond along as his assistant, he shrewdly fakes a message from Bond to M, saying that all is going to plan and that he has successfully infiltrated Goldfinger's organisation. Moneypenny reads the message, purrs contentedly and buzzes M with the good news.

When that scene was cut, Maibaum voiced his displeasure in a memo to **Saltzman**: 'Couldn't Moneypenny be briefing Bond? She's too good to only have her in one telephone conversation. And Bond ought to be trying to make her as she asks and he answers questions. Then when M enters you can have a nice funny moment.'

But Moneypenny is in only one scene of *Goldfinger*. There she is, shuffling files in that nice office with the floral prints on the wall alongside that silly wall map. Bond comes out of M's office – you might call Moneypenny the 'in-and-out' girl – there's some banter about gold wedding rings and she gets a peck on the cheek, the sort of sexual harassment that would land Bond in court nowadays. Then M's gruff tones come through the squawk-box and it's back to the plot.

We never see her write a memo, much less take dictation, and she probably couldn't handle being the secretary to a janitor, let alone the head of MI6. But she is a fixture, part of the safe womb that Bond returns to after each mission. She played the game of sexual temptress, knowing that Bond took great pleasure in resisting her, for she gave him what no woman in the field could ever give him: a sense of morality. Or maybe Bond just knew that she was M's girlfriend.

monkey puzzle

There is a sort of legend among fans of the Bond movies that Dr No was originally a monkey. A story went around that **Saltzman** and **Broccoli** first ordered up a spoof in which Bond infiltrates the island of Crab Key and discovers that Dr No is some sort of science-fictional mutant ape – **Ian Fleming** on Dr Moreau's island.

This is nonsense, of course, as a study of **Richard Maibaum** and Tom Mankiewicz's very first treatment reveals. However, this treatment, dated 7 September 1961, does have a simian element and precious little Ian Fleming beyond the basic plot premise of Bond's investigation of the disappearance of the Secret Service's representative in Jamaica.

To begin with, the plot which Maibaim and Mankiewicz devised has nothing to do with toppling America's space rockets. In their treatment, Dr No is planning to destroy the locks on the Panama Canal for reasons too silly to go into. Bond flies out to Jamaica, quickly meets Honey in a shop selling seashells and, together with Quarrel and **Felix Leiter**, sets sail for Crab Key.

In a previous scene we have met a shipping agent named Buckfield, who has a pet capuchin monkey named Li Ying. On Crab Key Bond and his party discover traces of the so-called dragon and at a Chinese cemetery they see a huge black statue of a monkey. Honey says that this means someone important is buried there.

In fact, Dr No is buried there. Later on, Bond dines with a man claiming to be Dr No. He removes both his claw hands and then his face mask, revealing himself as Buckfield. Apparently, Dr No had mystical powers; he hexed up the local Afro-Caribbean population and was to lead them to political power, financed by the Commies in Cuba.

After a rather pathetic chase on the island, Bond succeeds in blowing up Buckfield and his power base. The treatment ends on a wharf with the monkey, Li Ying, jumping on to Bond's shoulder, gibbering ironically.

Maibaum and Mankiewicz produced a second treatment less than three weeks later. There wasn't a monkey in sight.

Moore, Roger (b. 1927)

Let us simply say that he held his own.

Moore, Ted (1914–1987)

Ted Moore, the director of photography on *Goldfinger*, seems to have been shackled by Irving Allen and **Cubby Broccoli**, for it was not until 1966, when he shot *A Man For All Seasons* for Fred Zinnemann, that he fully escaped the protective custody of Warwick Films or the drab monotony of British B-movies.

Did Moore find this stifling or simply comfortable? In the early days he shot as many bad movies as anyone. Did he gaze enviously across the lot and see Christopher Challis, Geoffrey Unsworth, Robert Krasker or Freddie Young getting all the plums? Perhaps not, for Moore was drawing a regular paycheck and took pride in keeping those bargain basement actors in focus and minimising back-projection wobble. Clearly, Moore's loyalty to Allen and Broccoli paid off; the Bond pictures gave him a reputation by association. But if the Bond pictures have a distinctive visual style, it is less about photography than production design and location. After all, *You Only Live Twice* was shot by a master – Freddie Young, who won Oscars for *Lawrence of Arabia*, *Doctor Zhivago* and *Ryan's Daughter* – but it looks as if it could have been shot by anyone.

What Ted Moore did was to keep the Bond ball rolling. *Dr No* looks sharp and glamorous on location, and shoddy in the studio, betraying its budget. *From Russia With Love*, though, is the best photographed of all the Bond pictures because Moore, given a freer hand, creates a suitably Byzantine labyrinth out of Istanbul, delighting in the light and shade of the great bazaar and achieving some of the old Hitchcock magic from the belching, ominous smoke of the Orient Express. Perhaps because **Ken Adam** was absent, the picture has a look which sets it apart from the other Bonds.

Goldfinger, too, has a lustrous sheen, given a good print or, even better, a laser-disc version. The lighting for the opening sequence in Mexico has such a smoky exoticism that one expects Rita Hayworth or Marlene Dietrich to waltz into shot and plant her knee in Bond's crotch. After that, the picture looks fairly ordinary until the scenes in **Fort Knox**, where Adam's set is beautifully caught in Moore's glittery imagery, a paean to the beauty and power of gold, and the sort of thing that David Lean had in mind with silver when he was planning *Nostromo*. Moore's final Bond film was *The Man With the Golden Gun*, on which he was soon taken ill and was replaced by Oswald Morris. The join is undetectable.

Ted Moore was born in 1914 in South Africa and had emigrated to England by the time he was 16. He worked at the old British and Dominion Studios at Elstree and served as an RAF fighter pilot and later in the RAF's film unit during the war. After the war he was much in demand as a camera operator and worked on some impressive pictures, two of which – *Outcast of the Islands* and *The African Queen* – brought him into professional contact with **Guy Hamilton**, who was the assistant director. Having operated for cameraman John Wilcox, who was offered a job by Allen and Broccoli, Moore was present at the birth of Allen and Broccoli's Warwick Films.

He won an Academy Award for *A Man For All Seasons*, Zinnemann's film of Robert Bolt's play about Sir Thomas More, and later provided some evocative 1920s atmosphere for *The Prime of Miss Jean Brodie*. But despite the Oscar, Moore always remained a second-eleven cameraman and his later work is relatively undistinguished. He died in 1987 in apparently penurious circumstances, living with his wife in a small London flat and too proud to accept the offer of sheltered accommodation at one of the film industry's benevolent homes in the country.

Filmography
* *Films as camera operator:*
1951   *Outcast of the Islands* (phot. John Wilcox; dir. Carol Reed)
1951   *The African Queen* (phot. Jack Cardiff; dir. John Huston)
1953   *Genevieve* (phot. Christopher Challis; dir. Henry Cornelius)
1953   *The Red Beret* (phot. John Wilcox; dir. Terence Young)
1954   *The Black Knight* (phot. John Wilcox; dir. Tay Garnett)
* *Films as director of photography:*
1954   *A Prize of Gold* (dir. Mark Robson)
1955   *Cockleshell Heroes* (co-phot. John Wilcox; dir. Jose Ferrer)
1955   *The Gamma People* (dir. John Gilling)
1956   *Safari* (co-phot. John Wilcox; dir. Terence Young)
1956   *Odongo* (dir. John Gilling)
1956   *Zarak* (co-phot. John Wilcox and Cyril Knowles; dir. Terence Young)
1957   *Interpol* (dir. John Gilling)

1957 *How to Murder a Rich Uncle* (dirs Nigel Patrick (uncredited) and Max Varnel)

1957 *High Flight* (dir. John Gilling)

1958 *No Time to Die!* (dir. Terence Young)

1958 *The Man Inside* (dir. John Gilling)

1959 *Idle on Parade* (dir. John Gilling)

1959 *The Bandit of Zhobe* (dir. John Gilling)

1959 *The Killers of Kilimanjaro* (dir. Richard Thorpe)

1959 *Jazzboat* (dir. Ken Hughes)

1959 *In the Nick* (dir. Ken Hughes)

1960 *Let's Get Married* (dir. Peter Graham Scott)

1960 *The Trials of Oscar Wilde* (dir. Ken Hughes)

1961 *Johnny Nobody* (dir. Nigel Patrick)

1961 *The Hellions* (dir. Ken Annakin)

1962 *Mix Me a Person* (dir. Leslie Norman)

1962 *Dr No* (dir. Terence Young)

1962 *The Day of the Triffids* (dir. Steve Sekely)

1963 *Call Me Bwana* (dir. Gordon Douglas)

1963 *From Russia With Love* (dir. Terence Young)

1964 *Goldfinger* (dir. Guy Hamilton)

1965 *The Amorous Adventures of Moll Flanders* (dir. Terence Young)

1965 *Thunderball* (dir. Terence Young)

1966 *A Man For All Seasons* (dir. Fred Zinnemann)

1967 *The Last Safari* (dir. Henry Hathaway)

1968 *Prudence and the Pill* (dir. Fielder Cook)

1968 *Shalako* (dir. Edward Dmytryk)

1969 *The Most Dangerous Man in the World* (dir. J. Lee Thompson)

1969 *The Prime of Miss Jean Brodie* (dir. Ronald Neame)

1970 *Country Dance* (dir. J. Lee Thompson)

1971 *She'll Follow You Anywhere* (dir. David C. Rea)

1971 *Diamonds Are Forever* (dir. Guy Hamilton)

1972 *Psychomania* (dir. Don Sharp)

1973 *Live and Let Die* (dir. Guy Hamilton)

1974   *The Golden Voyage of Sinbad* (dir. Gordon Hessler)
1974   *The Man With the Golden Gun* (co-phot. Oswald Morris; dir. Guy Hamilton)
1977   *Sinbad and the Eye of the Tiger* (dir. Sam Wanamaker)
1977   *Orca* (dir. Michael Anderson)
1978   *Dominique* (dir. Michael Anderson)
1981   *Clash of the Titans* (dir. Desmond Davis)
1981   *Priest of Love* (dir. Christopher Miles)

Morland & Co.

'William, how do you get cigarette smoke out of a woman once you've got it in?'

It was 12 May 1952 and **Ian Fleming** was lunching at the Ivy with his friend William Plomer. He followed the question by saying he didn't think that 'exhales' or 'puffs it out' sounded right.

'You've written a book!' said Plomer, quickly twigging.

Fleming made a fetish of smoking, just as he made a fetish out of black knitted ties, boiled eggs and vodka martinis. He smoked cheerfully, obsessively and suicidally, usually seventy a day. Of course, everyone smoked in those days and those who did not were regarded as freaks, lepers, namby-pambys. Without a cigarette, stars like Humphrey Bogart, John Wayne and Bette Davis looked naked, and watching them was an audience wreathed in the wreaking smoke. Looking behind you in the cinema, the sight of the tobacco smoke floating across the beam of the projector was one of the most evocative sights in the world, despite the fact that the nicotine stained the screens and dimmed the image.

Fleming smoked Morland cigarettes, which he bought from a shop at 83 Grosvenor Street, just around the corner from Bond Street. And because Fleming smoked them, so did Bond, who carried them in a case made from gunmetal and lit them with a black, oxidized Ronson lighter.

When Fleming was asked if Bond was wise in smoking such a conspicuous brand, he said:

Of course . . . no self-respecting agent would use such things. He'd smoke Players or Chesterfields. But the readers enjoy such idiosyncrasies, and they accept them because they don't stop to think about it. The secrecy of my secret agent is pretty transparent, if you think about it even briefly. But the pace of the narrative gets one by these nasty little corners. It's a sleight-of-hand operation. It's overpowering the reader.

The shop on Grosvenor Street was tiny and its window display contained bowls of tobacco, smokers' paraphernalia and copies of the latest James Bond novel. Inside, the smell was heavily perfumed and there was always the manager Miss Cohen, a middle-aged woman with glasses and shiny black hair always tied in a tight bun. Sometimes you could glimpse a woman in the back room, rolling your very own. Until he became famous, Fleming would visit the shop every week and collect his weekly ration of five hundred at a cost, in 1963, of 37s 6d per hundred.

Morland cigarettes came, not in packs of twenty, like regular brands, but in boxes of fifty or a hundred. Because of the size of the boxes, you could never carry them in your breast pocket, so that if you were at a party and a friend offered a Piccadilly or a Capstan Full Strength, let alone a pathetic little Park Drive or a humble Woodbine, you couldn't produce your box of Morland and say 'Have one of mine', and savour the look of polite enquiry and the snobbish thrill of being a smoker who stood out − and smelt different − from the rest.

The boxes were stoutly made, deep blue with gold writing, as if they might have contained jewels, which, of course, they did. One got them home and 'decanted' them into cigarette cases of gold, silver or gunmetal. The cigarettes themselves were of regular length, not kingsize, and unfiltered, naturally. The name Morland never appeared.

Instead, they had three gold rings at one end and, along the edge, in tiny capitals, the word 'HANDMADE'. Each box contained a slip of paper which read:

> These cigarettes are made of the most choice and perfectly blended tobaccos, the dormant fragrance of which is preserved in our careful process of manufacture. Each cigarette is made by hand, one by one, and tobacco dust, so harmful to the throat is entirely eliminated.

However, despite their claims to the contrary, the cigarettes were variable in quality. Some were perfect, others poorly filled and some seemed to have less leaf than stalk, which meant they burnt like an explosive fuse and lasted less than a minute. The blend of Balkan and Turkish tobacco was also annoyingly inconsistent; they could be strong or weak, bitter or deliciously sweet, with hints of cedarwood, dark chocolate, vanilla or unadulterated tar.

These were the days when cigarettes were objects of desire and they came packaged like works of art. Morland's was just one of several specialist tobacconists based in Mayfair, St James's or Soho. But even regular shops offered a dizzying array of brands. W. D. & H. O. Wills had a remarkable cigarette called Passing Clouds, which was elliptical in shape and came in pink flip-top boxes decorated with Van Dyke's *The Laughing Cavalier*. Benson & Hedges could be bought in flat gold tins of twenty. Balkan Sobranie had a brand called Black Russian, with black paper and gold tips, and another brand called Cocktail, which came in a riot of different colours and was aimed at the ladies. Most expensive of all the proprietary brands, though, were Player's Perfectos Finos, which were unusually plump and strong buggers sold in embossed green boxes of twenty-five.

You could buy cigarettes from Egypt, from Russia, from Turkey and, most appealing of all, from America: King Size Chesterfield, Camel, Pall Mall, Lucky Strike, Lone Star and Philip Morris, all in pretty paper packs, all unfiltered, all expensive, all deliriously deadly. One of any of these with your first cup of coffee in the morning gave you such a terrific buzz, the nicotine coursing through your veins, that you could fall down the stairs.

Bond smoked for England. When abroad he favoured Chesterfields, or when in Turkey exotic things called Diplomats, which are still available. Gradually, the movie versions played down Bond's smoking and once **Broccoli** even had a health warning tacked on to the final credits. Ian Fleming died in 1964 and a few years later the little shop in Grosvenor Street was stubbed out as well.

See **product placement**.

O

Oddjob

As far as secondary villains or henchmen go, Oddjob goes further than most. In fact, in the novel he went even further, surviving the raid on **Fort Knox** and reappearing in **Goldfinger**'s requisitioned jet, only to be shot and blown out of the decompressed fuselage. The movie saved that fate for Goldfinger himself, having previously disposed of Oddjob by electrocution in the gold vault of Fort Knox. Amidst a shower of sparks, Oddjob falls to the floor like a slab of concrete.

In the novel, Bond casts his eye over this hulking presence, speculating on his race and his physical quirks much as Sherlock Holmes could identify your tailor from the way you undid your fly:

> Bond had had a good look at the chauffeur. He was a chunky, flat-faced Japanese, or more probably Korean, with a wild, almost mad glare in dramatically slanting eyes that belonged in a Japanese film rather than in a Rolls-Royce on a sunny afternoon in Kent. He had the snout-like upper lip that sometimes goes with a cleft-palate, but he said nothing and Bond had no opportunity of knowing whether his guess was right. In his tight, almost bursting black suit and farcical bowler hat he looked rather like a Japanese wrestler on his day off. But he was not a figure to make one smile.

Later on, after dinner at Goldfinger's Kentish mansion, Bond is treated to a demonstration of Oddjob's talents. First of all, Oddjob smashes a set of thick oak banisters with his bare hand. Then he demolishes a mantelpiece which stands seven feet off the ground. As a reward, Oddjob is given a cat to strangle and eat. Impressed, Bond asks to shake the man's hand, and when Bond's hand is returned to him safely, still connected to his wrist, he asks why Oddjob wears a bowler hat. And bang goes another piece of Goldfinger's interior decoration.

Sadly, the movie cannot compete with this. We are treated merely to the spectacle of Oddjob crushing a golf ball in his fist and then decapitating a marble statue with his metal-rimmed bowler. But the actor playing Oddjob, Harold Sakata, nevertheless has our undivided attention and our respect. He has proved his point. This man is dangerous.

Harold Sakata was seen regularly on British television on Saturday afternoons, as the Great Tosh Togo, a wrestler who traded armlocks and Boston crabs with the likes of Mick Macmanus and the Red Indian Billy Two Rivers, whose ritual war dance and tomahawk chop was lethal. Wrestling was a regular fixture on ITV, commanding a huge audience of men just back from the pub, full of beer, and their wives, who drooled over the mountains of muscle. As a sport it was distinctly dubious, but as entertainment it enthralled millions. The charisma of the wrestlers – some heroic, most downright evil – turned the sport into a weekly soap opera.

Sakata, who was born in 1926, was a Japanese American who lived in Honolulu. At first he was a light-heavyweight weightlifter, winning a silver medal for America in the 1948 Olympic Games. He then started training subsequent US weightlifting teams, before becoming a full-time professional wrestler. These men were not the twentieth-century equivalent of gladiators; they were more like circus performers who travelled the world for a modest purse. They were showmen who lowered the aesthetics of the Olympic sport to the level of a meat market lit up like Las Vegas.

Sakata was in and out of Britain throughout the late 1950s and early 1960s. He would sign contracts with Dale Martin Promotions, an organisation which monopolised British professional wrestling and licensed its events to ITV. It was during one of these TV broadcasts that Sakata was spotted by **Guy Hamilton** and invited to take a screen test.

Leslie Martin wrote to Eon's production manager, L. C. Rudkin:

> Roughly he is 5 ft. 8ins., weight 16 stones, of massive proportions and, of course, he is very agile. He has a very deep voice and, of course, speaks Japanese, and he is also very intelligent and a cultured individual with unending patience with the capability of accepting direction. . . . I will bring him to Pinewood at 10.00am on Tuesday 26 November and, if you wish, he can give you a demonstration of the art of 'Karate', ie, chop a brick in half with the edge of his hand, or break a plank of wood and kick a door panel in with his bare toe. He will bring his Wrestling outfit to the studios, and as to the bowler hat, I cannot wait to see him in that.

Goldfinger made Sakata a sort of celebrity, which he milked for all it was worth. Like Richard Kiel in later years, as well as countless '**Bond girls**', Sakata learnt that fame through a Bond film was a mixed blessing. He'd turn up at various casting agencies wearing his costume; he'd open supermarkets and appear in advertisements for Honda, Continental Airlines and even Range Rover on American TV. For years, he did the round of American talk shows, chopping bricks for the likes of Johnny Carson and Merv Griffin, and he even cropped up on *Rowan and Martin's Laugh-in*. He usually billed himself as Oddjob, and odd jobs is what he got. He was never going to be a movie star, much less an actor, though he maintained his dignity throughout and later worked tirelessly for various charities in Hawaii. His last significant public appearance – as Oddjob, of course – was at the Academy Awards ceremony in 1982 when **Broccoli** was given the Irving Thalberg Award. He died four months later, from cancer, in Honolulu on 29 July 1982.

Filmography

1964	*Goldfinger*
1966	*Dimension 5*
1966	*Danger Grows Wild**
1969	*The Phynx*
1973	*The Wrestler*
1974	*Impulse*
1975	*Mako – Jaws of Death*
1977	*The Happy Hooker Goes to Washington*
1977	*Death Dimension*
1978	*Goin Coconuts*
1981	*Safari of No Return*
1981	*Aces Go Places III: Our Man From Bond Street*

Operation Kid Brother

See **Connery, Sean**

---

* This curio was directed by Terence Young and was originally known as *The Poppy Is Also a Flower*. Based on an idea and a half-written scenario by Ian Fleming, it was made for the United Nations.

P

painted ladies

The shot of the golden girl lying on the bed was one of the iconic images of the 1960s, ranking alongside the four passport photos of the Beatles used in *A Hard Day's Night*, or the shot of Christine Keeler sitting naked astride a chair, or of **Sean Connery** with the **Walther PPK**, or of Harold Wilson on the steps of Downing Street, or of Jean Shrimpton snapped by David Bailey. These pictures announced to the world that, yes, Britain was emerging into modernity, that it was a sexy place, that it had a hint of decadence and danger. America at this time could offer only Deeley Plaza in Dallas, Troy Donahue and cans of Campbell's soup.

At first, it looked as if an actress named Margaret Nolan might play Jill Masterson. Nolan was a healthy-looking girl, with a big chest and a permanent pout. **Saltzman** took a shine to her and offered her the role of Dink instead, so that she had just one line:

BOND: Dink, meet **Felix Leiter**.
DINK: Hello.
BOND: Felix, say hello to Dink.
LEITER: Hi, Dink.
BOND: Dink, say goodbye to Felix. Er, man talk.

Bond then pats her behind and sends her packing. This may be the most sexist scene in the entire series, except perhaps for the moment in *The Man With the Golden Gun* when **Roger Moore**, after shagging Maud Adams, retrieves a jealous and undoubtedly moist Brit Ekland from the wardrobe and says, 'Forgive me, darling, your turn will come.' Even in 1974, you could hear the audience wince at that.

Having played Dink in the Miami sequence, Nolan was then asked to be the golden girl of the credit titles. She endured several days of being painted gold while the credit title designer, Robert Brownjohn, projected images on to her body. Unfortunately for Nolan, most people assumed it was Shirley Eaton.

'I don't say anything about that,' Miss Eaton told me:

> What they did was, they practised on her. They had to paint somebody gold before they painted me to see how it worked. And I suppose, thinking of money, they thought they'd use her for the credits. Actually, I was cross about it, but never mind. She was a stripper, she was so big and voluptuous, she was not at all my type of figure or face or anything like me.

Miss Eaton was among dozens of actresses who populated British movies of the 1950s, vaguely recognisable yet never graduating to leading roles or stardom. She was tall and pretty, with long blonde hair, and she made a fleeting debut in 1954 in *You Know What Sailors Are*. Also that year, she was a St Trinian's girl and could be glimpsed in *Doctor in the House*, the first of a successful comedy series. But it was in *Sailor Beware* that she got her first major role, as the bride-to-be and daughter of Peggy Mount, a coarse, plump comedienne whose *métier* seemed to be scrubbing the doorstep wearing an apron and hairnet. The picture was a popular hit and led Miss Eaton to appear in three of the early *Carry On* films – as a bit of constant crumpet and the target of innuendo from the likes of Sid James and Charles Hawtrey.

In fact, this was something of a dead end and she was dangerously typecast. She was in dire stuff like the Bob Monkhouse vehicle *A Weekend With Lulu* (Lulu was a caravan, Miss Eaton was Deirdre)

Ian Fleming, creator of James Bond. (Corbis)

Albert R Broccoli, known as Cubby, who turned a minor literary hero into a worldwide phenomenon. (James Bond Fan Club)

Richard Maibaum, who scripted thirteen of the Bond movies. (James Bond Fan Club)

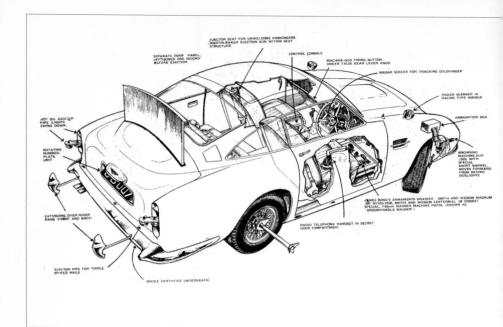

This Aston Martin DB5 had a lot of extra kit. (James Bond Fan Club)

The most famous car in the world poses at Pinewood. (James Bond Fan Club)

Pussy Galore's Flying Circus. (James Bond Fan Club)

Honor Blackman and the rear end of stuntman Bob Simmons. (James Bond Fan Club)

Shirley Eaton being prepared for the photo-shoot for journalists. (James Bond Fan Club)

On location at Andermatt, Switzerland. (BFI)

Connery takes some 8mm footage of Tania Mallet at Andermatt while Guy Hamilton watches the sky. (BFI)

Broccoli told Ken Adam, 'Build me a cathedral of gold.' He did. (James Bond Fan Club)

The exterior set of Fort Knox, built on the Pinewood backlot. (BFI)

Mobsters survey the model of Fort Knox which rises from the floor. (James Bond Fan Club)

The architect, Erno Goldfinger, from whom Fleming borrowed the name. (BFI)

A publicity shot with Connery, Eaton, Blackman and Mallet. (James Bond Fan Club)

The end of Oddjob. (James Bond Fan Club)

Honor Blackman, wearing a gold finger, attends the premiere. (BFI)

Mr and Mrs Ken Adam at the premiere. (BFI)

Soundman Norman Wanstall and his wife celebrate his Oscar victory. (Norman Wanstall)

and then suddenly she was in *The Girl Hunters*, in which the pulp private eye Mike Hammer was played by his own creator, Mickey Spillane. Eaton played the wife of a US senator – it was her first major dramatic role – who conspires in the murder of her husband and ultimately blows her own brains out. There was also *Rhino!*, her first Hollywood picture, in which she plays a nurse on safari. It was a nothing picture, but then came *Goldfinger*, which made her an international celebrity. She said:

I went to Harry Saltzman's office and wore a simple white dress with no sleeves. I hoped I looked . . . beautiful? Harry was a gruff, rough man and I didn't take to him particularly. He asked me what I thought about being nude and painted gold. I said I didn't mind as long as it was done tastefully. I didn't do a screen test or anything, my agent just called me a few days later to say I had the part. Then I met **Cubby Broccoli** who was a divine man.

I've got no axe to grind, unlike Sean, who I haven't seen for thirty years, but he's very naughty in not liking something that shot him to fame. He's done some wonderful work, he's a marvellous actor, but he won't have anything to do with Bond. I wore a black bikini for my first scene with him and he wore something which I called his Andy Pandy suit. Everybody was laughing at him but only Sean could get away with something like that thing he wore, that blue thing, his Andy Pandy suit.

Miss Eaton only met **Gert Fröbe** at the premiere and she only met Honor Blackman once, when their schedules crossed one morning:

She poked her head around my dressing room door and said

'Hi.' We both had our lovely morning faces on and she said, 'I'm not staying here. You look too good, Shirley.' Of course, Honor had the wonderful role, **Pussy Galore**, but it's me they always talk about. I've discovered I'm a sort of icon and I was only in the film for four minutes. That image of me will last forever. I was on the cover of *Life* magazine and then in March 1998 the same picture was used on the cover of *Fortune*. But when I did it I had no idea it would become such a classic. It was just hot and horrid to do. The paint was in a big fat tube, like sun cream, and a French make-up artist painted me all over. We did it quickly in a morning, then I was painted again the next day for publicity pictures.

After she made *Goldfinger* Miss Eaton toured America publicising it and was then left to get on with her career. 'It was the best thing that ever happened to me,' she said, 'because before *Goldfinger* the British cinema didn't know whether to make me a sex symbol or a girl next door. The Americans knew what I had.'

She made some American pictures, none of them especially notable, and then she suddenly vanished from the screen. She gave up acting for motherhood and went to live in the south of France with her husband of forty years, Colin, a building contractor. But in 1996 she was widowed, moved back to England and began writing her autobiography.

She had not been seen in public for years and then, in early September 1997, as the ocean of flowers spread across the lawn in front of Kensington Palace after the death of Princess Diana, she was plucked from the crowd of mourners by a TV camera crew and gave an impromptu interview, sharing in the grief of the nation yet still identified by the interviewer as 'golden girl, Shirley Eaton'.

See **gun barrel; Hamilton, Guy.**

premiere

On Thursday 17 September 1964 your author was present at the
world premiere of *Goldfinger*, and I still have my ticket and souvenir
brochure to prove it. Well, there was nothing on telly that night:
the BBC was offering *Compact*, a proto-soap opera, then a comedy
show with Lance Percival, the *News*, thirty-five minutes with Petula
Clark, a documentary about the Iron Curtain and, squeezed in before
the epilogue, Fanny and Johnnie Craddock cooked something which
was guaranteed to give you diarrhoea. Over on ITV you could see
Double Your Money, a pre-election programme on housing with Keith
Joseph, *The Richard Boone Show* and *What the Papers Say*.

So it was good to be Up West for the evening, smoking a **Morland**
and standing in Leicester Square watching the crowds and the stars
arrive. Of course, I chose my vantage point carefully and behaved
somewhat furtively. I was anxious not to be recognised but was fully
prepared to go into the 'parry defence against underhand thrust' if the
need arose.

I had paid for my ticket many weeks before. It cost two guineas for a
seat – S22 – in the dress circle, which would normally have cost 10s 6d.
Some of this money went to the charity, Old Ben, which helped street
news-vendors who yelled things like 'Gern-yer-newzan-stanner-rear'
which meant 'Get your *News* and *Standard* here'.

Outside the Odeon Leicester Square, among the *hoi polloi*, things
were a little chaotic, though not quite the near-riot which the papers
claimed the next day. After all, this was not Beatlemania. However,
in the crush one of the glass doors of the Odeon got smashed, and
not by **Oddjob**. I think I spotted the Aston Martin **DB5**, though it
was not allowed inside to see the film.

The papers estimated that the crowd numbered anything between
5000 and 10,000 people (10,001 if they spotted me). Although **Sean**

Connery was unable to attend – he was in Spain filming *The Hill* – everyone else of note was there. **Saltzman** and **Broccoli**, of course, **Hamilton** and all the girls. Your author remembers seeing Honor Blackman arrive wearing a white evening gown and a gold finger stall, studded with diamonds.

The premiere had been heavily hyped and the papers made great play of the fact that the film itself was taken to the cinema in gold cans. The screening was a triumph; there was loud applause as Connery emerged from under the seagull and yet more applause when he peeled off his wetsuit to reveal his white tuxedo. Then more applause when he said, 'Shocking, positively shocking.' By the time the picture ended our hands were raw.

'It was, I think,' Honor Blackman said later, 'the most glamorous night of my life.' Mine, too, **Pussy**, except that the train home was a bit of an anti-climax, even if my mouth did come ruthlessly down on a Mars Bar.

See **fish finger**; **hot stink**; **Houston, Penelope**; **Yokohama**

product placement

It's virtually impossible nowadays to watch a movie without being assailed by various products. Characters eat Cornflakes, go to McDonalds, drive Buicks, wear Nike trainers, stay at a Hilton, pack their Vuitton bags and look at their Seiko watches because those companies have paid for them to do so.

The Bond movies turned this into a full-time business and no credit roll was complete without its roster of corporations. It started with the Aston Martin **DB5** – the original and most elaborate piece of product placement ever devised – and escalated from there. If product placement is ever regarded as an element in the history of movies, then *Goldfinger* was the pioneer, the culprit. **Guy Hamilton** said:

The merchandising was strictly not my business. I couldn't care less. I used to get a little bit angry when **Harry [Saltzman]** used to come on the set. In the plane scene with **Pussy Galore**, when Bond shaves, suddenly the whole thing was a Gillette exercise. You never saw anything like it. There was Gillette foam, Gillette aftershave. . . . I said, 'Harry what are you doing? It's eight in the morning, the crew haven't arrived and you're dressing a set?' He'd done a deal with Gillette and we were going to get sixpence to use their stuff. By the time we got to *Diamonds Are Forever* it was very organised and I just asked Harry for a list of things, condoms down to zebras, and I'd just tick off what I could happily use.

See **fish finger; hot stink; Houston, Penelope; Morland & Co.; premiere; Yokohama.**

Pussy Galore

Few names are as provocatively upfront as Pussy Galore, or 'Poosy' as **Sean Connery** pronounced it. For **Ian Fleming** it was something of a lapse of taste, for he generally gave his female characters names which were merely exotic – Vesper Lynd, Solitaire, Gala Brand and so on. Calling a girl Pussy was blatant innuendo and we like to think he did it as a dare, challenging his American publishers to change it. And when the movie of *Goldfinger* opened in the States the name was embargoed on all publicity. Honor Blackman was tactfully described as 'Miss Galore' or '**Goldfinger**'s personal pilot,' though **United Artists** would have preferred her name to have been changed to 'Kitty' at the script stage. 'It's fun, it's tongue in cheek,' said Honor Blackman, 'and I was shocked that they were shocked. So I always used to say, "Oh, you mean Pussy"'

Calling a girl Pussy brought the Bond movie within punning distance of the *Carry On* films, and later Bond adventures maintained the smutty route – Plenty O'Toole in *Diamonds Are Forever* and Gobinda in *Octopussy*. But Pussy is a rare instance of an emphatic joke in Fleming, even if Bond's assault on her sexual preference is a case of rape.

The strongest-willed of the early movie heroines, the Pussy Galore in the novel was a rather marginal character, a lesbian gangster from Harlem who does not appear until three-quarters of the way through. Goldfinger tells Bond:

> She is entirely reliable. She was a trapeze artiste. She had a team. It was called 'Pussy Galore and her Abrocats.' The team was unsuccessful, so she trained them as burglars, cat burglars. It grew into a gang of outstanding ruthlessness. It is a Lesbian organization which now calls itself 'The Cement Mixers.' Even the big American gangs respect them. She is a remarkable woman.

And a few pages later Bond finally gets to see her:

> He felt the sexual challenge all beautiful Lesbians have for men. . . . Bond felt she would be in her early thirties. She had pale, Rupert Brooke good looks with high cheek bones and a beautiful jawline. She had the only violet eyes Bond had ever seen . . . the mouth was a decisive slash of deep vermilion. Bond thought she was superb and so, he noticed, did **Tilly Masterton** who was gazing at Miss Galore with worshipping eyes and lips that yearned. Bond decided that all was now clear to him about Tilly Masterton.

This is Fleming at his least imaginative, lamely building a character on the weakest of premises and on the corniest, Etonian ideas about America. The movie has none of this, dispensing early with Tilly and building up the character of Pussy so that she's a legitimate heroine rather than a sexy afterthought. The role required some skilful casting and, according to Hamilton, Honor Blackman was 'very obvious'.

And until Diana Rigg was cast as Tracy in *On Her Majesty's Secret Service* she was the only '**Bond girl**' to have a serious career behind her and in front of her.

Born in London in 1926, Honor Blackman made her screen debut in the controversial *Fame is the Spur* in 1947 and was the leading lady aboard the *Titanic* in *A Night to Remember*. A product of the Rank 'Charm School' – the British equivalent of the Hollywood studio system which turned out demure leading ladies – she alternated between the screen and the stage with modest success. Unlike her contemporary Jean Simmons, she never made it in Hollywood, but she became famous overnight when, in 1961, she was cast as Cathy Gale in the TV series *The Avengers*. Her contract was to run two years, and as the leather-clad judo expert she was a proto-feminist and cult figure. Blackman said:

> It's hard to go back to those types, but until that moment there were really only two kinds of women. There was the dyed blonde in black bra and stockings that the men were unfaithful to their wives with. Or there was the little wife who stayed at home and washed the dishes. Cathy Gale was the first woman who was the intellectual equal of the man and, above all, fought like a man, fought better than the man.

Blackman believes she was cast as Pussy because the role called for her to throw Bond over her shoulder and generally push him around. In fact, the early scripts, like the novel, do not have any judo in them and that element was only introduced after Blackman had been cast, a probably unique instance of an actress's talents significantly changing the development of a Bond script.

Seen in trousers throughout, Blackman gave *Goldfinger* an edge that was missing from other films in the series. Pussy was such a striking person, with such a shocking name, that she threatened to dominate the movie. Connery worried about this; he saw how his character was diminished by her and perhaps he worried, too, about playing opposite a real actress for the first time in a Bond movie. Pussy's predecessors, Ursula Andress and Danielle Bianchi, were hardly in Blackman's league, and she brought her own set of fans, with their own set of expectations, to the picture.

Rather than be dragged down by the predicament of being a 'Bond girl', Blackman went straight into *Life At The Top* and gave her finest screen performance. In 1968 she was reunited with Connery in *Shalako*, which was supposed to be Hollywood's answer to the spaghetti western. Shot in Spain by Bond regular **Ted Moore**, it also starred Brigitte Bardot, the movie prototype of the 'Bond girl'. The movie was dismal, as indeed are the rest of Blackman's pictures, which perhaps says less about her talent than about the state of the British film industry in the late 1960s and early 1970s.

Filmography

1947   *Fame is the Spur* (dir. Roy Boulting)
1948   *Daughter of Darkness* (dir. Lance Comfort)
1948   *Quartet* (dirs Ralph Smart, Harold French, Arthur Crabtree and Ken Annakin)
1949   *A Boy, a Girl and a Bike* (dir. Ralph Smart)
1949   *Conspirator* (dir. Victor Saville)
1949   *Diamond City* (dir. David Macdonald)
1950   *So Long at the Fair* (dirs Antony Darnborough and Terence Fisher)
1951   *Green Grow the Rushes* (dir. Derek Twist)
1954   *The Rainbow Jacket* (dir. Basil Dearden)
1954   *The Delavine Affair* (dir. Douglas Pierce)
1954   *Diplomatic Passport* (dir. Gene Martel)
1955   *The Glass Cage* (dir. Montgomery Tully)
1956   *Breakaway* (dir. Henry Cass)
1956   *Suspended Alibi* (dir. Alfred Shaughnessy)

1957 *You Pay Your Money* (dir. Maclean Rogers)

1957 *Account Rendered* (dir. Peter Graham Scott)

1957 *Danger List* (dir. Leslie Arliss)

1958 *A Night to Remember* (dir. Roy Baker)

1958 *The Square Peg* (dir. John Paddy Carstairs)

1961 *A Matter of Who* (dir. Don Chaffey)

1962 *Serena* (dir. Peter Maxwell)

1963 *Jason and the Argonauts* (dir. Don Chaffey)

1964 *Goldfinger* (dir. **Guy Hamilton**)

1965 *Life at the Top* (dir. Ted Kotcheff)

1965 *The Secret of My Success* (dir. Andrew Stone)

1966 *Moment to Moment* (dir. Mervyn LeRoy)

1968 *A Twist of Sand* (dir. Don Chaffey)

1968 *Shalako* (dir. Edward Dmytryk)

1969 *Twinky* (dir. Richard Donner)

1969 *The Last Grenade* (dir. Gordon Flemyng)

1970 *The Virgin and the Gypsy* (dir. Christopher Miles)

1971 *Something Big* (dir. Andrew V. McLaglen)

1972 *Fright* (dir. Peter Collinson)

1976 *To the Devil, a Daughter* (dir. Peter Sykes)

1977 *The Age of Innocence* (dir. Alan Bridges)

1979 *The Cat and the Canary* (dir. Radley Metzger)

Q

Q

Desmond Llewelyn, who sends Bond into the field fully kitted out, is now the longest-serving member of the Bond team. Absent only from *Dr No* and *Live and Let Die*, Llewelyn has outlived four different Bonds, three **M**s, three **Moneypenny**s, as well as **Saltzman** and **Broccoli**. He is to quartermastering what Dan Maskell was to incoming serving volleyers, what Murray Walker is to Schumachering, what Patrick Moore is to star-gazing. He is an affable and avuncular old cove, clearly a bit dotty and a permanent fixture in Britain's gallery of eccentrics.

Until he found his full-time job, Llewelyn was a familiar figure in British movies – he can even be glimpsed in *A Night to Remember*, marshalling the panic-stricken passengers (including **Honor Blackman**) on the *Titanic*. But he was never going to make it as a leading actor, and competition among character actors was always the stiffest. Bond made Llewelyn world famous and he's worn his fame lightly, living quietly on the South Coast, waiting for the next mission and – just the once, in *Licence to Kill* – rewarded with an unusually large part. He said:

> That was marvellous. I was on location in Mexico and for the first time in my life I made some real money out of a Bond film. But I've become so typecast, I'm never offered anything else at all. I get the occasional job here and there but it's always as Q, which is a bit boring for an actor.

Initially uninterested in or just plain bewildered by the gadgets he dispensed, Llewelyn began to get asked arcane questions by fans and became embarrassed when he wasn't able to give them the answers. It was when he was asked to go to America to help promote *Diamonds Are Forever* that he was ordered by **Eon**'s publicity director to bone up on them. But he always looked befuddled by the science, a bit of an absent-minded professor, which is, of course, the key to his charm:

> Oh gosh, the gadgets don't mean anything to me at all, and as I get older I have a problem learning lines. Especially when I've got long stretches of technical stuff to say and I don't have the faintest idea what I'm talking about.

At the age of 84 Llewelyn was a little wobbly and even more dithery in *Tomorrow Never Dies*, issuing Bond with his 7-series BMW, a car that drives itself. That may have been Llewelyn's final appearance as Q – he was the audience's sole link with the past, like a quill pen in the age of the laptop – and it looked back to his greatest moment, issuing **Sean Connery** with the **DB5** in *Goldfinger*.

It was a scene that had been written and rewritten many times, by **Maibaum** and by **Dehn**, and no one had it right. Then, on the set, **Hamilton** saw immediately what was wrong. He felt Q should be grumpy and diffident, and he gave Llewelyn an entirely new script, which the dismayed actor had to learn on the spot:

> In rehearsals, when Sean came in, I strode over to meet him. But Guy said, 'No no! Just ignore him.' I was puzzled by that because this was James Bond. But Guy was adamant and said, 'You don't like this man because he doesn't treat your gadgets with the respect they deserve. They always end up getting smashed. So you hate him.' The penny dropped and I've played Q like that ever since.

And Hamilton gave him the line that has stuck with him ever since: 'I never joke about my work, 007.'

Quiet de Luxe

When **Ian Fleming** completed the first draft of *Casino Royale* he celebrated by buying himself a new typewriter. Of course, this was no ordinary typewriter; its rarity and opulence would be symbolic of the riches and fame that would inevitably come its owner's way.

Fleming chose an American model, a gold-plated version of the Royal Quiet de Luxe which cost him $174. Fleming's biographer, Andrew Lycett, records that once Fleming had taken possession of the gleaming machine, he told friends that his 'personal goatherds in Morocco' were making 1000 sheets of special vellum paper which he planned to have studded with diamonds from Cartier.

Fleming's golden typewriter survived and in 1995 it was auctioned by Christie's in London for £50,000, many times its estimate price. The anonymous buyer was later revealed to be Pierce Brosnan.

R

racism

See **Fröbe, Gert**; **Oddjob**; **ugh!**.

reviews

See **Houston, Penelope**; **Johnson, Paul**; **Walker, Alexander**; **ugh!**; *Variety*; **whoops!**.

rivals and rip-offs

All movies, someone once said, are about other movies. From the cinema's earliest days producers and directors have been plagiarising each other – a shot, a cut, a whole scene, a story. Sometimes this is pure theft; at other times it can be regarded as homage.

Just as **Fleming** followed a tradition of clubland and detective heroes, so the Bond movies followed a long line of movie thrillers and sci-fi schlock. *Dr No* combined the British thriller of the pre-war era – *Bulldog Drummond*, say – with elements from sci-fi yarns like *Quatermass*, as well as the Red menace movies that Hollywood churned out in the paranoid 1950s. *From Russia With Love* seemed to be indebted to a whole raft of movies, which include *The Man Who Knew Too Much*, *The Lady Vanishes*, *Night Train to Munich*, *The Third Man* and *North by Northwest*.

Although the appearance of 007 was greeted as the arrival of a new screen hero in 1962, British TV was already screening two popular spy series – *The Avengers*, starring Patrick McNee and **Honor Blackman**, and

Danger Man, starring Patrick McGoohan, who was considered for *Dr No*. But the Bond movies generated a vast number of British and American TV spin-offs – *Get Smart*, *I Spy*, *The Man From UNCLE*, *The Saint* and *The Persuaders*, as well as a host of movie spy thrillers and spy comedies which were both rivals and blatant rip-offs. Some were good, some were decidedly awful, but all of them were rooted in the public's fascination with espionage. The list which follows is far from complete:

- 1964 *Carry On Spying*
  Typically British send-up with Charles Hawtrey playing secret agent Charlie Bind, number o-o-oh! Barbara Windsor plays Daphne Honeybutt and the villains work for STENCH – the Society for Total Extinction of Non-Conforming Humans. There's a nice in-joke in the opening sequence about **Sean Connery**'s earlier career as a milkman, though **Eon** threatened to sue the producers when it was revealed that the number 007 was a feature of the script. It opened a month before *Goldfinger*.

- 1964 *The Ipcress File*
  The first of the Harry Palmer films, starring Michael Caine and produced by **Harry Saltzman** from the novel by Len Deighton, who combined the espionage thriller with the social realism of kitchen-sink drama. Indeed, Caine is often seen at the kitchen sink, making real coffee or opening tinned mushrooms. The director, Sidney J. Furie, thought the plot so banal he decided to throw a smokescreen with fancy camera angles for every sequence. It is highly regarded, though, and **John Barry**'s music is superbly atmospheric. Two further Harry Palmer films were produced by Saltzman, *Funeral in Berlin* (1966) and *Billion Dollar Brain* (1968).

- 1964 *The Spy With My Face*
  The first of nine movie spin-offs from *The Man From Uncle* TV series, which ran from 1964–8, and starred Robert Vaughn as Napoleon Solo and David McCallum as Illya Kuryakin. The tongue-in-cheek humour, cheesy effects and the charisma of

the two stars earnt the series a cult following. Vaughn would have made a fine villain in a Bond movie.

- 1964 *The Intelligence Men*
  TV's most popular and gifted comedy duo, Morecambe and Wise, in a disastrous Bond send-up in which Morecambe, humming *Swan Lake* in a coffee bar, is mistaken for a Soviet agent. 'So appallingly mishandled,' said the *Monthly Film Bulletin*, 'that it emerges as an almost classic example of how not to amuse while apparently trying.'

- 1964 *Secret Agent FX18*
  A French attempt at a Bond send-up, with US import Ken Clark (who he?) as Francis Coplan, who travels to Mallorca with yacht and girl in tow to foil a plot hatched by Italian communists.

- 1965 *The Spy Who Came in From the Cold*
  Richard Burton plays the burnt-out agent Leamas in Sidney Lumet's film of John le Carré's novel about death and deceit on the Berlin Wall. Co-scripted by **Paul Dehn**, it smacks of authenticity, though the scene with **Bernard Lee** as a corner shopkeeper punched on the nose by Burton can be construed as an in-joke. Le Carré himself managed to transcend the genre of spy fiction by producing a series of novels which were regarded as literature.

- 1965 *Licensed To Kill*
  Tom Adams plays Charles Vine in a plot about a professor who has invented an anti-gravity machine. The film is more of a send-up than a thriller, with a Bondish moment when a nanny wheeling two babies in a pram produces a machine-gun and assassinates the professor's brother.

- 1965 *Alphaville*
  Jean-Luc Godard's comic-strip sci-fi thriller is not exactly a rival or a rip-off of James Bond, but no one was more aware than Godard of movie trends. His subtitle, 'Tarzan versus IBM', might have worked just as well for any Bond movie.

- 1965 *Our Man Flint*
  Like the Matt Helm movies, this is an Americanisation of the Bond ethos, with James Coburn as secret agent Derek Flint, who has to destroy Lee J. Cobb's plans for world domination. Cobb is the Blofeld figure, the head of ZOWIE – Zonal Organization World Intelligence Espionage. The film is daft and enjoyable mainly due to Coburn's lankily laconic presence.
- 1966 *Kaleidoscope*
  Warren Beatty plays an American gambler who breaks into a playing-card factory, marks the metals which print the cards, and sets out to make a killing in the casinos of Europe. The ambience of casinos, fast cars and willing women is very much in the Bond tradition.
- 1966 *The Silencers*
  The first Matt Helm movie, with Dean Martin as the suave American agent. The director, Phil Karlson, was offered *Dr No*, while the villain, Victor Buono, was proposed by **Richard Maibaum** as a possible Auric **Goldfinger**. Martin played Helm in three further, increasingly trashy pictures: *Murderer's Row* (1966), *The Ambushers* (1967) and *The Wrecking Crew* (1968). A TV series, starring Anthony Franciosa, followed in the 1970s.
- 1966 *Modesty Blaise*
  A cringe-inducing version of the comic-strip, decked out in psychedelic decor and with Dirk Bogarde drinking a martini with a live fish in it. Antonioni's inamorata Monica Vitti plays the female spy, Terence Stamp her cockney sidekick.
- 1966 *Where the Spies Are*
  David Niven plays an amateur spy embroiled in Middle East politics. This is the palest of imitations, co-scripted by Wolf Mankowitz, who co-wrote *Dr No*.
- 1967 *The Spy With the Cold Nose*
  It's a dog.
- 1967 *Deadlier Than the Male*

One of the few Bond rip-offs with a real literary pedigree, since Richard Johnson plays Dornford Yates's hero Bulldog Drummond. Sadly, resurrecting Drummond for the swinging sixties was a big mistake.

- 1967 *In Like Flint*
  This film has James Coburn in his second and final adventure as Derek Flint, still taking on Lee J. Cobb and ZOWIE, and still having the time to lay dozens of women, compile a dictionary of the dolphin language and perform at the Bolshoi ballet. The title is a pun on Errol Flynn's alleged sexual prowess.

- 1967 *Casino Royale*
  The only Fleming novel not owned by Eon became a vastly over-budget, over-schedule, over-everything spoof that made money despite its deserved reputation as one of the worst movies ever made. Dozens of writers and five directors contributed to the mess, in which David Niven – one of Fleming's original favourites – is just one of several James Bonds.

- 1968 *Operation Kid Brother*
  See **Connery, Neil**.

- 1981 *Aces Go Places III: Our Man From Bond Street*
  A Hong Kong Bond spoof, directed by Tsui Hark, which brought Harold Sakata and Richard Kiel together.

- 1983 *Never Say Never Again*
  Sean Connery's ill-considered re-return as Bond admittedly made 1983's 'official' Bond movie, *Octopussy*, look stale, but this rehash of *Thunderball* was a wasted opportunity.

- 1990 *The Russia House*
  This is an excellent adaptation of John le Carré's novel, with Sean Connery perfectly cast as the British publisher recruited by MI6 to smuggle secrets out of Moscow. Although Connery's tongue is never in his cheek, his history gives the film an additional layer of irony.

- 1994 *True Lies*

James Cameron's lavish spy romp begins with a brilliantly witty send-up of the pre-credits sequence of *Goldfinger* and then stretches the genre further than any Bond movie ever dared go. Arnold Schwarzenegger is perfectly cast as the über-Bond agent Harry Tasker.

- 1995 *Die Hard With a Vengeance*
  All the *Die Hard* pictures are indebted to Bond – Bruce Willis in the heating ducts of the first film owes a lot to *Dr No* – but this third film seems deliberately to mirror *Goldfinger* in its assault on New York's bullion reserves.

- 1996 *Spy Hard*
  The *Naked Gun* team send up the Bond ethos (plus the TV show *Get Smart*), with Leslie Nielsen as Agent WD40, Dick Steele, putting his foot in it where Bond would have put the boot in. Andy Griffith is an armless villain bent on world domination. The credit title sequence and song are a rehash of *Goldfinger*.

- 1997 *Austin Powers: International Man of Mystery*
  Mike Myers, of *Wayne's World*, sports a fetching chest wig and indulges in everything in this send-up of the swinging sixties, complete with a Blofeld villain with a cat in his lap, a Korean hatchetman who throws his shoes around and a female character called Allota Fagina. Instant cult status was assured.

See *ab initio* i; **scarlet letter, the**; **Goldfinger II.**

S

Sakata, Harold (1926–82)

Actor who played **Oddjob**.

Saltzman, Harry (1915–94)

We always talk of them as Saltzman and **Broccoli**. Harry came first because his name trips off the tongue more easily and because, in many ways, he was the initial driving force. It could be said that when Saltzman quit the Bond machine it lost much of its momentum and, anyway, Saltzman was always the more interesting man, more abrasive, more ambitious. Without Saltzman, the Bond movies became slickly anonymous, increasingly expensive forays into *Star Wars* territory, lacking the energy and style which made the early films so distinctive.

Saltzman was Canadian, born in St John, New Brunswick, on 27 October 1915. It was an area known for its massive tides, its fishing grounds and its freezing temperatures. One became a logger, a fur trapper, a fisherman, or one escaped as quickly as possible. Saltzman went to Paris and worked in *commedia dell'arte* and the circus but his hopes of becoming an impresario in French theatre were dashed by the war.

Saltzman served in the supply depot of the Royal Canadian Air Force. He always had an eye for the main chance and it was alleged that he made a bundle by smuggling jukeboxes to Europe concealed in Red Cross containers. After the war he settled in New York, threw away a job for Proctor & Gamble and by the mid-1950s he was a television producer, churning out episodes of *Robert Montgomery Presents* and *Captain Gallant of the Foreign Legion*, which was filmed in Italy.

Like many other marginal figures – Broccoli, for instance – Saltzman knew that if he could not easily make it in Hollywood he *could* possibly do it in Britain. His first effort, *The Iron Petticoat*, was a starry affair, an update of *Ninotchka* starring Bob Hope and Katharine Hepburn. Although the reviews were terrible, business was good and Saltzman was established as a producer. He returned to New York and was looking around for his next project when he met John Osborne.

Osborne's play *Look Back in Anger* had revolutionised the British theatre overnight, turning its young author into a celebrity. Its success was mirrored on Broadway, where Saltzman, whose first love was always the theatre, hoped he might produce Osborne's next play. But having swept the cobwebs away from British theatres – moving drama from the cosy drawing room to the grimy kitchen sink, as it were – Osborne's partner and director, Tony Richardson, now planned a similar assault on the British cinema. Saltzman seemed have most of the answers; anyway, Osborne took an immediate liking to him, admiring his 'fairground flair and uncanny taste', while Richardson liked Saltzman's enthusiasm for everything. 'You always knew he would somehow, somewhere, discover the magic carpet that would transport you to riches,' wrote Richardson in his memoirs. 'What we didn't know was that Harry hadn't a bean. He was a hustler, but a sublime hustler.'

Saltzman became a partner in Richardson and Osborne's Woodfall Films and moved to London, where he set up a lavish office with secretaries and chauffeurs. He was involved in the stage production of Osborne's *The Entertainer* and earnt a producer's credit on the film of *Look Back in Anger*, which flopped at the box office but which got some appreciative reviews. A film of *The Entertainer* followed, then *Saturday Night and Sunday Morning*, arguably the best of the kitchen-sink dramas, and which made a star of Albert Finney.

Saltzman's partnership with Osborne and Richardson was likely to come to an end. They had become so successful and so famous that Saltzman suddenly seemed superfluous to their plans, while his own schemes seemed far different from their own. But Saltzman also saw that the fad for social realism was coming to an end and that audiences wanted, in his words, 'something different, strong plots with excitement, fast cars, bizarre situations, drink and women'.

As *Saturday Night and Sunday Morning* went into production, to be followed by *A Taste of Honey*, Saltzman broke off his relationship with Woodfall and took a six-month option on the Bond novels, paying $55,000 for them. He had failed to get a deal and his six months were almost up when his friend the writer Wolf Mankowitz introduced him to Broccoli. An uneasy but financially equal partnership was forged, a further option was taken and then the deal with **United Artists** was struck. **Eon** was in business.

According to **Guy Hamilton**, 'Cubby was the tit and bum man and Harry was the gadget man'. Together, they made a formidable team. To begin with, Saltzman took the major responsibility for the scripts. Having worked with John Osborne, it's clear he thought that **Richard Maibaum** – Broccoli's man – was little more than a hack. Saltzman thought Maibaum's script for *Dr No* lacked the elements to make a viable and distinctive series, so he encouraged Terence Young and his assistant Johanna Harwood to rewrite it, dropping Maibaum's mid-Atlantic clichés for something specifically British. And there was also **Sean Connery**, a working-class hero, a sort of Jimmy Porter in a tuxedo and hand-stitched shoes, whose character had to be carefully considered and constructed, tailor-made for Connery. Maibaum's Bond could have been written for any of Broccoli's Hollywood stars on the skids.

Until *You Only Live Twice*, Saltzman and Broccoli were a team. But when Connery became disenchanted with the Bond series and started making financial demands, Saltzman himself began to get restless. He already had a **rival** series of his own – based on Len Deighton's novels – which starred Michael Caine, a sort of off-the-peg Bond who wore spectacles; these were spy thrillers which had everything, including the kitchen sink. Because Deighton never gave his spy a name, one had to be found for the screen version. Saltzman asked Caine what was the dullest, drabbest name he could think of. 'Harry,' said Caine, unthinkingly. And so Harry Palmer was born, starting spectacularly with *The Ipcress File*, and less so with the sequel, *Funeral in Berlin*, which was directed by Guy Hamilton. Then Saltzman produced *Battle of Britain*, a blatant, $14 million bid for the big time and a possible knighthood, which Hamilton also directed. The movie flopped and so did the final Harry Palmer picture *Billion Dollar Brain*.

Saltzman's finances were getting a little shaky and his ego had taken a serious bruising – he was unable to produce a hit without Bond and Broccoli. George Lazenby's Bond film, *On Her Majesty's Secret Service*, caused further friction with Broccoli, and by the time of *Diamonds Are Forever* and the first **Roger Moore** films Saltzman and Broccoli were hardly speaking to each other. *Live and Let Die* was produced by Saltzman and *The Man With the Golden Gun* was produced by Broccoli. It was the Lennon and McCartney syndrome, though the public was unaware of it at the time.

Saltzman was bored with Bond, and Roger Moore was always Broccoli's friend. Saltzman was also restless, keen to put his considerable fortune into new ventures, including the purchase of Technicolor, an idea which Broccoli turned down and which led to further complications since Saltzman used Danjaq's capital as collateral. UA's historian, Tino Balio, described Saltzman and Broccoli as 'two scorpions in a bottle', and because of their disputes plans for *The Spy Who Loved Me* were delayed. Finally, Saltzman bowed out permanently, with UA paying him $26 million, plus a hypothetical $10 million which released Saltzman from his contractual obligations to the studio. Saltzman apparently spent most of his money clearing his considerable debts.

His final picture was *Nijinsky*, starring George de la Peña as the dancer and Alan Bates as Diaghilev. A film about Nijinsky had long been a favourite among Hollywood sophisticates. In the 1950s Billy Wilder had wanted to make a film about him and went to Sam Goldwyn with it. Goldwyn was shocked by the idea of a movie about a ballet dancer who slept with his male teacher and who was carted off to a lunatic asylum because he believed he was a horse. 'No, no!' Wilder told Goldwyn. 'We've come up with a happy ending. He wins the Kentucky Derby!'

Saltzman pushed the project ahead. It was very much his pet project, though he backed out of his original plan to film it with Tony Richardson, from a script by Edward Bond, with Rudolf Nureyev and Paul Scofield. Eventually he hired Herbert Ross to direct, whose level-headed approach avoided the sort of fireworks that might have resulted if Richardson had made the picture. The picture was peculiarly bland and it bombed. Saltzman never made another film.

There were, though, other schemes. Saltzman bought the major theatrical agency H. M. Tennent, and had hopes of turning his stage hits into movies. But several costly failures and Saltzman's own failing health brought about his retirement and the dissolution of his business ventures. He moved to Paris, where he died on 28 September 1994.

Filmography

1955   *The Iron Petticoat* (dir. Ralph Thomas)
1959   *Look Back in Anger* (exec. prod.; dir. Tony Richardson)
1960   *The Entertainer* (dir. Tony Richardson)
1960   *Saturday Night and Sunday Morning* (co-prod. Tony Richardson; dir. Karel Reisz)
1962   *Dr No* (co-prod. Albert R. Broccoli; dir. Terence Young)
1963   *From Russia With Love* (co-prod. Albert R. Broccoli; dir. Terence Young)

1964   *Goldfinger* (co-prod. Albert R. Broccoli; dir. Guy Hamilton)

1965   *The Ipcress File* (dir. Sydney J. Furie)

1965   *Thunderball* (co-prod. Albert R. Broccoli; dir. Terence Young)

1966   *Funeral in Berlin* (exec. prod.; dir. Guy Hamilton)

1967   *You Only Live Twice* (co-prod. Albert R. Broccoli; dir. Lewis Gilbert)

1967   *Billion Dollar Brain* (dir. Ken Russell)

1968   *Play Dirty* (dir. André de Toth)

1969   *Battle of Britain* (co-prod. S. Benjamin Fisz; dir. Guy Hamilton)

1969   *On Her Majesty's Secret Service* (co-prod. Albert R. Broccoli; dir. Peter Hunt)

1971   *Diamonds Are Forever* (co-prod. Albert R. Broccoli; dir. Guy Hamilton)

1973   *Live and Let Die* (co-prod. Albert R. Broccoli; dir. Guy Hamilton)

1974   *The Man With the Golden Gun* (co-prod. Albert R. Broccoli; dir. Guy Hamilton)

1980   *Nijinsky* (exec. prod.; dir. Herbert Ross)

See **dealers**.

scarlet letter, the

James Bond was a creature of habit. Even though he had been retired for many years, he still woke early and gave himself a modest fitness regime followed by a dip in the pool, a cold shower and a shave. Then he went into the dining room where his faithful maid, Winnie, served him breakfast, which he ate with the *Daily Gleaner* propped up on the table. His breakfast was always the same: homemade yoghurt, wholewheat toast with a single boiled egg, honey and a pot of steaming Blue Mountain coffee. By glancing out of the latticed window, Bond could see the Blue Mountains themselves.

When he retired, Bond kept his London flat in the tree-lined square in Chelsea. In the 1950s and 1960s, when he was on active duty, it had been a perfect place to live: discreet, elegant and within easy reach of London's gaming clubs, restaurants and tailors. But it seemed that Bond's retirement – which he did not resist – coincided with the decline of the capital. Blades was the first to go. The club had taken on a new chef who eschewed plain grilled Dover sole and now served it in minuscule fillets with lime and kumquat sauce and brown rice timbales. Then the building was sold and converted into an all-suite hotel owned by Richard Branson and designed by Sir Terence Conran. Although Bond was never a member of Blades, dining there only when **M** invited him, it was a place of memories, notably that game of cards with Sir Hugo Drax which launched the Moonraker affair.

Even sadder for Bond was the demise of his favourite restaurant, Scotts, in Piccadilly Circus. The site was developed and Scott's itself transferred to new premises in Mount Street, Mayfair, just opposite the service's safe house where Bond once masqueraded as Charles Calthrop. But the new Scott's, which replaced a pretentious place called the Diplomat, was unwelcoming and seemed to cater to tourists. Bond frequented Wilton's for a while, seemingly the only place in London that could grill a sole or a cutlet satisfactorily, but it lacked the charm of Scott's and, frankly, the prices were appalling. Bond ended up eating at home.

Then there was that dreadful year of 1978, when the garbage was piled high in the streets, the year when England seemed to go mad. Mrs Thatcher's revolution brought about further turbulence, and the England that Bond loved and defended vanished forever. Japanese tourists clogged King's Road, parking was impossible, people gibbered into mobile phones (the scourge of the century, Bond thought), computers had taken over from people and the price of everything went through the roof. Bond's modest MoD pension no longer catered for his immodest tastes.

Bond sold his flat for a song and left for Jamaica, where he bought a small but lovely house in the hills above Ocho Rios. He had not been back to England since the memorial service for M. That had been a dreadful occasion. Bond had declined the invitation to speak (though he did write M's obituary for *The Times*) and at the reception afterwards the polite conversation with former colleagues bored him rigid. He realised then how much he felt like an exile in his own country.

In Jamaica he was alone. He preferred it that way. The sun always shone, and the humidity was good for his lungs and muscles. Every three months he would fly to Miami for a medical check and sometimes he would see old friends like **Felix Leiter**. And in Jamaica there were plenty of opportunities for female company, mainly American widows and their daughters, who gathered at Jamaica Inn or Strawberry Hill, the only hotels on the island with any style. Once, a long time ago, Bond had even invited **Miss Moneypenny** to stay. That proved to be a big mistake and she left in a flood of tears; Bond was morose for a month.

Bond also received occasional visits from young scriptwriters who wanted to film his life story or publishers who wanted him to write his memoirs. He saw them all, gave them lunch and sent them away empty-handed; unlike that disloyal, lower-echelon shit Peter Wright, Bond would never break the Official Secrets Act. The movies were made, willy-nilly, though Bond never saw any of them.

Nevertheless, he had to endure a peculiar kind of fame. It was not the fame of a movie star; Bond was a more mysterious and thus a more glamorous figure than that. And if someone – usually a tourist – claimed to recognise him, he would say, 'I'm terribly sorry. I'm not *that* James Bond. I'm an ornithologist.' If pressed, he could even produce a book, *Birds of the West Indies*, to prove it.

Bond had been through a long period of self-doubt and remorse, when he wondered if it had all been worth it, whether England had been worth fighting for, especially now that it was an offshore province of Europe run by faceless bureaucrats, reptilian spin doctors and a prime minister who was a grinning, walking contradiction – a bland megalomaniac named Blair. Bond detested the sanctimonious little creep. But a course of therapy and life in Jamaica had cleared his mind. Now aged 76, Bond was still a man who looked forward, rarely back.

It was his postman, an amiable man named Nelson, who sometimes forced him to reflect on his life. This morning the post included a letter which had been forwarded to him from London. Bond studied the envelope carefully. It was handwritten and postmarked in Boston a month earlier. None the wiser, Bond slit open the envelope, which contained a long letter and a smaller sealed envelope, which was slightly heavy. There was obviously a small object inside it, hard and rectangular, about an inch long. He looked at the signature on the letter: Moorea Rutland. The name meant nothing to him.

Bond poured himself another cup of coffee, picked up his Oliver People's glasses and settled down to read:

Dear Mr Bond,

My name is Moorea Rutland and I am writing to advise you of the death of my mother, whom you knew as **Pussy Galore**. I'm sure this news will come as a great shock to you, although I know that you and my mother knew each other briefly and that was thirty-five years ago. But she spoke about you often and I believe she loved you very much. She passed away on 14 March. I miss her very much.

My mother told me everything about you, about how you and she met, and about Mr **Goldfinger**. My mother was a very open and honest person who had no regrets about her past life. As you know, she was the victim of an unhappy childhood and was raped by her uncle, which made her uncomfortable in the company of men. She became a stunt pilot and then fell in with some bad people and, well, you know the rest. When I was old enough and had boyfriends, she told me that it was you who made her feel like a real woman, which may be a sexist thing to say nowadays, but it's true. And after those bad times, she told me that your influence in London and Washington saved her from being arrested for being an accomplice to terrorism. She said that betraying Goldfinger and saving so many lives was the best thing she ever did.

You may like to know what became of her. Well, after the American government let her go without charging her, she found a little place to live in the Bahamas, which she paid for with some of Mr Goldfinger's gold – is that so bad? She lived alone on the beach, in a hut really, and started up an aerial sightseeing company, flying tourists around in an old seaplane. She was a little crazy then, I think, and she called herself Bonnie Lee after a character in an old movie about flyers that she liked.

Then, in 1966, she received news that her father had died. She hadn't seen him for years and had completely cut herself off from her family, as you can imagine. But her father left her everything, which amounted to several million dollars. He was a shrimp fisherman who'd made it big on the Gulf Coast, and her brother, who was his partner, had drowned when his boat went down.

My mother left the Bahamas and moved to Louisiana to run the shrimp business. She also started to lease out boats for game fishing. That was how she met my dad, Mark Rutland. He was in publishing and ran a large company in Boston which specialised in educational textbooks. He was then married to a woman named Margaret Edgar. He didn't talk about her much but I know she was blonde and pretty, that she had serious psychological problems, that she adored horses and that she once tried to steal Mark's money. This made him all the more attracted to her and they got married in late 1964. The marriage was a disaster from the start. I don't think it was ever consummated. It was when Mark was in New Orleans on business that he met my mother. He was five years older than my mother and she told me she was attracted to him because, she said, he reminded her of you, Mr Bond. She said you looked uncannily alike and that you both had the same charm, elegance and authority. Anyway, they became friendly and soon started an affair. When Mark had to fly to Los Angeles on business, my mother joined him, and then they flew to the South Pacific, which is where I was conceived and which is how I got my name, Moorea.

Mark decided to tell his wife what had happened and that he was in love with Bonnie Lee. As I said, she was mentally unstable – she hated the thought of sex – and I think the shock of discovering that my mother was pregnant drove her to suicide. One night at their upstate farm she shot her horse, Forio II, and then shot herself.

My mother married Mark Rutland in 1967 and I was born four months later. Mother sold the shrimp business and went to live in Boston. That's all there is to tell, really, for I think she found true happiness with Mark because they had both lived through a lot and had to come to terms with similar problems. Sadly, my father died on that TWA flight which crashed off Long Island and my mother started to decline immediately afterwards. I think she died of a broken heart.

When she was dying, she told me that she always intended to write to you, to see if you were well, to see if you ever thought of her and wondered what she was doing. But she never did, not even when she learnt about the tragedy which befell your wife. However, when I was going through her things I found this letter, which was addressed to you, and attached to it was this little envelope. I have no idea what is in it but the least I can do is to send it to you.

Respectfully yours,
Moorea Rutland

Bond put the letter down and let out a deep sigh. He had not often thought of Pussy, or Honeychile Rider, or Solitaire, or any of the other girls he had met. If any woman dominated his thoughts it was Tracey.

Bond took a final sip of coffee, which had gone cold and bitter. He picked up the little envelope and put it down again. At first he considered throwing it away, even burning it. He got up and went down into the garden to inspect his hibiscus and oleander, pruning them where necessary with his Spear & Jackson secateurs. He asked his gardener to mow the lawn. Returning to the house, he went into the kitchen, where Winnie was preparing his favourite lunch of crab quiche and rocket salad. To her astonishment, he started to wash up his breakfast things. He switched on his Sony television and watched CNN for a moment or two. He was agitated.

The little envelope was where he had left it. He snatched it up and tore it open. Inside was a short note and yet another, smaller envelope. He read the letter:

Hi, handsome!
I don't have the words to express what I feel. I think of you often and hope you are well and at peace with the world. I am unwell but I have found peace. All I have to remind me of you is this little memento of our time together. Silly isn't it?
All my Love, my darling James,
Pussy

Bond opened the little envelope. Inside was a small metallic object and a piece of paper. He knew immediately what they were. The tiny **Homer** was slightly buckled and the piece of paper even had **Mr Solo**'s dried and faded blood on it. The paper was the note which Bond had scribbled hastily, so long ago, just before Pussy had stolen the floor from under him:

007 TO C.I.A.

AERIAL NERVE GAS

PRECEDES DAWN RAID

FORTKNOX.

TOMORROW

Bond held the Homer and the piece of paper for a long time, staring into space and not resisting the tears which flooded into his eyes.

See **Connery, Sean**.

screenplay

Iowa City is a pleasant place in one of the coldest parts of America, where farming is the major occupation. Most of the original, prairie Victorian town has been demolished to make way for the sprawling University of Iowa, which Iowa City gained in compensation for losing its prominence as the state capital. Because of the university, which spreads itself over several blocks, Iowa City is a youthful place filled with cheap restaurants, movie theatres and bookstores, which gives it an unexpected vibrancy.

Iowa City also has a remarkable secret. It is without doubt the world's most important centre for the study of the James Bond films. The reason for this is simple: **Richard Maibaum**, who wrote or co-wrote thirteen of the Bond movies, graduated from the University of Iowa in 1931, and it is there, in the Special Collections Department, that his papers have been deposited. Here are all the treatments and screenplays which Maibaum wrote, together with a wealth of correspondence and rare press cuttings, all superbly collated and catalogued. It is because of Maibaum's and his widow Sylvia's foresight and generosity that we can trace the development of the *Goldfinger* script and assess the individual contributions of Maibaum and his successor on the project, **Paul Dehn**.

Maibaum started work on *Goldfinger* in early April 1963 and in a long letter to **Saltzman** and **Broccoli**, dated 30 April 1963, he outlined his ideas and the problems created by the novel:

> As you know there are lots of problems. Not enough action for Bond in the early part and not enough love-stuff. So we'll have to do some inventing. Also the whole **Leiter** business is not very satisfactory – merely pulling him in at the end during the ambush at **Fort Knox**. However, with these areas covered in some way, I think we can essentially keep the book.
>
> Let me first give you some of my basic thoughts. Whereas *Dr No* was a mystery (a man is killed, who did it? – and why?) and *Russia* was a straight suspense story (we know almost all of the plot against Bond and want to see how he foils it) *Goldfinger* is what I call 'a duel.' Bond versus **Goldfinger**. It is not, I repeat not, a story about a robbery, although the Fort Knox heist is the most important section of the book and will be treated as such in the film. Usually in films where robbing a Brink truck or looting the Bank of England (as was done in Jules Buck's picture for which I did the adaptation) the planning occupies the first several reels and they are done in almost documentary style. This is not what we should do with *Goldfinger* because it is both old stuff and doesn't properly tell our story – the clash between two supermen, Bond and Goldfinger.

Maibaum worried about **Fleming**'s very obvious plot contrivances, especially the element of coincidence, even though the novel is deliberately structured on 'happenstance', 'coincidence' and, lastly, 'enemy action', which is the consequence of the first two. In particular, Maibaum disliked Fleming's device of having Bond encounter Goldfinger before **M** assigns him the case. In the early stages, Maibaum proposed that Bond meet **Jill Masterson** (Masterton in the novel – Maibaum's slip was never corrected) at Miami Airport and that when he discovers Goldfinger's method of card-cheating he should also discover some smuggled gold bars in the room, a device which allows Bond to enter the case right from the start.

Maibaum also wanted to preserve Bond and Jill's brief tryst on the train to New York and her subsequent return to London, where she is murdered, coated in gold paint by **Oddjob**. However, Maibaum wanted Bond, and therefore the audience, to *see* Jill's body and not to be told about it – as in the novel – by Jill's vengeful sister, **Tilly Masterson**.

'The business of Jill's death and the manner of it is too good and startling to be thrown away as it is in the book,' Maibaum wrote. Right from the start, the dead girl covered in gold paint was envisaged as the film's motif, its most striking image.

But Maibaum's biggest problem was Goldfinger's motive for stealing the gold from Fort Knox. Hitchcock would not have bothered about the motive at all. The gold would have been the McGuffin, the pretext for the plot, which emphasised – as in, say, *North by Northwest* – character and action over logic. Perhaps those in the Bond team were more prosaic in their approach and had less confidence in their technique; anyway, Maibaum and his colleagues burst blood vessels making the plot make sense.

In the novel Goldfinger is working for the Russian security department, SMERSH, and the motive is clear: by taking possession of the stolen bullion, the Russians will monopolise the gold market and destroy the American economy. But because Saltzman and Broccoli insisted that the SMERSH element be removed from the story the motive was removed as well. Maibaum told his producers:

Taking SMERSH out of the picture reduces Goldfinger's lust for gold to merely that – a psychopathic obsession. What does he do with his gold? Without a purpose he becomes nothing more than the greatest miser since Croesus. Perhaps we can infer that he is flying to a country, never expressly mentioned, perhaps a new nation which desperately needs gold, with whom he can make a deal never to be extradited.

Maibaum also threw in an idea which became one of the most famous scenes in the film:

> That BUZZ SAW *must go.* It's the oldest device in cheap melodrama. It's comic by now. Instead, I am dreaming up a machine which utilizes the new LASER BEAM. It was featured in LIFE magazine. . . . I visualize a demonstration of the beam, showing it cutting through steel, and then used as the buzz saw was in the book, threatening to cut Bond in half. This out-Flemings Fleming. Using the very latest scientific discovery in the old proven way of scaring the wits out of people.

Maibaum ended his letter with a note of caution and a casting suggestion. At the time he wrote this letter, *From Russia With Love* was on location in Istanbul and Maibaum had heard worrying rumours that Terence Young was turning it into a comedy. He had also recently seen the actor Victor Buono, and thought he would make a 'tremendous Goldfinger. [He's] six feet four and weighs three hundred pounds. He has been called a combination of Charles Laughton and Laird Cregar.'

Maibaum's first job was to write a detailed treatment, an outline of the plot together with sample lines of dialogue. He delivered his fifty-four pages on 20 May 1963, and in his covering letter to Saltzman and Broccoli he admitted it had been 'a tough nut to crack. For instance, Goldfinger's plan to knock off Fort Knox simply won't stand up. Especially the business of drugging the water supply. NOT EVERYBODY DRINKS WATER AT THE SAME TIME.'

Maibaum solved the water problem by introducing nerve gas, which was still delivered through the water supply. And at this stage

Goldfinger is still planning to take the gold away with him, at first on trucks, then by train and then aboard a Soviet submarine. Knowing that Broccoli was a dedicated tit and bum man, Maibaum also added: 'We have six girls in this one . . . Bonita, the Mexican dancer, the red head at the Miami airport, Jill, **Moneypenny**, Tilly and **Pussy**. I've kept the Lesbian angle, but played it as "man-hating," a perfectly acceptable, recognizable proclivity.'

In this first treatment, the pre-credit sequence exists in embryonic form and is framed in a flashback as a rather melancholic Bond recalls events for Felix Leiter at Miami Airport. We do not see Bond blow up the heroin factory, though he is involved with the Mexican dancer, reflected in whose eyeballs he sees the assassin stealing up on him. And, after the assassin is electrocuted in the bath, Bond's celebrated parting quip – 'Shocking, positively shocking' – is already in place and can most assuredly be ascribed to Maibaum.

After the Miami sequence, when Goldfinger is caught cheating at cards, Bond and Jill take the overnight sleeper to New York, as in the novel, but it is Bond himself who discovers Jill's body in her London flat. Following a briefing with M, Bond then goes to collect the Aston Martin, which has no machine-guns, nor an ejector seat, just the **Homer** device and reinforced bumpers. At this stage, there is no scene with the Governor of the Bank of England.

After the game of golf, Maibaum preserves the novel's key sequence when Bond has dinner with Goldfinger and is given a demonstration of Oddjob's strength – the Korean smashes the mantelpiece and banisters.

Maibaum's problems begin in Switzerland, when the plot, as in the novel, starts to unravel. Maibaum preserves the sub-plot involving Tilly Masterson, who is not killed by Oddjob but accompanies Bond to Kentucky, where she becomes Bond's secretary. And the torture scene, with its laser beam, is far too long and complicated, ending with Bond crying out, 'Go to hell, Goldfinger!' before a dramatic fade-out. Maibaum, as well as Fleming, is unable to provide a convincing reason why Goldfinger doesn't just kill Bond off on the torture table.

The ending is a terrible muddle, though Maibaum knew that the film had to end as all Bond stories end – 'His mouth came ruthlessly down on hers'. Although Maibaum bravely gives the hero precious little to do in the last quarter of the picture, he seems reluctant to make sweeping changes to the novel, so that the gangsters participate in the raid on Fort Knox, and Pussy Galore, who is just one of the gangsters hired by Goldfinger, is a rather minor character. The raid itself is exciting, except that there are no scenes in the bank vault, simply a fire-fight outside. At the climax, Bond, Goldfinger, Oddjob and Pussy escape on their private jet, as they do in the novel. Oddjob is sucked out of the window and Goldfinger is strangled.

This first treatment is little more than a boiling down of the novel to its essential components, many of which fail to work in screen terms or contain so many flaws as to be incoherent. By the time Maibaum delivered his second treatment, on 8 July 1963, significant changes had been made, although he had yet to dispense with Jill Masterson in Miami. And, puzzlingly, the Aston Martin had been scrapped in favour of Bond's vintage Bentley. Tilly is now killed by Oddjob in the forest, which improves things, but the laser scene is still needlessly complicated, with Bond contriving a false identity as a criminal adventurer in the hope that Goldfinger will hire him as a confederate. The scene ends with Goldfinger asking Bond if he can drive a tank. When Bond says, yes, of course he can, Goldfinger offers him a job and $1 million. 'Whatever you're cooking up,' says Bond, 'it must be the biggest caper ever planned.' 'It will make history Mr Bond,' says Goldfinger, 'and you will be part of it.'

With Tilly out of the picture, Bond's relationship with Pussy is expanded and improved, and the Fort Knox raid is now planned to include the aerial nerve gas attack executed by Pussy's Flying Circus. But, most importantly, Maibaum has solved the problem of the motive for the raid on Fort Knox. In what must be considered a brainwave, Maibaum devised the idea of the atomic device, which not only enabled Goldfinger to reap the bounty of the gold without actually removing it, but also improved vastly on Fleming by bringing the story scientifically up to date.

However, Maibaum still persists with the gangsters – it's likely that, as an American, he enjoyed writing their corny B-movie slang. Consequently, the gangsters still participate in the raid, though one of them – Mr Springer – decides to opt out. He is shot by one of Goldfinger's men and then his Cadillac, with Mr Springer's corpse inside it, is pushed off a cliff. Conveniently, Leiter's men find the body and Bond's SOS message inside Springer's clothing.

The climax now has Bond driving the tank which contains the atomic device. There are still no scenes inside the bank vault, just the FBI ambush outside. Bond is taken away by Goldfinger, Pussy and Oddjob aboard a private jet bound for Cuba. When Pussy discovers that Goldfinger was perfectly willing to kill 60,000 people, she experiences a moral reverse and kisses Bond on the lips. But this turns out to be far from a sexual advance: as their mouths come together Pussy passes him a note which says 'I'm with you'. Bond smashes a window, Oddjob is sucked out and then Bond strangles Goldfinger. Pussy and Bond land the plane and end up in bed.

Maibaum's next job was to convert his treatment into a full, first-draft screenplay. The pre-credit sequence still lacks Bond's act of sabotage and, a little later, Bond and Jill still take the train to New York after Goldfinger has been humiliated at the card table. Then Maibaum tackles one of the key scenes:

INT. JILL'S FLAT. LONDON

BOND closes the door behind him. Camera pans with him, staring, to studio couch. JILL, naked, lies on it, her body entirely covered with gold paint. The rays of the sun shimmer on it.

BOND(bewilderedly): Jill?

He stops, bends down, picks up her wrist, feels her pulse, realises she is dead. He stares at the gold paint on his fingers. In her hand is a card. He takes it out of her fingers, looks at it. The same one he sent her in the lounge of the Floridiana: JAMES BOND, UNIVERSAL EXPORTS, LONDON.

He puts the card in his pocket, looks down at the dead girl, his face grim. Then he turns, walks quickly to the door, walks out of the scene. As his footsteps die away, CAMERA PANS IN OPPOSITE DIRECTION, HOLDS as a bulky dark figure moves out of a shadow. The man steps forward into more light: ODDJOB, a squat, powerful Korean in an almost burstingly-tight suit, yellow gloves and an odd-looking bowler. CAMERA MOVES IN TO HIS FACE. Slanting, dramatic eyes, glittering like a gorilla's, over a broad flat nose and a snout-like upper lip that sometimes goes with a cleft palate. As face FILLS SCREEN . . . DISSOLVE.

After being briefed by M – there is still no scene at the Bank of England – Bond sees Mr Brackett (there is no **Q** at this stage) and is shown his converted Bentley, which has reinforced bumpers and a homing device, but still no guns or ejector seat. After the golf and the scene at Goldfinger's house, there is the drive across Switzerland when Bond meets Tilly – whom he rams from behind in the Bentley. Later they share a bed at a Swiss inn before Tilly sets off to shoot Goldfinger. Bond follows her, the Koreans arrive and Tilly is killed.

The laser scene remains a huge problem. Maibaum is still unable to think of a reason why Goldfinger allows Bond to fly out to Kentucky. With Tilly out of the picture, Maibaum was obliged to enlarge Pussy's role and it is now – in a radical departure from Fleming – that she becomes Goldfinger's personal pilot. Goldfinger introduces her to Bond somewhere over the Atlantic:

GOLDFINGER: This is Mr Bond. Miss Pussy Galore, Mr Bond.

BOND: My pleasure, Miss Galore.

PUSSY: Anything else, Mr G?

Goldfinger shakes his head. Pussy goes into the cockpit, ignoring Bond.

BOND: I approve your taste in pilots.

GOLDFINGER: I employ Miss Galore because she is a superb flyer – not for her looks.

BOND: I hope you don't disapprove of your employees socialising. After business hours, of course.

GOLDFINGER: I'm afraid you'll find her singularly uninterested.

What follows is some thirty pages – around 20–30 minutes of screen time – in which Maibaum does precisely what he decided against doing when he wrote his first notes on the subject. He goes into almost documentary detail about the planning of the raid on Fort Knox. After Goldfinger briefs the gangsters, Mr Midnight says: 'Mr Goldfinger, you are the greatest since Cain invented murder. Count me in.'

It is at this meeting that Bond makes his first move towards Pussy:

BOND: I need a large drink. Will you join me?

PUSSY: Never touch it.

BOND: Smoke?

She shakes her head.

BOND: No weaknesses of any kind? Mah Jong? Marijuana? Men?

PUSSY: You're getting colder.

BOND: Money, obviously. I'm in for a million. What about you?

PUSSY: I never flash a roll in public.

BOND: As strictly junior partners we ought to join forces to protect our interests.

PUSSY: I'll take care of my end. You handle yours.

Mr Springer still opts out of the plan and his fate – pushed off a
cliff in his Cadillac with Bond's message in his pocket – remains
unchanged. In his previous treatment, Maibaum cut straight to the
raid on Fort Knox, but now he adds a bizarre, erotic interlude in
which the remaining gangsters are entertained by Pussy, who dances
naked, covered in gold paint.

When Pussy's act is finished Bond follows her to her room, where
he finds her removing her gold paint. His attempts to flirt are rebuffed
in a long dialogue scene which explains Pussy's dislike of men.

As always, Maibaum's raid on Fort Knox involves the gangsters and
there is still no scene inside the depository. Having decided to detonate
an atomic device, Maibaum saw no reason why the gold itself should
be seen, a somewhat surprising lack of dramatic judgement. After all,
Goldfinger is obsessed with gold – its colour, its texture, its beauty, its
talismanic power (this story is almost the *Nostromo* of the Cold War
era) – and Maibaum's refusal to let the audience see the stuff, stacked
in millions, is baffling.

When Bond, Goldfinger, Oddjob and Pussy are aboard the plane,
the following dialogue exchange occurs, which is a rather lame
attempt to provide a motive for Goldfinger switching off the laser:

GOLDFINGER: Why didn't I crush you like a beetle! I was mad to
   have taken the chance – but I *liked* you Mr Bond.
BOND: I hate your guts, Goldfinger. You're a murderous swine.
GOLDFINGER: Please . . . let us observe the amenities. In due course
   you will suffer excruciatingly.

In the climactic struggle on the plane, Oddjob is sucked out and
Goldfinger is strangled by Bond as the plane depressurises. As Pussy
struggles at the controls, she asks where Goldfinger has got to. 'He
went off the gold standard, permanently,' says Bond, in a clever

one-liner which sadly never made it into the finished film. And in this version, Maibaum brings the story full circle by having Bond and Pussy about to share a room at the Floridiana Hotel in Miami.

Time was getting rather short if they were to make the deadline of a world premiere in London in September 1964. Saltzman and Broccoli knew the story still required serious surgery, and they sensed that they needed a fresh mind to work on it. Having made so many changes to the novel – notably the killing of Tilly and the introduction of the atomic bomb – Maibaum seemed unable to make that extra imaginative leap to tighten and simplify the plot. It was at this point that **Guy Hamilton** came aboard as the director and Paul Dehn was brought in to rewrite the script. At first they simply replaced the flaws in Maibaum's script with new ones, although Dehn's fertile imagination certainly improved many of the sequences.

Paul Dehn's first script, dated 23 December 1963, began in high style. Dehn had studied the opening to *From Russia With Love* and had wanted to come up with something even better as a pre-credit sequence. He took the bare bones from Fleming and Maibaum and added a note of sardonic, sartorial surrealism:

EXT. WHARFSIDE. SOUTH AMERICA. NIGHT
Featuring 'RAMIREZ EXPORT CO' with its plant installation and storage houses surrounded by a high wall. Armed uniformed guards, torches in hand, can be seen patrolling as the CAMERA descends to water level.

Its surface is scummed with flotsam, refuse and vegetable rind. The hairless, distended cadaver of a dog, legs pointing stiffly skyward, drifts across the frame towards the jetty steps.

The dead dog rises clear of the water to reveal JAMES BOND's face, his teeth clamped to the cadaver's underbelly. Peering cautiously around, he removes a stopper from a small nozzle attached to the dog and with a hiss the cadaver deflates. BOND drops it into the water and we watch it sink.

BOND glides into the picture. He is wearing a black waterproof suit, zip-pocketed all over and a waterproof rucksack. He vanishes into the shadows at the base of the wall.

And a little later:

BOND clears the wall and reaches comparative safety. In one smart gesture, he unzips the top of his waterproof suit, revealing a white dinner jacket complete with red carnation.

After he read this scene, Maibaum told Saltzman and Broccoli that he thought the dead dog was a 'dubious gimmick' and 'too repulsive'. Just before shooting started, Guy Hamilton ordered that the dog be changed to a seagull.

The remainder of the pre-credit sequence proceeds very much as in Maibaum's script, except that the Mexican dancer now asks why Bond wears a gun. 'For sentimental reasons,' he says in this first version. 'It was my grandmother's.' Dehn later changed this to the satisfyingly Freudian 'I have a slight inferiority complex'.

Dehn adds a lengthy dialogue sequence – later cut completely – between Leiter and Goldfinger's card stooge – before getting Bond to enter Goldfinger's suite. Their initial dialogue – 'Who are you?' says Jill. 'The house detective?' 'Am I dressed like a house detective?' says Bond – subsequently reverted back to Fleming, which enabled **Sean Connery** to say 'Bond, James Bond'.

Dehn saw how the train sequence slowed things up, though he still has Jill murdered in her London flat. Bond is briefed by M in a car en route to the Bank of England, the scene written by Dehn exactly as it appears in the finished film. Then Bond visits **Q**

Branch and sees the car, no longer the old Bentley which Maibaum preferred:

ASTON MARTIN.
The car looks totally innocent.

Q: Aston Martin **DB5**.
BOND: She looks a beauty. Can I have the keys?
Q: It's not quite as simple as that, 007. Come in beside me and don't touch anything. I want your undivided attention, please, for three-quarters of an hour.
BOND: Of course.
Q: The Homer's quite a novelty. A neat little transmitting device, magnetised of course, which you can conceal anywhere on the car you're tailing, so you can let it out of your sight.
BOND: Reception?
Q: Audio-visual. On your dashboard.
BOND: Range?
Q: One hundred and fifty miles.
BOND: I could stop and have lunch while the other fellow drives on. Pick him up again after the brandy.
Q: You could, 007, if you were prepared to take the car into the dining-room, or to earn a reputation for incontinence through having to leave the dining-room so frequently during luncheon. This is not a toy. It's an operation device perfected after years of research by our . . .
BOND: I'm sorry.
Q: The car has some interesting modifications. Here's an amusing little wheeze . . .

He presses a dashboard button.

DISSOLVE TO BOND swinging the Aston Martin through the main gates of St Mark's Golf Club.

★   ★   ★

Dehn had the idea that it would be more tense in screen terms if none of the Aston Martin's refinements – beyond the Homer – were revealed to the audience at this stage, an argument with which Hamilton agreed until Broccoli persuaded them otherwise. But Q's dialogue about incontinence led Maibaum to draw a firm line through it and append the words 'This is silly'.

It is after the game of golf that Dehn makes the first significant change by cutting the long dinner scene with Goldfinger and by having Oddjob demonstrate his prowess by decapitating the statue and crushing the golf ball in his fist. That speeded up the story considerably, establishing Oddjob immediately and leaving Goldfinger's megalomania to shine later in Kentucky.

The pursuit across Switzerland is as Maibaum wrote it, except that Bond no longer dallies with Tilly overnight. Whereas Maibaum had Bond's Bentley ram her from behind, the Aston Martin is now equipped with the scythes which cut her tyres to shreds. Dehn also killed her off – as Maibaum had done – but comes unstuck soon afterwards. In Dehn's script, Bond plans to plant a grenade at Goldfinger's factory but is prevented from doing so by Tilly's assassination attempt. Dehn then finesses the car chase, adding the little old lady with the machine-gun, the ejector seat and the mirror which causes Bond to crash, but he still fails to come up with a decent motive for Goldfinger's sparing of our hero when he's threatened with the laser beam. Dehn, like Maibaum before him, gives Goldfinger and Bond a huge amount of explicatory dialogue, but at least Dehn came up with one of the most celebrated dialogue exchanges in the entire series. Lying prone on the laser table, Bond asks why he needs so many safety belts:

GOLDFINGER: Choose your next witticism carefully. It may be your last.
BOND: D'you expect me to talk?
GOLDFINGER: Dear me, no, Mr Bond. I expect you to die.

*　　*　　*

From the laser torture, Dehn cuts to the plane, on which Bond makes a pass at Pussy's co-pilot, Susan. Goldfinger tells him, 'You mustn't do that to Pussy's girls.' Oddjob is also aboard the plane, applying his chopsticks to a plateful of fried mice.

In his first draft, Dehn is still far from solving the problems of the raid on Fort Knox, and, in particular, what to do with the gangsters and how to enable Bond to get word out to Felix Leiter. When we first meet the gangsters they are playing croquet on the lawn when Goldfinger arrives at the stud farm by helicopter. Bond is still Goldfinger's assistant, a participant in the subsequent briefing, and he believes Goldfinger's story that the atomic device will not harm anyone and is being used simply to blow open the door to the depository. But Dehn has come up with the idea of the model rising from the floor. It is still Mr Springer who opts out of the heist, but now they had a better idea of how to get rid of him.

Wolf Mankowitz, who co-wrote the first drafts of *Dr No*, claimed he was talking with Saltzman when the problem of Mr Springer came up. Having him shot and then sent over a cliff in his car did not seem good enough for a Bond film. Mankowitz said:

I'd been looking at that day's *Times*, and there was an article about the Mafia disposing of bodies by sticking them in the boots of cars and getting the cars trashed in one of those things. I said, 'Look, I'll give you an idea but it'll cost you £500 in cash.' They said OK so I said, 'Well, this is it. They put the body in an old car and they put the car into a crusher. A big machine comes down and bang, smash, wallop. There's a square of dirt with a little blood coming out of it. Any good?' And it's a very famous scene. There were lots of other things like that which gave me loose cash in my pocket.

Having got the idea of crushing the car, Paul Dehn then added a joke about someone having a 'crush' on Mr Springer.

Meanwhile, back at the stud farm, aware they are under CIA surveillance, Goldfinger suggests that Pussy take Bond to the hayloft, where she demonstrates her karate technique, the first time that Pussy is revealed as an expert in martial arts, doubtless because Honor Blackman was on the verge of being signed for the role. Bond makes another pass at her and he is quickly thrown to the ground. 'Say please when you touch my statistics, buster,' she tells him. And in a strange, voyeuristic touch, Oddjob is spying on them from below, with hay falling on to his bowler hat.

Next up is the air raid, with the nerve gas delivered by Pussy's pilots. The bomb arrives, the door is blown open with the laser, and, in a major departure from Maibaum, Dehn finally gets Bond and Goldfinger inside the bank vault, where the gold sits gleaming in thousands of stacks. It is here that Bond finally tumbles the whole plan:

BOND: Goldfinger, you're mad. This is a bloody dirty bomb. If it goes off it'll contaminate every bloody bar of gold in the vault.

GOLDFINGER: My dear Mr Bond. It will go off. And it will contaminate every bloody bar of gold, making them unmarketable for at least three generations and so quintupling the market value of my small, personal fortune of twenty-three million pounds in bullion. There will be economic chaos in the west. There will even be revolution. Revolution in the west means the evolution of the east. You are watching, Mr Bond, the birth and emergence – as the world's richest and strongest great power – of Communist China. You didn't think I was going to be so silly as to steal the gold, did you?

Goldfinger inserts the male 'primer' into the bomb's female 'aperture.'

GOLDFINGER   (bellowing as orgiastically as Hitler):   I'm going to

kill it! And I'm going to kill you! You're expendable now, 007.
Oddjob, take him down and rejoin me.

It is now that the Seventh Cavalry arrives, in the form of Leiter and
the Fort Knox marines. In the ensuing fight Goldfinger and Pussy
escape in their helicopter, leaving Bond and Oddjob to fight it out
in the gold vault. Dehn conjures an electrocution for Oddjob, as in
the finished film, though it is Bond himself who is able to disarm
the bomb.

In the aftermath, Leiter tells Bond that his SOS message reached
them in time. While Maibaum had this message planted on the
gangster, Mr Springer, Dehn pulls a surprise by having Leiter reveal
that Bond had a back-up plan and had planted a second message on a
veterinary surgeon who was treating one of Goldfinger's race horses,
a sub-plot which seemed to last forever.

Bond is flown to Washington, only to discover that the plane has
been hijacked by Pussy and Goldfinger, who accidentally fires his gun
and is sucked out of the plane. Pussy manages to ditch in the sea and
the final scene is one of arch theatricality:

CLOSE TWO-SHOT, BOND SMILING AT PUSSY
He looks up, straight into camera and 'sees audience.'

BOND: We made it.

Tableau, on which RED VELVET CURTAINS FALL.
After a beat, they rise again to disclose Pussy and Bond alone in a
stupendous clinch. CURTAINS begin to fall (tactfully!) behind:

ROLL-UP CAPTION:
'Next comes (forthcoming title)'

By the time Maibaum had digested this version – and it says much for his influence and Saltzman and Broccoli's loyalty that Maibaum was still very much part of the team – some major changes had been made. Realising the weaknesses of the plot, Dehn and Hamilton decided to have Bond imprisoned in Kentucky, enabling him to escape his cell and overhear the briefing from inside the model. They also realised how cumbersome it was to have the gangsters present at the raid, so they are murdered during the briefing in order to demonstrate the power of the nerve gas, and to emphasise Goldfinger's thirst for power and the pleasure he takes in killing. Realising that Bond does little at the climax on the plane, Dehn and Hamilton introduced a struggle during which Bond forces Goldfinger to fire his pistol, thus depressurising the aircraft.

A month after Dehn delivered his script Maibaum sent his suggestions and comments to Harry Saltzman. While Maibaum's judgement of structure and plot coherence was exemplary, he rejected the new, flippant tone of the picture:

> As I told you over the phone this morning, I was pleased by most of the continuity changes you made. However, I'm concerned about the overall tone of the script. It tends to get very Englishy now and then, coy, arch, self-consciously tongue-in-cheek. It's lost the aspect of dead seriousness we had in the other two – except for a few carefully chosen tip-offs – that we were really kidding about the whole thing. It's always fatal if the audience gets the idea that we *think* we are being funny. Nowhere in *No* or *Russia* does Bond really lose his essential dignity. Here he is just a patsy, and a comic one at that. Parts of the script sound as if it were written for Bob Hope and not Sean Connery. There are *too many* gags and gadgets. Don't forget, you hope to make more films after *Goldfinger*, so don't sell Bond short in terms of character. Even if he is the great superman, superlover, superagent, he still must be identifiable to audiences. Don't reduce him to a cartoon comic ever. Some of the things you

told me will help. Goldfinger not telling him about the plot
against Fort Knox but his over-hearing it from inside the model
is good. Also his *forcing* Goldfinger to shoot window out. But
Pussy still does nothing to warrant ending up in Bond's arms.

There remained two major flaws in the story: Goldfinger still had no
compelling reason to spare Bond's life on the laser table and Pussy
remained a marginal character. Dehn solved the first problem quickly
and deftly having Bond reconnoitre Goldfinger's Swiss factory and
overhear the words 'Operation Grand Slam', so that when he repeats
them to Goldfinger it is enough for the laser to be switched off.
And when Honor Blackman was confirmed as Pussy Galore the
role expanded considerably and led to Pussy betraying Goldfinger
by alerting the CIA about his plan. That not only saved time by
eliminating the veterinary surgeon's role, as well as the complications
regarding Mr Springer – later **Mr Solo** – but also gave weight to
Pussy's sexual reorientation, a vast improvement on Fleming, who
never saw the symbolic value of it.

The script was now almost complete, with all its major flaws ironed
out, even though Maibaum still worried about certain aspects: 'How
does Goldfinger get away in the helicopter?' he asked Saltzman.
'Wouldn't all the military planes be after him? Maybe you simply
have to duck that one and brazen it out. Maybe he got away.'

No one liked Dehn's theatrical ending, with its chintzy curtains and
final romantic clinch. It was Saltzman who suggested they parachute
out of the plane, but no one could figure out what would happen
next. Maibaum advised Saltzman:

Don't altogether discard some version of the parachute idea.
Perhaps that is Pussy's way of saving him. Her chute, and they
fall out of the plane in each other's arms. After the chute opens
... well ... it can be the first instance in history of a dame
screwed in mid-air. I've seen two men on a chute before but

never a guy and a gal in flagrante delicto. Coitus in the clouds. I'm only half serious but the idea intrigues me. The main thing now is to achieve the proper balance between the suspense and the sex and the fun. As of now I feel it's out of whack on the side of the fun.

On 3 February 1964, just a month before shooting was due to start, Maibaum attended a meeting with Broccoli and Sean Connery, whose financial involvement and creative influence was by now considerable. No longer the hunk who came cheap, Connery had become an international star, one of the most famous actors in the world, and he wanted to ensure that the film suited his own interests just as much as the producer's. Maibaum's notes on the meeting are preserved at the University of Iowa:

> Connery feels tone of script all wrong. Wants serious approach with humor interjected subtly as in other films. Feels that Bond's involvement with Goldfinger in Miami is too casual. He should be starting his investigation of Goldfinger there after finishing assignment in South America.
>
> He feels present script has lost Bond's mission, which was to find Goldfinger's gold hoard of twenty million pounds. That is why he goes along with Fort Knox hoping continued association with Goldfinger will lead him to the gold illegally smuggled out of England. Otherwise, why doesn't he just shoot him?
>
> Connery also feels that Bond should convince Goldfinger he is a criminal. Suggests (independent of first script which he says he never read) that bogus background be prepared for Bond which Goldfinger 'discovers.' However, Cubby replied that this was dubious as the 'hostage' idea seems to work.
>
> Connery is very much against Pussy bouncing him around. He said make something out of their relationship or drop her

out of the script. He hates scene in hay while Oddjob watches hay fall from loft.

He feels that Bond is overshadowed completely by Goldfinger throughout. Thinks script is in bits and pieces and not 'full,' so far as playing scenes are involved.

He thinks the gangsters at the Stud Farm are Guys and Dolls characters. Instead they should be real menaces. He thinks squeezing the golf ball is ludicrous.

Paul Dehn was prevailed upon a write a second draft, which became the final shooting script, incorporating the ideas and suggestions of Saltzman and Broccoli, Guy Hamilton, Connery and Maibaum. Hamilton refined many of the scenes on the spot, notably the superb helicopter introduction to Miami, as well as the scene with Q and the Aston Martin.

By March 1964, when the film started shooting, Maibaum had returned to California. He did, though, make one or two final contributions to the script, notably the pay-off line when Mr Solo's body is brought back to the Stud Farm, compressed into the body of the Lincoln Continental. Paul Dehn had contrived a joke about someone having a 'crush' on Mr Solo. Maibaum had a better idea. 'I think I have a better sick joke,' he told Broccoli. 'So: GOLDFINGER: Forgive me, Mr Bond – but I must arrange to separate my gold from the late Mr Solo. BOND: Yes – you said he had a pressing engagement.'

Maibaum's contribution seems to have ended there and he set to work on *Diamonds Are Forever*, which was then intended as the next film. But the surviving correspondence hints that Maibaum felt rather bruised by the whole experience. As he wrote to Cubby Broccoli:

It occurs to me that Harry, Guy and yourself mentioned something about my staying on an additional week because Sean may have wanted something fixed up – but *nobody* asked me. I hope that whatever is done preserves the tone of the script as we finally got it. And for God's sake, don't forget to keep Guy sticking a go-fast pill up Froebe's [**Fröbe**'s] ass. He may be great, but German actors give everything the full treatment – and slow. I know you'll sound off at the crucial moments as you always do. Good luck and all the best to all of you.

sexism

See **painted ladies**; **ugh!**.

sexuality

See **come again (1)**; **come again (2)**; **come again (3)**; **Johnson, Paul**; **Pussy Galore**.

Slim

It is one of the greatest and most famous scenes in the movies. Humphrey Bogart is sitting in a chair, looking strangely small and vulnerable as Lauren Bacall, wearing a tight-fitting suit, leans against the doorframe on the other side of the room. There is tension in the air, as well as cigarette smoke and romance.

Bacall moves over to Bogart and kisses him. Then she kisses him again, more seriously this time. 'It's even better when you help,' she says. She moves back to her perch by the door, standing languidly, her lips wet, her thighs trembling. Bogart asks her why she did that. 'I've been wondering whether I'd like it,' she says. Then she makes as if to leave, telling Bogart that if he wants anything he only has to whistle: 'You know how to whistle, don't ya Steve? You just put your lips together and blow.'

Bacall was playing a character called Marie Browning, though Bogart called her Slim. The movie, *To Have and Have Not*, was directed in 1944 by Howard Hawks, whose own wife was called Slim, though her real name was Nancy Raye Gross. She was just the sort of woman Hawks adored: witty, sexy, a woman at ease in Hawks's world of drinking, hunting and sailing.

Hawks met his own Slim on 30 August 1939 at the Clover Club on Sunset Boulevard. She was dancing with another man, **Albert R. Broccoli**, whom everyone knew as Cubby. Hawks asked Broccoli if he could meet his partner and, to cut a long story short, they married on 11 December 1942. In gratitude to Broccoli, Hawks made him an assistant director on *The Outlaw*, thus launching Broccoli's career, although it is arguable that – through indirectly causing that scene in *To Have and Have Not* to be written – in introducing Hawks to Slim and, by extension, Bacall to Bogart, Broccoli's major contribution to film history had been achieved before he had even heard of James Bond.

Solo, Mr

Mr Solo, played by Martin Benson, is the man who has a pressing engagement. **Ian Fleming** had suggested to an American TV producer, Norman Felton, that he name the hero of his new espionage TV series Napoleon Solo. Felton liked the name so much he decided to call the series *Solo*. When **Eon** protested that the name of the character was already in use, Felton was forced to change the name of his series to *The Man From UNCLE*. Benson himself was a well-established British actor whose dark, Italianate looks made him ideal for shady characters or even more exotic roles. In *The King and I* he played a Siamese and in *Cleopatra* he played a eunuch who grovelled before the young Pharoah until Caesar had him executed.

song

See **title number**.

soundman

It was a week before Christmas when Turner flung his ruby red
Mercedes-Benz C36AMG through the Worcester bypass and into
a blanket of fog. Yesterday there was heavy snow, blown in from
Siberia, but it vanished as soon as it appeared, and now night had
descended and fog engulfed the land below the Brecon escarpment.

Turner and his friend Tony Sloman were going to visit a plumber
named Norman Wanstall. Norman could fix your lavatory, he could
install your central heating boiler, he could unblock your drains and
he could make your pipes stop gurgling like a demented Wurlitzer.
Norman was a special person.

At Bromyard, Turner turned north and crept along the narrow
road, looking for the sign which announced Norman's remote house.
But after five miles Turner thought he was lost. Intending to turn
round, he swung left into a lane, then sharp right into someone's
drive. But Turner misjudged the angles and was unable to reverse out
to make the turn. Looking down the beam of his headlights, he saw a
gate and the tufted grass of a field. Turner sensed disaster but drove
on. A panther on the open road, the C36 wallowed like a buffalo on
the sodden grass and dug itself deep into the mud. Turner was stuck.
In the middle of nowhere. He started to curse.

Images of *Straw Dogs* and the opening of *An American Werewolf
in Paris* passed through Turner's mind as he watched Sloman, who
was of a much calmer disposition, disappear into the fog towards the
lights and a barking dog. In a moment or two Sloman reappeared with
the owner of the house, who offered to tow Turner's car out of the
morass. But the mud was too thick for the Subaru estate, despite its
four-wheel drive. Then the man said he had a brother with a Land
Rover. That would do the trick. Would you like a cup of tea?

The man was about 30, with two pretty young daughters who came
into the kitchen to see the strangers, giggled nervously and then ran
away again. The man introduced himself as Roy Harris.

'Where have you come from?' he asked.

'From London,' said Sloman. 'We're going to see someone who lives up the road. Norman Wanstall.'

'Norman?' said Harris. 'Norman Wanstall? He's my plumber.'

Turner was leaning against a large and beautifully warm central heating boiler.

'That's Norman's boiler you're leaning on,' said Harris, proudly.

'That's amazing!' said Sloman.

'Norman is a very special plumber,' said Turner. 'He's the only plumber in the world with an Oscar.'

'I knew he worked in films,' said Harris. 'Didn't know he had an Oscar.'

'He won it for *Goldfinger*,' said Sloman. 'But he gave up movies and became a plumber. Do you farm the land around here?'

'No, I'm in poultry,' said Harris. 'I catch turkeys.'

It turned out that Harris and his partner make a living rounding up turkeys and chickens. In a way, they are to the British poultry industry what John Wayne and Montgomery Clift were to *Red River*. They started small, driving from Herefordshire to the Home Counties every day to catch the birds which fossicked in huge indoor pens, waiting to be separated from their giblets. The business expanded and now they work for McDonald's and Marks & Spencer, raiding their vast poultry pens every night, grabbing the birds by the dark meat – that is to say, by a leg and a wing – and forcing them into crates, ready for the conveyor belt of death. Harris said:

We don't kill 'em ourselves. We just catch 'em. You have to be careful, mind, as they can be pretty angry, which is why we do it at night, when they're a bit dozy. It's a year-round job. People eat turkey all year, not just at Christmas and Easter. But this is our busiest time, of course. I'll catch around 100,000 turkeys next week. Are you in the film industry yourselves? What stars have you worked with? Have you seen *The Full Monty?*

Sloman started to tell Harris of the time he worked with Brad Pitt and of the travails of the British film industry. He might have told Harris about the British Film Institute, too, and its erstwhile satanic host, Wilf Stevenson, but the Land Rover arrived and the Mercedes was plucked from the field as easily as one could snap a wishbone.

Turner and Sloman drove away, laughing at the almost surreal absurdity of their little adventure. On their way to meet an Oscar-winning plumber, they had got stuck in the mud and were rescued by a turkey-catcher whose boiler had been installed by that selfsame plumber. There is still an England, they thought, out there in the furthest reaches of the country, still strange, still surprising and full of utterly splendid people.

'Be not afear'd,' whispered Turner, as he turned into Norman's driveway, 'the isle is full of sound effects.'

Norman Wanstall came to the door dressed in tight jeans which were torn at the knee; he is wiry, with thinning and unruly hair. He must be over 60 but he has bags of energy. We quickly get the impression that he welcomes the chance to chat about his former life in the movies. Norman says:

> An audience always thinks that what they hear on the soundtrack was what was there when the scene was shot. Putting stuff on afterwards, and all the post-synch, well, that doesn't come into their minds and it's just as well it doesn't. The best work I've ever done was for Yorkshire TV, when we put together a dialogue track from stuff that was unusable. I'm very proud of some of my dialogue work. I think, probably, I'm as good as anyone in the world at dialogue, but I think at sound effects there's a lot of guys who are as good as me and probably better. I've seen some films, like *Top Gun*, when the dialogue track and sound effects just blew my mind, to be honest.

When he was 14 Norman visited a movie set and fell in love with the industry. By an odd coincidence, the film being shot was one of **Cubby Broccoli**'s Warwick epics, *Hell Below Zero*.

> I was at a co-ed grammar school, and I had a sort of girlfriend whose mother, Lana Stevens, was secretary to the production controller at Pinewood. She invited us to spend a day at the studios and I went on the set and saw Alan Ladd in a replica of a ship. And wherever you walked you saw Dirk Bogarde or John Gregson, all these people. I never forgot it, and when I finished my national service I wrote to Lana Stevens to ask how people got jobs in the film industry. I went to see her, we chatted and she offered me a job in the cutting rooms, which I thought was the most God-awful place. I thought I was going to be on the set, with all these people, looking through a camera. I started with a cutter called John Guthridge on a Frankie Howerd picture called *Jumping for Joy*. It took me weeks to figure out what was going on but the atmosphere in the cutting room was so good I just hung in there.

Norman was given a three-year contract and, among other things, worked on the *Titanic* movie *A Night to Remember*, on which he was assistant to Harry Miller, who later became Norman's assistant on the Bond films. Then, as Norman's contract was about to expire, he was invited to be assistant to the legendary Winston Ryder:

> Win Ryder was probably the greatest sound editor who ever lived. I did three films with him. *John Paul Jones*, then *Solomon and Sheba* and then *Sink the Bismark!* Win was extraordinary because he never taught you anything. He never said, 'Look, this is the way how things are done.' He might ask your opinion but he'd never teach you anything. But after three pictures with him I learnt the most basic thing about sound editing. That was, you

never create a sound in its entirety. The whole thing was made up of components. I learned from Win that providing you have the ingredients you can create anything. He was a magician.

There was a scene in *Solomon and Sheba* when the soldiers turn their shields to the sun and blind the opposing army, which plunges down a ravine. I'd watched Win for weeks winding all these sounds in, a bit of this, a bit of that, then King Vidor goes and puts music all over it. That's the sound editor's nightmare. I was in tears for Win, who told Vidor that he'd fucked it up. Then Vidor said, 'Yeah, that's what I've come all this way for.'

Norman's last picture for Win Ryder, *Sink the Bismark!*, was edited by Peter Hunt, at that time the most up-and-coming editor in Britain. Norman remembers:

I had made it known that I wanted to become an editor and get out of this sound game. Anyway, I became Peter Hunt's first assistant and worked on *There Was a Crooked Man*, which was the only film where Norman Wisdom played a real part. After that, we did *The Greengage Summer*, then *HMS Defiant*, with Dirk Bogarde and Alec Guinness. The picture was produced by Lord Brabourne, who had to raise some extra finance and needed to have a screening. They'd shot this huge battle, partly real galleons, partly models, with cannons and all the gear. But we hadn't done the sound and we couldn't just show a cutting copy with all that spacing and silence.

So Peter Hunt said, 'You worked with Win Ryder, just do something with it.' I instinctively knew the ingredients I needed and laid in all these cannons, crowds, muskets and swords, and we quickly did a dub. Then they came back and said I'd done them a huge favour.

It was then that Peter Hunt said we'd be working on *Dr No*, which had a very tight budget. But because it was such a busy film, we divided it up. Peter cut the picture, we got a dubbing editor for the dialogue and I did all the sound effects. For a novice like me, it was terrifying, and of course I had to work with Gordon McCallum, the chief mixer at Pinewood, who was a very difficult man to work with.

'Not if it was your first picture,' said Sloman. 'Mac would have been good to you.'

'Oh, is that why it was?' said Norman. 'That's good psychology because we became very close. Mac really loved *Dr No*. He rubbed his hands and said, "This is really making movies."'

Norman set to his task, starting with the credit titles and the sound of the gun echoing down the **gun barrel**. Then he tackled the sound of the silenced **Walther PPK**, which he created by firing airguns. The electronic door, the radar devices and all the gadgets had to be invented from scratch.

Until he started work on *Dr No*, Norman had never heard of James Bond or **Ian Fleming**. But after *From Russia With Love* he was in the Bond business, a key member of the technical team which went from one picture to the next. And running the show were **Saltzman** and Broccoli. 'Saltzman', said Norman, 'was the only man I ever addressed as Mister. Cubby was Cubby but Saltzman was always Mr Saltzman. He was an ominous-looking character and I never got too close to him, even though I did *Ipcress File* for him.'

Goldfinger was a massive job for Norman. Athough the budget was bigger, the technology was primitive by today's standards; there were no computers to reproduce the sound of a laser beam, the screeching tyres of an Aston Martin **DB5** or the sound of a spinning bowler hat:

Well, where do we start? For the laser beam when Bond is lying on table we recorded a whipcrack for when the laser is switched on. We also laid in this other metallic sound, but then they put music over it and ruined it.

The spinning hat is my pride and joy. I'm very proud of it because it was made up of the most unbelievable ingredients. I looked at the hat and knew I had to have certain elements to create the sound it made. My assistant was Peter Pennell, who did *Blade Runner*, and I sent him out to a toy shop. One of the toys we bought was a propeller which kids would spin and which would twist up a piece of metal and make this strange whirring sound. The other toy was a cardboard disc with a string through it which kids would spin. And because the hat was metallic and really vicious, we needed something for when it leaves **Oddjob**'s hand. That had to be really frightening. So we got an ordinary carpenter's wood saw, put it on a bench and just twanged it. Those two toys and the saw gave us what we wanted; we played around with the sounds, and it worked a treat.

The sound when the hat hits the statue at the golf course was a doddle, but the scene when it gets stuck in the bars of **Fort Knox** was interesting. I had never seen a set like it and I heard that the only reason why **Ken Adam** didn't get an Oscar for it was because he insisted on being called production designer, not art director. We went on to that set every day, and once we dropped something on to the metal rungs of the floor and it gave off this tremendous metallic, echoing sound. So that gave us the sound of the hat getting stuck in the bars, and when we combined that with the sound of the hat flying through the air we had the full monty.

The crushing of the golf ball was a very hard sound to create. That would have had at least four tracks on it. Then there was the Aston Martin. Because it was such a high-performance car we had an expert from the factory with us. We got the car on a test track, huddled in the back with our tape recorders, and off we went. The way this guy changed gear was amazing, so we had all these exciting sounds of gear changes. Then we had all those sounds of the revolving number plates, the bullet-proof shield and the oil slick.

The crushing of the car was shot in the States. It was shot with sound but the tracks I had were very limited. I had the basic ingredients, but if you remember there were these huge jaws which kept coming up and over the car, crushing and gripping, but the sounds I had didn't match those shots. I was working away one lunchtime and heard the sound of these workmen working on a set on the lot at Pinewood. It was a compressor which was making great hissing and whooshing sounds. I thought, that's exactly what I need. I rushed over to our sound mixer, Dudley Messenger, but the only thing he had available was a little recorder, probably battery run, which he'd bought for his kid. So we took this out and put a mike on it and we knocked it off. The workmen didn't know what the hell we were up to. Then I added lots of glass breaking, which we did by just smashing lots of bottles. And for the car itself being buckled and bent, we just crushed lots of beer cans and stuff.

There was one final sound we wondered about. **Goldfinger** being sucked out of the aircraft:

We hadn't a clue what to do with that. No one knew what it would sound like, so we just did it verbally. We all made sucking sounds, puckered our lips and so on. The great advantage of having a hi-tech theatre was that you had the mikes to do it.

That was the fun of working on the Bond films. Everything had to be invented and I'd go in to Mac with these sounds and he'd mix them all together. Today we have something we called rock and roll, where you can go back and forward, but then we had to create each one separately until we got a version we liked. Only when we finished it did we show it to Saltzman and Broccoli, and hoped they liked it.

In January 1965 Norman learnt that his work had been nominated for an Academy Award. He stood a fifty-fifty chance of winning since only one other film – *The Lively Set* – had been nominated in the category of sound effects.

'Cubby Broccoli paid for me to go to the ceremony,' said Norman. 'I told him I wanted to take my wife and he said OK as long as I paid for her. I said, well, she's earnt it, and when we came back with the Oscar, Cubby paid for her, which was nice of him.'

Norman has a video copy of the entire ceremony, which he puts on for us. It is in black and white, a little fuzzy, but absolutely riveting. The show is brought to us courtesy of Head & Shoulders shampoo, Timex and Honda – 'The greatest thing on wheels'.

Bob Hope wanders on to the stage and welcomes the audience to 'Santa Monica on Thames', in view of the dominance of British nominees. 'Hollywood's handing out the foreign aid,' says Hope, and the audience's laughter sticks in its throat.

There are shots of Rex Harrison, Julie Andrews, Richard Burton and Elizabeth Taylor, and behind Julie Andrews sits a glowering Jack Warner. Then Steve McQueen and Claudia Cardinale walk on stage to present the first award. Then Angie Dickinson announces Norman's name and he skips on to the podium.

'I'm a technician,' he says, 'so perhaps I'll leave the eloquence to the actors who'll follow.' He is, nonetheless, eloquent himself, clutching the Oscar which now stands beside the TV. Seeing the show gives him an obvious thrill and he still gets an annual Christmas card from Bob Hope.

After the Oscars Norman was offered *Alfie*, which he was unable to do. He worked on Truffaut's *Fahrenheit 451* and *The Ipcress File*, as well as all the Bond films. Norman, though, wanted to become an editor and, hopefully, a director. He fell in with Mike Sarne, an actor and pop singer who wanted to become a film director. And he did become a film director, of some of the worst movies ever made. But Norman liked Sarne and he won some good

reviews for salvaging the material. 'I so admired Mike's enthusiasm,' he said.

By the early 1970s Norman was becoming disenchanted with the
movies. Although he was being offered some plum films – Norman
Jewison flew to London just to offer him *Fiddler on the Roof* – he
found the industry changing for the worse.

'Being a film technician,' he said, 'is like being in the army. There's
always someone above you, telling you what to do, which is why
people hate working for Kubrick. I worked for Kubrick, on *Barry
Lyndon*, but I didn't get a credit. Ugh . . . yeah . . . but give Kubrick his
due, one man leads the team. That's the only way to make a movie.'

It was shortly after that experience that Norman quit the movie
industry. An amazing thing to have done, just quit like that, I said.
Norman replied:

Really? I don't think it's amazing at all. I think twenty years is
a long time in that game. I'm not underestimating the drastic
nature of it, because I didn't really know what I was going to
do. We came to live out here without any plans. Win Ryder
had retired to Shropshire, so I clocked that, and then my best
friend said, 'Why are you looking in the West Country? Go
to Shropshire or Herefordshire. That's real country.' So we
came here.

The only thing I knew that existed in those days were these
courses called TOPS – Training Opportunities – and I'd heard
about them but I didn't know which one I'd pick. I had a share
in a sound effects company, so I sold my share and had a few
bob to keep me going. And when the course came up I really
enjoyed it.

I thought if I stayed in the industry my epitaph would be 'He
loved the job but hated the industry'. I really loved the job and
couldn't believe I was being paid to do it. But the industry I
absolutely hated. I hated the freelancers always searching for

work, all the back-stabbing, the lack of loyalty. Even your best mate, if there was a job going, forget it. . . . Anyway, I looked back on those twenty years and asked myself if I wanted to spend the next twenty like that. I really did ask myself that question and the answer came up no.

Norman did, though, work on one last movie, which was *Never Say Never Again*. He was called back for that because it was felt that **Sean Connery** would like to have someone from the old days on the team. Norman got the buzz again and he needed the money. But he went back to being a plumber and hasn't touched a piece of film since.

As we left Norman I asked him if he'd heard of Brian G. Hutton. He hadn't.

'The director,' I said. 'He made *Kelly's Heroes* and *Where Eagles Dare*, and then he retired to become a plumber.'

'You're joking!' said Norman.

'No, seriously,' I said. 'Hutton works in America, installing swimming pools. You and he are the only film people who have become plumbers.'

'But Hutton doesn't have an Oscar,' said Sloman.

stand-ins

See **his *Meister*'s voice**; **Wilson, Michael G.**

Sweet Movie

Sweet Movie was a French-Canadian production directed by Dusan Makavejev in 1974, and starred Carole Laure, Pierre Clementi, Anna Prucnal and Sami Frey. At its premiere at the Cannes Film Festival the film's sexual frankness caused quite a stir, especially Makavejev's homage to *Goldfinger*.

In Cannes at least, the one scene that really seemed to shock the audience was that of Prucnal, in the near nude, attempting to seduce a group of prepubescent children, a disturbing but valid metaphor. Even former Makavejev supporters were confused and disappointed by the film. The French, as usual in such cases, came up with vague rhetorical reviews but since the picture was being talked about it was decided to release it immediately. When it opened in Paris filmgoers were treated to a process rarely seen on the screen since the early days of *Fatima's Belly Dance*: black stripes, vertical or horizontal according to the case, covered the offending parts so that a visual pun on *Goldfinger* was totally lost along with many a plot point.

(Edgardo Cozarinsky and Carlos Clarens, *Film Comment*,
May–June 1975)

The virgin, played with winsome innocence and then phlegmatism and eventual awakening by Carole Laure, finds her rich husband has a golden phallus. Then she is hustled off by the family muscleman to Paris from Canada in a suitcase. There she ends up in the Eiffel Tower where she falls for a romantico singing Mexican and losing her virginity. The ex-virgin is adopted by a sort of commune that indulges in horrific table orgies of vomiting, urinating etc and then deficating [sic] in plates which they whirl about. Pic is thus not the clearest [sic] but does have a brio and shock scenes sans being scabrous due to a sly but never exploitative presence recording all these weirdo shenanigans.

(*Variety* review of *Sweet Movie*, 22 May 1974)

The director, Makavajev, observed all this with a laconic eye and planned more on-screen erections which he saw as the world's secret weapon against Communism, something which 007 might have agreed with.

'*Sweet Movie* gets away with the first cock on a French screen, perhaps because it's a gallant quote from *Goldfinger* – the "goldcock". (Dusan Makavejev, *Film Comment*, May – June 1975)

See **history of the cinema; Houston, Penelope; Johnson, Paul; *Time Out*; Walker, Alexander; ugh!; *Variety*; whoops!**.

T

theme tune

See **title number**.

Tilly

See **Masterson, Tilly**.

Time Out

In the week *Goldfinger* opened, London's West End cinemas offered a choice of art movies, Hollywood blockbusters and dramas, a range of movies far wider than anything today. Satyajit Ray's *Devi* was at the Academy, Peter Brook's *Lord of the Flies* was at the Cameo-Poly and Ingmar Bergman's *The Silence* was at the Berkeley; *The Fall of the Roman Empire*, *Cleopatra*, *Becket* and *Lawrence of Arabia* had settled into long runs in 70mm at the Astoria, Dominion, Plaza and the Metropole, while *How the West was Won* and *It's A Mad, Mad, Mad, Mad World* could be seen in Cinerama at the Casino and Coliseum. And in Leicester Square itself, *Goldfinger* replaced Hitchcock's *Marnie*, starring **Sean Connery**, at the Odeon, facing John Ford's western *Cheyenne Autumn* at the Warner, John Huston's *The Night of the Iguana* at the Empire and Franklin J. Schaffner's (pardon me, Gore Vidal's) *The Best Man* at the Leicester Square Theatre.

Evelyn Waugh topped the bestseller lists with *A Little Leaving*, followed by H. Montgomery Hyde's *Norman Birkett*, C. V.

Wedgewood's *The Trial of Charles I*, Elizabeth Longford's *Victoria RI*, Len Deighton's *Funeral in Berlin* and Christopher Isherwood's *A Single Man*.

The weekly newspaper *The New Musical Express* published its Top Ten: 'I'm Into Something Good' (Herman's Hermits), 'You Really Got Me' (The Kinks), 'Rag Doll' (The Four Seasons), 'Have I The Right' (The Honeycombs), 'I wouldn't Trade You For The World' (The Bachelors), 'Where Did Our Love Go' (The Supremes), 'I Won't Forget You' (Jim Reeves), 'The Crying Game' (Dave Berry), 'As Tears Go By' (Marianne Faithfull) and 'Oh, Pretty Woman' (Roy Orbison). The Beatles, who were on tour in America, had slipped to number 18 with 'A Hard Day's Night'.

In the theatre, in the era before Andrew Lloyd Webber and Cameron Macintosh, Londoners had a choice of four big musicals – *Camelot* at Drury Lane, with Laurence Harvey as King Arthur; *The Sound of Music* at the Palace; and two Lionel Bart productions, *Oliver!* at the New and *Maggie May* at the Adelphi. American imports included *12 Angry Men* at the Lyric and, at the Globe, *Who's Afraid of Virginia Woolf?*, starring Constance Cummings and Ray McAnally. Franco Zeffirelli's production of *Hamlet*, in Italian, was playing at the Old Vic; Joe Orton's black comedy *Entertaining Mr Sloane* was settled in for a long run at Wyndham's and *Beyond the Fringe* ground on at the Mayfair. The Royal Shakespeare Company offered Pinter's *The Birthday Party*, Peter Brook's controversial *Marat-Sade*, with Glenda Jackson, and Beckett's *End-game*. More suburban tastes were catered for by the comedy *Boeing-Boeing*, with Leslie Phillips, at the Apollo and by Agatha Christie's *The Mousetrap*, then in what was described as its 'Twelfth Shattering Year' at the Ambassadors. The policeman did it.

See **history of the cinema**; **Houston, Penelope**; **Johnson, Paul**; *Sweet Movie*; **Walker, Alexander**; **ugh!**; *Variety*; **whoops!**.

title number

Anthony Newley was the first person to make a recording of the title song to *Goldfinger*. He didn't belt it out, though, he just trotted it out as if it was background music for a teashop in Frinton, and it remained unheard until 1992, when it appeared on the album *The Best of James Bond*, as well as the laser edition of the picture.

'I'd got a recording of Mack the Knife,' said **Guy Hamilton**, 'that seemed to be gritty and **Goldfinger**-ish. I played it for John Barry and I think it keyed him in.'

John Barry himself, who had scored the first two films and had also rewritten the James Bond theme when Monty Norman's original proved unworkable, took Hamilton's idea to the lyricists Anthony Newley and Leslie Bricusse. All they had to do was to write a song called 'Goldfinger', with its three syllables and its meaning obscure until one saw the picture. Barry said:

> *Goldfinger* was the weirdest song ever. We couldn't have written that song as a song. I remember I went to Tony Newley and he said, 'What the hell do I do with it?' I said, 'It's Mack the Knife.' It just worked. Shirley Bassey didn't know what the song was about but she sang it with such extraordinary conviction that she convinced the rest of the world that it meant something.

For the orchestral score, John Barry had precious little time to compose the music and make it fit. Film composers invariably have to deal with impossible deadlines – while their music is often a core element of any picture, they seem to be treated in a cavalier fashion, coming last in the pecking order. Nevertheless, under extreme pressure to meet the deadline, Barry created a marvellously inventive score, including a musical motif for glittering gold, a jazzy, big-band version of the title song and a dramatic countdown for the raid on **Fort Knox**. He said:

I would take a day without even writing a note. I'd just have manuscript paper, look at the film and say, yeah, it's got to hit there. I'd map out a structural line before I got down to writing the music. Then I'd sit and compose, using that graph with the highs and lows. It was a lot of work and then they'd drive you nuts. I'd write a two-and-a-half minute action sequence, say, with great precision, down to a third of a second, and somebody from the cutting room would call and say they'd just taken eight frames out. I'd go nuts because the whole structure had to be changed. The whole Fort Knox sequence was a nightmare. I didn't receive that sequence until the Friday night and we had to record the music on the Monday. You just bled. But that's the nature of the beast.

See **Midas touch**.

U

ugh!

The week that *Goldfinger* opened, many of London's film critics were attending the Venice Film Festival, where Joseph Losey's *King and Country* and Pier Paolo Pasolini's Marxist view of Christ, *The Gospel According to St Matthew*, were the major talking points. But back in London one critic soldiered on – Nina Hibbin of the *Daily Worker*, the only newspaper, it was claimed, that was owned by its readers. The mouthpiece of the Communist Party, and bankrolled by the Kremlin, the *Daily Worker* could not be expected to approve of James Bond's latest exploits, and Miss Hibbin seemed to be kitted out with Rosa Kleb's shoes as well as typewriter. However, Miss Hibbin did not attack for the film for having a hero who was the puppet of the capitalist-industrial complex or an agent of imperialism; she just thought the film was morally repugnant:

> The sickest and slickest James Bond film of them all – that's 'Goldfinger,' opening at the Odeon, Leicester Square tomorrow.
>
> The cult of James Bondism is a vicious one, a symptomatic sickness of the age, and the latest in the film series is well in the mould of its predecessors, 'Dr No' and 'From Russia With Love.'
>
> Bondists are expected to shriek with laughter even before the first victim is kicked in the guts or battered against a wall.

They must gurgle with relish whenever their nonchalant hero, created by the late **Ian Fleming**, rolls a girl he's hardly met and certainly hates into the nearest bed.

Above all, they must be ready (as soon as they are given the magical wisecrack signal) to roll in the aisles as a man is electrocuted and disintegrates in a flame-coloured flash.

'But it's not for real,' they'll tell you merrily. 'It's only meant for a giggle.'

And it's true that the sleek and glossy, streamlined packaging and the knife-edged electronic nightmares are not for real. The much vaunted James Bond girls – **gold paint** and all – are not real.

The maniac plot to drop an H-bomb on the American gold reserves and so by irradiation to deflate all the gold in the West, is definitely not for real.

But all this is a vast, gigantic confidence trick to blind the audience to what is going on underneath.

The constantly lurking viciousness, and the glamorisation of violence – they are real enough. So too are the carefully timed peaks of titillation and the skilfully contrived sensationalism – they're real, too.

The racialism (inscrutably smiling villains of Oriental countenance), the cold-war implications of the plot – they are not in the film for a joke.

All this is the underlying menace of the film which gives the laughter a dangerous and sinister ring.

Those who have been conned can laugh away, if they want to, while a car goes hurtling over a cliff and bursts into flames. The idea of four people being burnt to cinders is, oh, such glorious fun – especially if you are not given time to ponder on their charred faces and distorted limbs.

After the Press show, a well dressed damsel with a posh accent – a fanatical Bondist – was chattering excitedly in the foyer. 'I'd simply love to see the whole thing again!' she twittered.

As for me – ugh! I was glad to get out on to the freshly-rain-washed pavements of Leicester Square.

(Nina Hibbin, *The Daily Worker*, 16 September 1964)

Incidentally, Nina Hibbin's daughter, Sally, wrote the **Eon**-sponsored *New Official James Bond Movie Book* (Hamlyn, 1989) before becoming Ken Loach's regular producer.

See **history of the cinema**; **Houston, Penelope**; **Johnson, Paul**; *Sweet Movie*; *Time Out*; **Walker, Alexander**; *Variety*; **whoops!**.

United Artists

When United Artists (UA) decided to finance the first Bond film, *Dr No*, the company made one of the most important decisions in its long and strange history. It was David Picker who made the deal. Sent to run the London office with Bud Ornstein, Picker – and which studio executive ever had a better name – found himself at the forefront of the revival of British cinema in the 1960s. He not only gave the green light to *Dr No*, he also financed *Tom Jones*, which won four Oscars, and *The Knack*, which won the *Palme d'Or* at Cannes in 1965. Picker also backed the first Beatles movie, *A Hard Day's Night*, and Saltzman's *The Ipcress File*. Everything Picker picked seemed to reap critical praise and box-office gold. In France, UA was backing François Truffaut and Alain Resnais, in Sweden Ingmar Bergman and in Italy Federico Fellini. For five years UA was unquestionably the most daring and culturally important studio in Hollywood.

Except that UA was never a proper studio, for, unlike MGM or Paramount, it had no sprawling sound stages or backlot. The company was founded in January 1919 by Charlie Chaplin, D. W. Griffith, Mary Pickford and Douglas Fairbanks, an alliance of the four most powerful creative artists in Hollywood, who decided they could have more control over their pictures and make more money from them if they distributed them independently. The alliance, which was never expected to last, led Richard A. Rowland, an otherwise forgotten president of Metro Pictures, to remark that 'The lunatics have taken over the asylum'.

By the time pictures started to talk, in 1926, UA had gone through a period of immense profitability to near insolvency. Griffith's career was virtually over; Fairbanks and Pickford were divorcing and never survived the arrival of sound; and Chaplin made more scandalous headlines than he made films. The original alliance had ended, although one company president, Joseph Schenck, brought in fresh talent, such as Gloria Swanson, Ronald Colman and producer Sam Goldwyn. By the 1930s the company founded by the 'lunatics' had been taken over completely by the executives. Goldwyn, Howard Hughes, David O. Selznick and Alexander Korda would all steer what had become an amorphous company through the 1930s and 1940s. For Hughes, UA had become the film-industry equivalent to publishing's vanity press, an outlet for his personal fetishes, notably Jane Russell's chest in *The Outlaw*, which also happened to be the first feature that **Cubby Broccoli** worked on.

By 1950 UA was deeply in the red, haemorrhaging about $100,000 a week. The company was saved by two far-sighted executives – Arthur Krim of Eagle Lion and Robert Benjamin of Rank – who borrowed $3 million from a Chicago financier and $500,000 from Spyros P. Skouras of 20th Century-Fox, who was once called by Billy Wilder 'the only Greek Tragedy I know'. *The African Queen* and *High Noon* put the company into the black, enabling them to buy out Chaplin's and Pickford's remaining stock.

Krim, in particular, gave the company a fresh impetus. While the other major studios were floundering, unable to maintain the battle against television, Krim guided the studio towards the independent sector and the new wave of American directors emerging from live TV: Stanley Kubrick, John Frankenheimer and Sidney Lumet were all distributed through UA, as were Billy Wilder and Otto Preminger. In 1955, 1956, 1960 and 1961 UA won the Best Picture Oscar for *Marty*, *Around the World in 80 Days*, *The Apartment* and *West Side Story*. Lacking its own studio, which had seemed a severe handicap in the 1930s and 1940s, now seemed the key to the company's success. As the market for motion pictures contracted, the other studios were desperate to unload their vast tracts of real estate and their vast wardrobe and prop departments. Staff were laid off, studio orchestras were disbanded and props were auctioned. All UA had was Arthur Krim and a few other suits sitting at their desks saying, Yes, go and make that for us and you won't need to pay us the vast overhead you pay at Fox or Metro. People looked at UA and saw the end of the old studio system, and they saw that it worked.

By 1957 UA had become a public company and ten years later was making $20 million a year. UA had become an attractive investment and in 1968 the company was bought by TransAmerica, a San Francisco-based insurance group. Krim continued running the company until 1969, when David Picker was made president, despite the fact that he had just financed Tony Richardson's satirical epic *The Charge of the Light Brigade*, a costly blunder and a masterpiece which few appreciated at the time. But Richardson's film, more than any other, signalled the end of the boom in British production. After that, UA withdrew from Europe and returned to Hollywood, which had revitalised itself with hits like *Easy Rider, The Graduate* and *Bonnie and Clyde*.

UA maintained its custody of the Bond pictures, helping to buy out **Harry Saltzman**'s share of the franchise. In fact, it was Bond alone which kept the company afloat through the late 1970s when Krim and his cohorts left to form Orion Pictures, taking with them such luminaries as Woody Allen. The new team at UA, hired by TransAmerica, then became embroiled in *Heaven's Gate*, the costs and losses of which brought about the sale of the studio to MGM.

See **dealers**.

V

Variety

The American trade paper *Variety* gave an effusive review to *Goldfinger* which would have delighted the American cinema owners who regarded the paper as their bible. If *Variety* nixed a picture the all-powerful theatre chains got distinctly nervy:

> Another boxoffice bonanza for third James Bond film from the **Broccoli–Saltzman** stable; splendidly witty and zestful slice of fantastic hokum, with **Sean Connery** relishing every dame and fight.
>
> There's not the least sign of staleness in the Bond 007 formula, and this third sample looks like matching the mammoth grosses of *From Russia With Love* and maybe exceeding them. In addition to its ample quota of action and girl-fancying, this film has extra piquancy from a script that's not afraid to laugh at its own conventions and from a production that uses a number of mechanical and electrical gimmicks to spice the mayhem. And the whole thing is given an affluent gloss that makes it ideal for escapists.
>
> Some liberties have been taken with **Ian Fleming**'s original novel by scripters **Richard Maibaum** and **Paul Dehn**, but without diluting its flavor. The mood is set before the credits show up, with Connery making an arrogant pass at a chick and spying a thug creeping up from behind; he's reflected in the

femme's eyeballs. So he heaves the heavy into a bathful of water
and connects it deftly to a handy supply of electricity.

Thereafter the plot gets its teeth into the real business, which
is the duel between Bond and **Goldfinger**. The latter plans to
plant an atomic bomb in **Fort Knox** and thus contaminate the
US hoard of the yellow stuff so that it can't be touched, and
thus increase tenfold the value of his own gold, earned by
hard international smuggling. The first half-hour is gloriously
sly 24-carat pleasure. Bond meets up with Goldfinger in Miami,
where he's playing crooked poker [*sic*]. He's planted a blonde
with a telescope [*sic*] in his hotel bedroom, and she can spy
the other guy's fistful of cards in the patio below. And she
tells Goldfinger what he's holding by transistor radio, which
he listens to through a hearing aid.

But the blonde tries to run out on Goldfinger, so he snuffs
her out. And this launches Bond on a chase, with plenty of
fanciful trimmings. He's given an Aston-Martin [**DB5**] that is
equipped with radar, machine-guns, an ejector seat that hurtles
unwanted passengers through the roof, and a smokescreen
device. With this, he traces Goldfinger to a Swiss hideout,
where he's captured after a car chase that wouldn't have been
despised by the Keystone Kops. Hi-jacked back to the States
where Goldfinger runs a stud farm, Bond meets up with **Pussy
Galore**, with cleavage to match the monicker. And the entire
preposterous affair comes to a dizzy climax with Bond foiling
the Fort Knox coup, leaving himself three seconds [*sic*] before
the bomb is timed to go off.

Sean Connery repeats his suave portrayal of the punch-
packing Bond, who can find his way around the wine-list as
easily as he can negotiate a dame. But, if backroom boys got
star billing, it's deserved by **Ken Adam**, who has designed
the production with a wealth of enticing invention. There's
a ray-gun that cuts through any metal, and threatens to carve

Bond down the middle. There's Goldfinger's automobile –
cast in solid gold. And his farm is stocked with furniture that
moves at the press of a button. Perhaps the most memorable
visual incident is the crushing of a limousine, with a body
inside, at a scrap yard. It's then put in the boot of another
car [*sic*] and driven back to Goldfinger; he wants to rescue
the gold it's made of [*sic*].

Honor Blackman, with a large local rep for her tele success
in *The Avengers* skein, makes a fine, sexy partner for Bond. As
Pussy, Goldfinger's pilot for his private plane, she does not
take things lying down – she's a judo expert who throws
Bond until the final k.o. when she's tumbled herself. Gert
Frobe [**Fröbe**], too, is near-perfect casting as the resourceful
Goldfinger, an amoral tycoon who treats gold-cornering as a
business like any other. And Harold Sakata scores as **Odd-job**,
his chief henchman, who kills by throwing his bowlerhat at
the jugular vein like a discus; it has a razor concealed in the
brim [*sic*]. **Shirley Eaton** looks appropriately edible as the girl
who gets bumped off. A neat cameo as Bond's Secret Service
boss, M, is supplied by **Bernard Lee**. Cec Linder, **Tania
Mallet** and Nadja Regin are also okay in minor roles.

Guy Hamilton's direction is first-class, especially in the
earlier scenes, but he tends to loiter a little in the middle
stretches. The script, by Maibaum and Dehn, is a professional
blend of excitement and offhand humor. After the battle of
Fort Knox and [after] Bond has been saved in the nick
of time, his payoff is 'And what kept you, then?' [*sic*].
It's this tongue-in-cheek attitude that gives the script an
extra kick.

Ted Moore's lensing does full justice to Adam's astute sets,
which are great for Technicolor. The musical soundtrack is
slickly furnished by John Barry, who also composed the **title
song** (to lyrics by Anthony Newley and Leslie Bricusse) which

is sung over the closing and opening credits by Shirley Bassey, with the expected intensity.

(*Otta*)

See **history of the cinema**; **Houston, Penelope**; **Johnson, Paul**; *Sweet Movie*; *Time Out*; **Walker, Alexander**; **ugh!**; **whoops!**.

villains

See **Goldfinger**; **Oddjob**.

W

Walker, Alexander

This review of *Goldfinger* by Alexander Walker is revealing of the way movies were reviewed in 1964. It is highly unlikely that Walker would ever write a review like this today, witty and stylish as it is and written for the influential *Evening Standard*. Walker is one of the very few major British newspaper critics to have also made his mark as a serious film historian; his 1974 book, *Hollywood, England*, remains one of the finest studies of the British cinema ever published and contains the first serious attempt to analyse the Bond phenomenon. But this review, with its minor errors of fact, is strange for its avoidance of any comparison with the two previous Bond films, and for its avoidance of any analysis of the film's political and cultural significance. Although Walker is uncritical of the film's blatant sexism and undercurrent of racism, he does at least pinpoint the way that future Bond films are to develop – their dependence on gadgetry and their reduction of Bond himself to a servant of technology, a trend which **Sean Connery** soon reacted against:

> Even before the credit titles get on the screen, Agent 007 has stripped off a frogman's suit to reveal a crisp white tuxedo, planted his toecap in an assassin's teeth and apologised to a lady he embraced straight from her hot bath while wearing a cold automatic in his sky-blue shoulder holster.

Bond is back and Goldfinger is his most thrilling sortie yet.

But let me now state that the inevitable has happened. Sean Connery, alias **Ian Fleming**'s deathproof hero, has at last met his match.

For the first time the man with a licence to kill has an equally deadly rival for our pop-eyed imagination.

No, it is NOT the wickedly enjoyable performance of the German star Gert Frobe [**Fröbe**] as **Auric Goldfinger**, the **Midas**-motivated master criminal who is so besotted by the stuff that he uses a gold putter at golf and wears a crew-cut head of hair of a colour I can only call caraty.

And it is NOT our own ravishing **Shirley Eaton**, even though her black-undie-clad figure is a premium draw for Bond till Goldfinger vengefully does a spray job in gold paint on her voluptuous bodywork.

And it is NOT a cool newcomer called **Tania Mallet** who gets in Bond's way when he is tracking Goldfinger through Switzerland. Even more fatally, she gets in the way of a razor-edged bowler hat.

The gent who flings the bowler like a boomerang is **Oddjob**, played by Harold Sakata with the leaden menace of a Korean Tweedledum.

But even though the gold bricks that Bond lobs at him during Goldfinger's raid on **Fort Knox** bounce off his chest like mothballs, Oddjob does NOT steal the scenes from 007.

Honor Blackman comes closest to doing that. I don't know whether this tawny beauty was told to play Goldfinger's mistress, **Pussy Galore**, as a female James Bond but that's what she does. And fine and feline she looks.

I purred with pleasure watching her chuck Bond playfully under the chin with her pistol and drawl, 'You like close shaves don't you?' Or throw him in the hay for what must be the only love scene played by judo holds. Needless to say, Bond knows his defences.

And so does Sean Connery against anything in Goldfinger that is flesh and blood. What he has a harder job doing is holding his own against all the film's mechanical gimmicks and automated gadgets. They really are eye-stealing.

They range from a transmitter in the heel of Bond's shoe that pinpoints his whereabouts with a radar bleep, to an Aston Martin [**DB5**] that lays down a smokescreen, fires hidden machine-guns and ejects unwanted passengers through the roof.

The jolly rumpus room in Goldfinger's racing stud converts itself at the touch of a button into a deadly gas chamber. And the FBI men tailing a car with a corpse in the back seat are baffled when car and body vanish – mechanically compressed into a cube the size of a tea chest.

There are karate fights, exciting car chases and all the usual hells for Bond to go through, including being handcuffed to a cobalt bomb. But sometimes he seems to be just standing there while the marvellous gadgets do the work.

Production designer **Ken Adam** deserves a hero's cheer for sets that make Goldfinger a magnificent tongue-in-cheek spectacular. It is a safe bet that the guards at the real Fort Knox who see Adam's glittering gold repository will cry with envy all the way to the vaults.

Director **Guy Hamilton** draws a bead on every scene and the script by **Richard Maibaum** and **Paul Dehn** crackles with literate wit and Hitchcock surprises like the dear old lady in Goldfinger's gate lodge who suddenly handles a Sten gun like a Stormtrooper.

Shirley Bassey rasps out the Goldfinger song as if she was biting the top off cartridges. And Robert Brownjohn's credit titles are dazzlingly projected on the anatomy of Shirley Eaton,

who seems not only to have been gold-painted for that purpose,
but wax-polished as well.'

(*Evening Standard*, 17 September 1964)

See **history of the cinema**; **Houston, Penelope**; **Johnson, Paul**;
Sweet Movie; *Time Out*; **ugh!**; *Variety*; **whoops!**.

Walther PPK

James Bond nearly died in *From Russia With Love* when his trusty
Beretta automatic jammed on him. In fact, this was not Bond's fault
at all since **Fleming** had issued him with sub-standard equipment.

In 1956 Fleming received a letter from a Lancashire firearms
enthusiast named Geoffrey Boothroyd. Boothroyd wrote to say how
much he liked the novels and that he only wished Bond would get
rid of the Beretta, which Boothroyd described as a 'lady's gun and
not really a nice lady at that'. Impressed by Boothroyd's knowledge,
Fleming made the change in his next novel, *Dr No*, in which a
'Major Boothroyd' is introduced as the armourer of the Secret
Service. Bond is issued with a Walther PPK, which was one of
the weapons the real Boothroyd had recommended. But even then
Fleming bungled things; Bond set off for Jamaica with the right gun
but the wrong holster. By the time Fleming wrote *Goldfinger* Bond
was properly equipped. The movies, though, turned the Walther
PPK into Bond's favoured weapon; not only that, they made a cult
out of it, they fetishised it, cleverly combining its outline into the
trademarked 007 logo.

The Walther Company was founded in Zella St Blasii in 1886.
The Carl Walther Waffenfabrik was an immediate success, supplying
pistols and rifles to the German army and to the police forces from
the beginning of the twentieth century. By this time the revolver
had reached a plateau of development and the next challenge was to
produce an automatic, a weapon which could fire more quickly and
efficiently. Most of this development took place in Europe, especially

by the Mauser and Luger companies. After some experiment, which produced some bizarre-looking pistols, it became apparent that cartridges of 7.65 mm or 9 mm calibre were best suited to the new mechanism. By 1910 the technology had been considerably refined and all the world's leading manufacturers were producing automatics.

Walther itself was a relatively late entry into the field, though when it did enter the market in the late 1920s its Model PP (*Polizei Pistole*) was an immediate success. This was quickly followed by the PPK – the *Polizei Pistole Kriminal* – which was slightly smaller than the PP and designed to be worn by plainclothes policemen, or fictional secret agents. During the war it saw service on all sides, and in its homeland its small size made it the handgun of choice for tank corps and fighter pilots.

The PPK has been in virtually continuous production ever since, with various refinements. But there is one curious anomaly: when Fleming gave Bond the Walther it seems that it was not in production – at least, not in the West.

In 1945 the area around the Walther factory was occupied by the US Army and the factory itself was virtually destroyed by rioting refugees and by the survivors of the concentration camp at nearby Buchenwald. When the war formally ended, the area was ceded to the Soviet Union and Walther's business – its guns and its calculating machines – were licensed to two companies in the communist east, Hämmerli and Manurhin, the latter company manufacturing the PPK. This remained the position until the late 1950s, when Walther resumed production in its new premises at Ulm. Thus, when Major Boothroyd issued 007 with a Walther PPK, Bond was being given a gun designed by capitalists but made by communists and other bootleggers. How could **M** possibly have stood for that?

See **gun barrel**.

Wanstall, Norman

See **soundman**.

Whicker, Alan

If James Bond was fictional, a fantasy, was there not on God's Earth, or at least the section of it called the United Kingdom, a man of flesh and blood who embodied the same dash, the same sex appeal, the same values, the same willingness to fly to the uttermost regions of the earth to do battle with dragons?

Indeed there was such a man and he now resides on Jersey, an island hideaway where one must be very rich, very conservative and very discreet. Let us enter a magical kingdom called *Whicker's World*. That's Whicker. Alan Whicker.

I have no idea if Alan Whicker has modelled himself on Bond and have no wish to spoil a fantasy by writing to ask him if it is even partially true. Why run the risk of Whicker replying to say, Thank you, but no, in fact I modelled myself on Cliff Michelmore or Fyfe Robertson or Walter Cronkite.

Whicker is Bond on his day off. He wears a disguise – thick-rimmed spectacles and a pencil-thin moustache. He wears suits and ties; his black hair is glossily immaculate, and one can smell the aftershave and it isn't Old Spice. He is elegant in a clubland sort of way and he has mastered the art of being able to walk and talk at the same time, something which few television presenters can do. He never seems at a loss as to what do with his hands and arms, and he is supremely relaxed in front of the camera. But most of all there is his accent – regionless, classless, yet inimitable. No one talks like Whicker. The Monty Python team once sent him up affectionately, all of them wearing Whicker-wear, wandering around a far-flung beach, intoning with deadly earnest into a microphone. And there is a fan club, naturally, where Whickers of the world unite.

Whicker came to prominence at the same time as Bond. And when 007 was dispatched to the Caribbean to do battle with Dr No, Whicker flew off to the same region to interview Papa Doc Duvalier, the Haitian tyrant. Whicker goes to all the world's hot spots, yet he is perhaps most at home hobnobbing with the rich and famous, the surgically enhanced, in their green-baized, be-pooled enclaves in Monaco or the Bahamas. In his long career Whicker has interviewed everyone, talking to them on seemingly equal terms about the price of everything and the value of nothing. But when we say that Whicker interviewed everyone, we must make an exception of **Ian Fleming**, who declined the invitation in what Whicker later described as the rudest letter he had ever received. Could it possibly be that Fleming dared not look his hero in the face?

whoops!

1 The latest edition of Halliwell's *Filmgoer's Companion* claims that **Guy Hamilton** died in 1986.

2 '[Dr No] was badly made and **Connery**, a solid clod-hopping lump, was grossly miscast' (David Shipman, *The Great Movie Stars*).

3 '**Ken Adam**'s Aston Martin convertible had everything a super-agent would desire' (Andrew Yule, *Sean Connery*).

4 'They put a gleamingly polished Thunderbird through the works' (**Penelope Houston**, *Sight and Sound*).

5 At the end of the **Fort Knox** sequence the bomb is disabled when the counter reaches the number 007. However, the script had the counter at 003 and was changed only when **Harry Saltzman** thought that 007 would be far more satisfactory. But no one thought to change Connery's next line: 'Three more ticks and Mr **Goldfinger** would have hit the jackpot.'

See **Houston, Penelope**.

Willis, Austin

Actor who played **Felix Leiter**.

Wilson, Michael G.

Michael G. Wilson is the producer, with Barbara Broccoli, of the current Bond movies. Back in 1964 he was a law student who was on vacation in Kentucky, where he was hired as a teaboy who also doubled for Harold Sakata when **Oddjob** takes **Mr Solo** for his pressing engagement. 'I think that was Michael's first adventure in the movie trade,' said **Hamilton**.

Y

Yokohama

> Bond eased the door open. She was sitting on the far side of the room, her pink tweed suit open over a matching silk shirt, her legs curled under her. Never before had Bond met a girl who wore clothes all the time, and he had become aware, since the night when he had first seen her across the hotel dining room in Yokohama, that there was some mystery about those perfect clothes, perfectly made. Earlier, he had heard the quiet humming of a precision-made machine, but now the room was quite still. Her gaze shifted from him to the table in front of her. On it stood a Singer electric sewing machine, Model No. 327.

> (advertisement in *Goldfinger* World **Premiere** brochure)

See **product placement**.

Z

Zeitgeist

All of the above.

Bibliography

Amis, Kingsley, *The James Bond Dossier*, Jonathan Cape, 1965.

Balio, Tino, *United Artists*, University of Wisconsin Press, 1987.

Barnes, Alan and Hearn, Marcus, *Kiss Kiss Bang Bang*, Batsford, 1997.

Bennett, Tony and Woollacott, Janet, *Bond and Beyond*, Macmillan, 1987.

Booker, Christopher, *The Neophiliacs*, Pimlico, 1992.

Burgess, Anthony, *Live and Let Die* (Preface), Coronet, 1988.

Burgess, Anthony, *Ninety-Nine Novels*, Allison & Busby, 1984.

Callan, Michael Feeney, *Sean Connery: The Untouchable Hero*, Virgin, 1993.

Chierichetti, David, *Hollywood Director: The Career of Mitchell Leisen*, Curtis Books, New York, 1973.

Freedland, Michael, *Sean Connery*, Weidenfeld & Nicolson, 1994.

Gardner, John, *Licence Renewed*, Jonathan Cape, 1981.

Haining, Peter, *James Bond: A Celebration*, W. H. Allen, 1987.

Harvey, Chris, *Aston Martin & Lagonda*, Oxford Illustrated Press, 1995.

Hibbin, Sally, *The New Official James Bond Movie Book*, Hamlyn, 1989.

Hogg, Ian and Weeks, John, *Pistols of the World*, Cassell, 1992.

Lycett, Andrew, *Ian Fleming*, Weidenfeld & Nicolson, 1995.

McCarthy, Todd, *Howard Hawks*, Grove Press, 1997.

McFarlane, Brian, *An Autobiography of British Cinema*, Methuen, 1997

Pearson, John, *The Life of Ian Fleming*, Jonathan Cape, 1966.

Petrie, Duncan, *The British Cinematographer*, British Film Institute, 1996.

Walker, Alexander, *Hollywood, England*, Michael Joseph, 1974.

Yule, Andrew, *Sean Connery*, Little, Brown, 1993.

Acknowledgements

The author would like to Scott Curtis at the Academy of Motion Picture Arts and Sciences; Shirley Eaton; Derek Elley; Guy Hamilton; Susan Hansen and Robert McCown at the University of Iowa; Waltraud Loges; Andrew Lycett; Sylvia Maibaum; Dottie Pack at the US Army Armor Center, Fort Knox; Graham Rye and the James Bond International Fan Club and Archive; Tony Sloman; Norman Wanstall.

Transport: Mercedes-Benz/AMG; Ford Motor Company; Maserati; Pontiac; British Airways; British Midland; Avis.

Hotel accommodation: Villamil, Palma de Mallorca; the Ritz-Carlton, Marina del Rey; Holiday Inn, Iowa City.

Others: Cartier, Sony, Apple Macintosh, NEC and Umax.